INSPIRATION COFFEE & WISDOM TEA

Daily Delights at the Divine Coffeehouse

Reverend Peter G. Vu

First published by Dog Ear Publishing
8888 Keystone Crossing
Suite 1300
Indianapolis, IN 46240
www.dogearpublishing.net

ISBN: 978-145757-043-8

This book is printed on acid-free paper.
Printed in the United States of America

I would like to dedicate this book to the following groups:

- My wise and loving God, who has created this magnificent world to show us the divine wisdom, knowledge, beauty, and love in an attempt to help us desire the eternal life in the Kingdom of God.
- My family, friends, teachers, counselors, coaches, and religious figures, who have taught me and passed on knowledge and wisdom to help me be the light for the world and uplift others in times of trouble and turmoil.
- People who are feeling lost or discouraged in modern-day culture. Your commitment and hope in divine power tells us to search for the guiding light of God and joy in our daily life amidst our daily challenges.
- Global citizens who are members of the human race, despite your different cultures, traditions, religious beliefs, races, and backgrounds. Your desire to be good and make our world a better place for the next generations has encouraged me to write this book and find one more way to help us enjoy our life to the fullest and bring us close together as a human family.

I'm forever grateful to our omniscient God and indebted to you all. May our wise and loving God help you enjoy every moment of your day and make the right decisions every day of your life.

Introduction

Every morning, we wake ourselves up with a cup of coffee or latte. Its intoxicating aroma helps push us along in our daily tasks, even though we might not be quite awake yet. In the middle of the day, we might pick up a cup of tea to calm our nerves down and help us finish up our day. As we go through this daily routine and rely on those external stimulants to get us through our day, I imagine how much more our spirit might need encouragement to stay focused and get inspired each day. That is how I have come up with the concept of having two sayings each day for this book. One is to inspire us like coffee or latte in the morning, while another is like tea, giving us some wisdom to help us face our daily decisions with confidence. I give context and a short interpretation of each saying before wrapping it into a small package with a bow either called **In-Flavor** (Inspiration Flavor) or **Wi-Flavor** (Wisdom Flavor). Then I help mix that flavor and turn it into **Inspiration Coffee** or **Wisdom Tea** for you to enjoy each day.

Like our daily coffee and tea, I try to keep the two daily sayings and their reflections short and sweet. We do not have all day to read page after page on how we should make the right decisions or what we need to do to have a meaningful life. Another book would have to deal with that. This book is designed simply to give us a quick spiritual boost as we try to run from one task to another in our busy schedule.

Although the short-term goal of this book is to help us get through each day with joy and purpose, its long-term focus is to fine tune our characters and make us better people at home, at work, at worshipping place, in the neighborhood, and in other places. This world would be like Heaven if there were less fighting, arguing, and killing. We cannot get our cup of coffee, latte, or tea these days without worrying that a crazy lunatic will come in with a deadly weapon to gun us down like an animal or a bomb to blow us up. We certainly cannot enjoy anything in a world like that. This situation needs to be stopped, and it begins with us. We need to talk and act differently than what we see on the news or witness in our world every day. When we can do that, we help change the world one person at a time, and others hopefully will follow our example. This transformation will not only make our world a better place but also make us feel much better about ourselves.

Another reason for me to write this book is because I have observed that many decent people, who might not be quite religious, still have strong beliefs on certain values and want to share them with the world at every chance possible. The best way for them to do that is by putting one of those values in a short saying at the bottom of their signatures or under a logo of a company. Check that out for yourself! In fact, I have seen two recent television interviews in which people have quoted the sayings of inspiring figures who have changed their lives or helped them make important decisions. Furthermore, many of us enjoy reading a short message from a fortune cookie, which often makes us pause and think a little bit. That is what I hope this book will help us do each day: just to pause for a few minutes and think about those two daily sayings.

Finally, we have seen how national identity has been emphasized all over the world and turned people against one another. The truth is that we all belong to one human family, regardless of our races and religions. We need to learn to get along and help out one another. This book highlights that important point by collecting inspiring and wise sayings from the Bible, Koran (Muslim sacred book), Talmud (Jewish sacred book), and many human traditions. Some of the famous figures are Jesus, Confucius, Muhammad, Mahatma Gandhi, Aristotle, the Dalai Lama, Thich Nhat Hanh, St. Mother Teresa, Billy Graham, Abraham Lincoln, Benjamin Franklin, Thomas Edison, Martin Luther King Jr., Eleanor Roosevelt, Susan B. Anthony, and many more.

I have used five resources to select the two famous quotes for each day for the entire year and recorded each of them as following:

(Practical ...) for taking from *The Complete Book of Practical Proverbs and Wacky Wit*.

(Quotations ...) for taking from *The Whole Book of Quotations: Wisdom from Women and Men around the Globe throughout the Centuries.*

(Religious ...) for taking from *The Treasury of Religious & Spiritual Quotations: Words to Live By*.

(Wise ...) for taking from *The Wise and Wacky Wit: A Potpourri of Proverbs from A to Z*.

(Wit ...) for taking from *The Words of Wit and Wisdom: A Random Collection of Memorable Quotes*.

Here are some of the quotes that you will find in this book:

"I do the best I know how, the very best I can; and I mean to keep on doing it to the end. If the end brings me out all right, what is said against me will not amount to anything. If the end brings me out wrong, ten angels swearing I was right would make no difference" (Abraham Lincoln, under the description Practical, Action, pg. 4).

"Cautious, careful people, always casting about to preserve their reputation and social standing, never can bring about a reform" (Susan B. Anthony (1820–1906), American suffragist, under the description Quotations, Reform and Reformers, pg. 230).

"Opportunity is missed by most people because it is dressed in overalls and looks like work" (Thomas Edison, under the description Practical, Opportunity, pg. 174).

"The most important thing in any relationship is not what you get, but what you give" (Eleanor Roosevelt (1884–1962), American humanitarian and First Lady, under the description Quotations, Relationships, pg. 232).

"Riches are not from an abundance of worldly goods, but from a contented mind" (Muhammad (570–632 AD), prophet of Islam, under the description Quotations, Wealth, pg. 303).

"We must use time creatively, and forever realize that the time is always ripe to do right" (Martin Luther King Jr. (1929–1968), American civil rights leader, "Letter from a Birmingham Jail," under the description Quotations, Time, pg. 278).

"After crosses and losses, men grow humbler and wiser" (Benjamin Franklin, under the description Practical, Adversity, pg. 7).

"True happiness flows from the possession of wisdom and virtue and not from the possession of external goods" (Aristotle (384–322 BC), from *Politics (Book VII of the Analysis)*, under the description Religious, Happiness, pg. 221).

"The present world crisis ... is a crisis of man's spirit. It is a great religious and moral upheaval of the human race, and we do not really know half the causes of this upheaval" (Thomas Merton, from *The Way* (June 1963), under the description Religious, Human Spirit, pg. 252).

"If you have a particular faith or religion, that is good. But you can survive without it if you have love, compassion, and tolerance. The clear proof of a person's love of God is if that person genuinely shows love to fellow human beings" (Dalai Lama, *For the Love of God* (1990), under the description Religious, Love, pg. 305).

"I object to violence because when it appears to do good, the good is only temporary; the evil it does is permanent" (Mahatma K. Gandhi, from *Selections from Gandhi* (1945), under the description Religious, Nonviolence, pg. 362).

I hope you will enjoy this book each day as much as I have enjoyed putting it together. I hope it will transform you to be a better person and slowly change our world to become a piece of Heaven that the next generations can appreciate for all the wonderful effort we have put into it for our human family.

Fr. Peter Vu

JANUARY

January 1

If you wait for perfect conditions, you will never get anything done. ... Keep on sowing your seed, for you never know which will grow—perhaps it all will. (Ecclesiastes 11: 4–6) (Practical, Achievement, pg. 1)

In-Flavor: Take chances in life and be not too cautious. Start with big dreams and keep working on them until you see the good results. That is the key to your future success and achievement.

Inspiration Coffee: Wonder Counselor, help me dream big, take chances, and keep working on it until I see great success. Thank you, Lord.

Don't try to disclaim responsibility by saying you didn't know about it. For God, who knows all hearts, knows yours, and he knows you knew! And he will reward everyone according to his deeds. (Proverbs 24:12) (Practical, Action, pg. 3)

Wi-Flavor: Some people like to avoid responsibility by making excuses. But God knows every human heart. If you want God to reward you in the end, then own up to your responsibility and fulfill it.

Wisdom Tea: Wisdom of God, when I am tempted to dodge my responsibility, remind me that you know my heart and I need to fulfill it. Thank you, Lord.

January 2

I do the best I know how, the very best I can; and I mean to keep on doing it to the end. If the end brings me out all right, what is said against me will not amount to anything. If the end brings me out wrong, ten angels swearing I was right would make no difference. (Abraham Lincoln) (Practical, Action, pg. 4)

In-Flavor: You should always do your best in everything and work hard. Carry on your task to the end and do not worry about the end result or your critics. That is how you should act and live.

Inspiration Coffee: Wonder Counselor, help me do my best in everything and not worry about the end result or my critics. Thank you, Lord.

He who doesn't know where he is going may miss it when he gets there. (Practical, Aim, pg. 11)

Wi-Flavor: If you do not know where you are supposed to go, you will never get there. Likewise, if you do not have any hope or dream, you might miss the opportunities to make it come true.

Wisdom Tea: Wisdom of God, when I feel lost in this world, I need your help to find my dream and direction to get there. Thank you, Lord.

January 3

Aims and ideals are like tuning forks; you must sound them frequently to keep your life up to pitch. (Practical, Aim, pg. 11)

In-Flavor: Don't forget to review your aims and ideals frequently. That is how you can keep your chin up and remain hopeful amidst your busy and challenging life.

Inspiration Coffee: Wonder Counselor, help me look up and remind myself of my aims and ideals to keep me hopeful in my busy and challenging life. Thank you, Lord.

The bamboo that bends is stronger than the oak that resists.

(Japanese proverb) (Practical, Change, pg. 26)

Wi-Flavor: Oak, which is strong, will break if it resists. But bamboo, which seems weak, shows its real strength when it bends. So, if you can adapt or change with a situation, you will be strong like the bamboo that bends.

Wisdom Tea: Wisdom of God, when I find change in a situation difficult, I need your help to bend myself and adapt with it so that I can be strong and healthy in this life. Thank you, Lord.

January 4

Gentle words cause life and health; griping brings discouragement. (Proverbs 15:4) (Practical, Discouragement, pg. 55)

In-Flavor: Use gentle words in dealing with others to bring them peace and life. Griping only causes resentment and discouragement. That is how you can lift up others and avoid discouraging them.

Inspiration Coffee: Wonder Counselor, help me use gentle words to lift up people I might encounter today and avoid discouraging them with my griping attitude. Thank you, Lord.

We must all hang together, or assuredly we shall all hang separately. (Benjamin Franklin) (Practical, Cooperation, pg. 42)

Wi-Flavor: Since creation, human beings have discovered the power of unity and learned to cooperate for survival. If you can see the strength and blessings of unity, you must convince others to cooperate.

Wisdom Tea: Wisdom of God, when I want to do things on my own, I need to see the importance of cooperation and working together to make a strong community and successful result. Thank you, Lord.

January 5

When we do what we can, God will do what we can't. (Practical, Faith, pg. 72)

In-Flavor: You need to do your part and work hard, but leave the rest for God to take care. That is how you put your faith in God and let God take care of what you cannot do.

Inspiration Coffee: Wonder Counselor, help me not to worry too much and just do my best. For you will take care of the rest for me. Thank you, Lord.

The glory of young men is their strength; of old men, their experience. (Proverbs 20:29) (Practical, Experience, pg. 64)

Wi-Flavor: Young people count on their strength to bring them glory, while old people rely on their experience. If you want to double your glory, you can count on both your strength and experience.

Wisdom Tea: Wisdom of God, I might not know all my gifts in dealing with my daily challenges. But I need you at least to let me see the gift of strength in being young and of experience in being old. Thank you, Lord.

January 6

It's nice to know that when you help someone up a hill, you're a little closer to the top yourself. (Practical, Help, pg. 106)

In-Flavor: Encourage yourself to help someone in tough times. When you do, you will feel like a champion—or at least stronger and wiser. That is how you should view helping others in their challenging times.

Inspiration Coffee: Wonder Counselor, give me a courageous and caring heart to reach out and help people in tough times, for that caring and humble work will make me be a better person, like my loving God. Thank you, Lord.

Friends are God's life preservers. (Practical, Friendship, pg. 84)

Wi-Flavor: Some people share social time with their friends, while others count on them as counselors. You might see friendships as existing for other reasons, but hopefully, friends will be there for you in desperate times.

Wisdom Tea: Wisdom of God, I thank you for sending the right people throughout my life to be my friends. They have been my life preservers and cheerleaders. I need to cherish and pray for them often. Thank you, Lord.

January 7

The man who has a good opinion of himself is usually a poor judge. (Practical, Judgment, pg. 123)

In-Flavor: Be humble and consider others' opinions to give yourself a whole view of an issue. That is how you can confidently make a fair and wise judgment on any issue and be a good judge.

Inspiration Coffee: Wonder Counselor, help me to keep my head down and listen well to others' opinions on every issue. That is how I can be a fair judge and deliver good judgments. Thank you, Lord.

Gossips burn so much oxygen at the mouth that there's never any left for the brain. (Practical, Gossip, pg. 98)

Wi-Flavor: People who spend time on gossips never have enough time to ponder on their truthfulness and consequences. If you choose to spread rumors, think about their destructive power first.

Wisdom Tea: Wisdom of God, I might be tempted to get involved in gossips about someone or some issue. I need your grace to resist that temptation and think hard about their destructive power. Thank you, Lord.

January 8

All the roads to success and achievement are uphill. (Practical, Leadership, pg. 138)

In-Flavor: Some think they can achieve success without having to face hardships and disappointments. But you must work hard and expect challenges if you want to succeed and achieve great things.

Inspiration Coffee: Wonder Counselor, help me see that the roads to success and achievement are full of hardships and disappointments. But with your help, I will work hard and conquer all the challenges. Thank you, Lord.

Man was given five senses: touch, taste, sight, smell, and hearing. The successful man has two more: horse (sense is stable thinking coupled with the ability to say nay) and common. (Practical, Horse Sense, pg. 112)

Wi-Flavor: The five senses give humans the ability to collect facts and data, but the senses do not formulate a decision. If you want to be a successful person, you must know how to use the five senses—and two more.

Wisdom Tea: Wisdom of God, I might have five senses like ordinary people, but if I want to be a successful person, I need two more senses—horse sense and common sense—to make my dreams a reality. Thank you, Lord.

January 9
Parents who are afraid to put their foot down usually have children who step on their toes. (Practical, Parents, pg. 181)

In-Flavor: Be firm on your expectations and show your children the right ways. Otherwise, they will ignore and disrespect you in the future. That is how you can be good and responsible parents.

Inspiration Coffee: Wonder Counselor, help me to be a good and responsible parent by not being afraid to put my foot down and still loving my children wholeheartedly. Thank you, Lord.

He who graduates today, and stops learning tomorrow, is uneducated the day after. (Newton D. Baker) (Practical, Learning, pg. 140)

Wi-Flavor: Education is the key to success. It gives a person knowledge of the world and helps formulate good decisions. If you do not keep on learning, you will soon be left behind and become uneducated.

Wisdom Tea: Wisdom of God, I might think learning stops after my graduation. But it is actually a lifelong process. I must keep on learning, for education is the key to success. Thank you, Lord.

January 10
A prudent man foresees the difficulties ahead and prepares for them. (Proverbs 22:3) (Practical, Preparation, pg. 193)

In-Flavor: Life is full of challenges and uncertainties. You should be prudent and prepare for them today, instead of waiting to see them tomorrow. That is how you can survive and stay ahead of the game.

Inspiration Coffee: Wonder Counselor, help me to be prudent and prepared for the difficulties and uncertainties ahead. That way I can survive this life and succeed. Thank you, Lord.

Troubles in marriage often start when a man is so busy earning his salt that he forgets his sugar. (Practical, Marriage, pg. 150)

Wi-Flavor: Marriage begins and remains with two people. If one of them is busy earning a living, the other one will feel neglected. So, if you want your marriage to succeed, you must take good care of it.

Wisdom Tea: Wisdom of God, I do not want any trouble in my marriage. I need you to help me take good care of it by knowing how to balance my work and family. Thank you, Lord.

January 11
This year's success was last year's impossibility. (Practical, Success, pg. 211)

In-Flavor: You must work hard on your idea and be persistent with it. Then whatever is impossible in the past will become your present success. That is how you can conquer the impossibility and succeed.

Inspiration Coffee: Wonder Counselor, help me work hard on all my ideas and never give up. That way I can turn an impossible idea to a present success. Thank you, Lord.

An ounce of mother is worth a pound of clergy. (Spanish proverb) (Practical, Mother, pg. 164)

Wi-Flavor: People come to the church and the clergy for moral guidance. They do not see the importance of a mother. But if you have the loving care of a mother, it is worth ten times more than moral guidance.

Wisdom Tea: Wisdom of God, I might underestimate the importance of the tender, loving care of a mother. But you help open my eyes to see that it is worth ten times more than moral guidance. Thank you, Lord.

January 12
I never did anything worth doing by accident, nor did any of my inventions come by accident; they came by work. (Thomas Edison) (Practical, Work, pg. 247)

In-Flavor: Hard work and courage brought about all worthwhile things and great inventions for Thomas Edison. Nothing happened by accident. If you want any achievement, you must work.

Inspiration Coffee: Wonder Counselor, successes and achievements do not come by accident. They come by work and courage. Help me work hard on my ideas and make them a reality. Thank you, Lord.

Give your troubles to God; he'll be up all night anyway. (Practical, Prayer, pg. 188)

Wi-Flavor: Life is full of troubles and moments of sadness. People often come to God to ask for help. Perhaps next time you think of your troubles, you just need to hand them over to God in prayer.

Wisdom Tea: Wisdom of God, my life might be full of troubles and sad moments, but I just need to hand them over to you in prayer. Thank you, Lord.

January 13

The good neighbor looks beyond the external accidents and discerns those inner qualities that make all men human and, therefore, brothers. (Martin Luther King Jr., *Strength to Love*) (Quotations, Brotherhood and Sisterhood, pg. 30)

In-Flavor: Be a good neighbor and judge if someone can be your brother or sister by their inner qualities, not their exterior features.

Inspiration Coffee: Wonder Counselor, help me be a good neighbor who can judge a person by their inner qualities and not their external features. Thank you, Lord.

A quarrelsome man has no good neighbors. (Benjamin Franklin) (Practical, Quarrels, pg. 203)

Wi-Flavor: Some people like to pick a fight with everyone on everything and do not reach out to help a neighbor. If you keep quarreling with people, you cannot make peace or a good neighbor with anyone.

Wisdom Tea: Wisdom of God, I might get easily irritated and like to quarrel. I need you to help me be a good neighbor and avoid quarreling. Thank you, Lord.

January 14

Distance tests a horse's strength; time reveals a man's character. (Chinese proverb) (Quotations, Character, pg. 35)

In-Flavor: You know a horse's strength by its traveling distance. But it takes time for you to learn about a person's character. If you want to learn about a friend's true character, only time will tell.

Inspiration Coffee: Wonder Counselor, although time will tell about someone's character, help me to be honest about mine so that everyone can tell who I am at the first hour. Thank you, Lord.

Gratitude is the heart's memory. (French proverb) (Practical, Thankfulness, pg. 222)

Wi-Flavor: The heart remembers all sorts of things, from sad moments to happy ones. You can help the heart remember one more thing—namely, gratitude—by having a thankful attitude.

Wisdom Tea: Wisdom of God, gratitude is a very special virtue. I need you to carve this virtue into my heart so that I will always have a thankful attitude. Thank you, Lord.

January 15

The worst man is the one who sees himself as the best. ('Ali (600–661 AD), first Imam of the Sh'ia branch of Islam; fourth caliph) (Quotations, Pride, pg. 215)

In-Flavor: When you see yourself as the best, you tend to look down on everyone around you and miscalculate the future challenges. That is how pride can become a problem, and you must avoid it.

Inspiration Coffee: Wonder Counselor, help me to be humble and continue to work hard for my future success without looking down on anyone or thinking I am the best. Thank you, Lord.

A wise person has an open mind and a closed mouth. (Practical, Wisdom, pg. 239)

Wi-Flavor: A person with an open mind will listen to other suggestions, while the one with a closed mouth will think clearly on a decision. If you are a wise person, you will listen more and talk less.

Wisdom Tea: Wisdom of God, I ask you to help me to be a wise person by having a closed mouth to think clearly and an open mind to listen to other suggestions. Thank you, Lord.

January 16

Respect yourself, and others will respect you. (Confucius (551–479 BC), Chinese philosopher, *Analects*) (Quotations, Respect, pg. 238)

In-Flavor: Being respectful means to act with care and consideration in spite of a situation. When you do that with yourself, people will imitate it and respect you. That is how you get respect from others.

Inspiration Coffee: Wonder Counselor, help me learn to respect myself by acting with care and consideration regardless of a situation. In doing that, others will come to respect me. Thank you, Lord.

A hurtful act is the transference to others of the degradation which we bear in ourselves. (Simone Weil (1909–1943), French philosopher) (Quotations, The Golden Rule, pg. 112)

Wi-Flavor: People often take it out on others when they experience something wrong in their lives. So, when your life is messed up somehow, be careful not to say or do anything hurtful to others.

Wisdom Tea: Wisdom of God, when I feel hurt inside from a bad past experience, help me not to pass it on to others by saying or doing hurtful things to them. Thank you, Lord.

January 17
To win, one must be big enough to see the worth in others, big enough to cheer when others score. (Lucie Campbell Williams (1885–1962), American educator) (Quotations, Victory, pg. 294)

In-Flavor: Everyone wants to win. But it takes heart and humility for a true champion to cheer for the opponents and treat them with respect. That is the way you should approach victory.

Inspiration Coffee: Wonder Counselor, give me the heart of a champion to cheer for my opponents and treat them with respect as I welcome a victory or a win. Thank you, Lord.

Ignorance is the night of the mind, a night without moon or star. (Confucius, *Analects*) (Quotations, Ignorance, pg. 136)

Wi-Flavor: An ignorant does not have any idea about the world and remains in the dark night of his/her mind. You must avoid being ignorant and continue to learn about the world every day.

Wisdom Tea: Wisdom of God, I do not like to be in the dark night of the mind. I need to see your light to dispel darkness and ignorance from my life by my continuous learning. Thank you, Lord.

January 18
Adversity in the things of this world opens the door for spiritual salvation. (A. J. Toynbee, in the *New York Times*, December 26, 1954) (Religious, Adversity pg. 19)

In-Flavor: Be strong and persistent when you encounter daily adversity, for it helps prepare you for the spiritual world. That is how you should view adversity and, hence, come to see the need for divine help.

Inspiration Coffee: Wonder Counselor, adversity is part of this world. Help me to persevere through it and realize the need for your help. Thank you, Lord.

God is merciful to those who are merciful to others. (Talmud, ancient body of Jewish civil and canonical law, Sifre 117) (Quotations, Mercy, pg. 182)

Wi-Flavor: Everyone wants others to be merciful to them, but often find it difficult to reciprocate. So, if you want God to be merciful to you on the Last Day, you must treat others mercifully in this life.

Wisdom Tea: Wisdom of God, I need to learn to be merciful to others so that you will be merciful to me on the Last Day. Thank you, Lord.

January 19
Temptation is the voice of the suppressed evil, conscience is the voice of the repressed good.
(J. A. Hadfield, *Psychology and Morals*, 1923) (Religious, Conformity, pg. 100)

In-Flavor: Listen to the voice of conscience because it tells you good things, and resist temptation because it does the opposite. That is how you learn to get yourself to do the right things.

Inspiration Coffee: Wonder Counselor, help me listen to the voice of my conscience to do the right things and avoid the lure of temptation to follow the evil acts. Thank you, Lord.

The conquest of oneself is better than the conquest of all others.
(*Dhammapada*, collection of ancient Buddhist poems and aphorisms) (Quotations, Self-Discipline, pg. 255)

Wi-Flavor: Humans have gone to the ends of the earth, even the universe, to conquer other humans and foreign lands. But it takes great self-discipline and much more to be able to conquer yourself.

Wisdom Tea: Wisdom of God, I want to spend my whole life trying to conquer the whole universe. But it is better for me to conquer myself than all others, which can be done through self-discipline. Thank you, Lord.

January 20
In this world, aspirants may find enlightenment by two different paths. For the contemplative is the path of knowledge; for the active is the path of selfless action.
(Bhagavad Gita, ancient Hindu scripture) (Religious, Enlightenment, pg. 158)

In-Flavor: You will be happy and content when you experience enlightenment by way of knowledge or doing selfless acts. That is how you can find enlightenment and meet God in this world.

Inspiration Coffee: Wonder Counselor, help me experience enlightenment by path of knowledge or/and path of selfless actions and come to meet you right here in this life. Thank you, Lord.

If she [woman] is weak in striking, she is strong in suffering.
(Mahatma K. Gandhi) (Quotations, Women, pg. 309)

Wi-Flavor: Women are not well-known for their powerful striking or impressive attack. But you have to admire that they are strong in suffering and remarkable in endurance amidst challenges.

Wisdom Tea: Wisdom of God, I might be weak in my physical power like the fairer gender, but you will make me strong in my ability to suffer and endure. Thank you, Lord.

January 21
Nobody hath found God by walking his own way. (Guru Ram Das (1580), in M. A. Macauliffe's *The Sikh Religion*) (Religious, Finding God, pg. 189)

In-Flavor: It is a great joy and blessing to meet God. If you want that, you must get out of your own way and head in God's direction. That is how you can meet God and find lots of wonderful things.

Inspiration Coffee: Wonder Counselor, I might want to go my own way, but I need you to help me follow your way and find you and your wonderful blessings. Thank you, Lord.

Anger deprives a sage of his wisdom, a prophet of his vision. (Simeon, in the Talmud) (Religious, Anger pg. 28)

Wi-Flavor: Anger always brings out the worst in people and causes a sage to lose his wisdom and a prophet, his vision. You must do your best to avoid anger and search for peace instead.

Wisdom Tea: Wisdom of God, anger can cause lots of damages, such as depriving a sage of his wisdom or a prophet of his vision. I want you to help me avoid anger and find peace every day. Thank you, Lord.

January 22
Idleness is the enemy of the soul. (St. Benedict of Nursia (480–533 AD), *Rule of St. Benedict of Nursia*) (Religious, Idleness, pg. 259)

In-Flavor: Your soul needs to be preoccupied with a mission. Idleness will cause it to be tempted and get involved in bad things. The best way for you to combat idleness is to always keep yourself busy.

Inspiration Coffee: Wonder Counselor, idleness will tempt me to get involved in many bad things that are the enemies of the soul. Help me keep myself busy and put an end to my idleness. Thank you, Lord.

Come to me, all who labor and are heavy laden, and I will give you rest. (Matthew 11:28) (Religious, Comfort, pg. 87)

Wi-Flavor: Humans are often heavily burdened with daily responsibilities and much in need of relief. You might feel the same way, but the only one who can bring you comfort and relief is the Lord Jesus.

Wisdom Tea: Wisdom of God, I may be heavily burdened with daily responsibilities and other life stress. I need you to help me find some rest and relief. Thank you, Lord.

January 23

Greater love has no man than this, that a man lay down his life for his friends. (John 15:13) (Religious, Love, pg. 307)

In-Flavor: Love causes you to do lots of crazy things. But your true love for a friend will inspire you to make great sacrifices, including offering your life for him/her. That is what true love looks like.

Inspiration Coffee: Wonder Counselor, help me experience true love for a friend by my willingness to make sacrifices and offer my life for him/her. Thank you, Lord.

Destiny waits in the hand of God. (T. S. Eliot, *Murder in the Cathedral*, 1935) (Religious, Destiny, pg. 133)

Wi-Flavor: Everyone knows their lives are in the hand of God. God knows what will happen to everyone. If you think you are in control of your destiny, think again, and come home to God.

Wisdom Tea: Wisdom of God, I want you to help me realize that my destiny is in your hands and stop pretending that I am in charge of my life. Thank you, Lord.

January 24

Work as if you were to live 100 years. Pray as if you were to die tomorrow. (Benjamin Franklin, *Poor Richard's Almanac*, 1758) (Religious, Prayer, pg. 414)

In-Flavor: If you want to live long, you must work hard to save for it. Similarly, if you know you will die tomorrow, you will pray a lot to prepare for it. You should view work and prayer that way.

Inspiration Coffee: Wonder Counselor, help me learn to work hard to save for a long life and pray intensely as if my last day on Earth is imminent. Thank you, Lord.

Education is the leading of human souls to what is best, and making what is best out of them; and these two objects are always attainable together, and by the same means. (John Ruskin, *Stones of Venice*, 1853) (Religious, Education, pg. 155)

Wi-Flavor: All humans want what is best and try to make what is best out of themselves. What leads humans to all of that is education. If you desire what is best for your future, education is the key for you.

Wisdom Tea: Wisdom of God, I may not realize the importance of education, but I need your help to keep on learning to achieve what is best for myself and my potential. Thank you, Lord.

January 25

It is only through the mystery of self-sacrifice that a man may find himself anew. (C. G. Jung, *Two Essays on Analytical Psychology*, 1928) (Religious, Sacrifice, pg. 497)

In-Flavor: Self-sacrifice forces you to think about a cause greater than yourself. You will learn to let go of yourself and find new causes to live for. That is one of the blessings self-sacrifice will do for you.

Inspiration Coffee: Wonder Counselor, it is certainly not easy for me to make a self-sacrifice for a cause. But by letting go of myself, I will find a new birth and vision for my life. Thank you, Lord.

If you have faith [as small] as a grain of mustard seed, you will say to this mountain, "Move hence to yonder place," and it will move; and nothing will be impossible to you. (Matthew 17:20) (Religious, Faith, pg. 178)

Wi-Flavor: The power of faith is discussed a lot in the Bible because it can do the impossible and bring about great miracles. If you want to experience the impossible, embrace the power of faith.

Wisdom Tea: Wisdom of God, I might not have experienced the power of faith yet, but if I have faith even as small as a grain of mustard seed, you assure me that I can move mountains and see the impossible. Thank you, Lord.

January 26

Progress will be carried forward by a series of dazzling visions. (Victor Hugo, *William Shakespeare*, 1864) (Religious, Vision, pg. 597)

In-Flavor: Making progress on something requires you first to have great visions and then work to transform them into a reality. That is how you make great progress from dazzling visions.

Inspiration Coffee: Wonder Counselor, I need to have good visions and turn them into my real, wonderful work. Help me acquire those visions from you and make good progress with them. Thank you, Lord.

To err is human, to forgive divine. (Alexander Pope, "An Essay on Criticism," 1711) (Religious, Forgiveness, pg. 193)

Wi-Flavor: Humans often make mistakes that cause hurt and pain for themselves and others. They need God to forgive them. You can blame yourself for your errors or try to be divine and learn to forgive.

Wisdom Tea: Wisdom of God, I might err for being human and cause hurt to myself and others. I need you to forgive me and teach me to be divine and do the same to others. Thank you, Lord.

January 27

The merits of each one depend not directly on what sort of soil God has given him to cultivate, but on what use he makes of what God has given. (Edward F. Garesche, *Ever Timely Thoughts*, 1925) (Religious, Work, pg. 621)

In-Flavor: You might not be born rich or with great talents. But if you know how to make good use of what you were given, your success will be sweet. That is how you should view work and success.

Inspiration Coffee: Wonder Counselor, you might have given me certain talents and resources, but my success depends on how I make good use of those. Help me be a good steward of your gifts. Thank you, Lord.

He who conceals hatred has lying lips, and he who utters slander is a fool. (Proverbs 10:18) (Religious, Hatred, pg. 224)

Wi-Flavor: Hatred brings hurt and destruction. Lying causes suspicion and mistrust. Slander creates scandal and division. None of those are good things, and you must avoid them by all means.

Wisdom Tea: Wisdom of God, I ask you to help me avoid carrying hatred and false statements in my heart. Otherwise, I will have to lie about them or say foolish things. Thank you, Lord.

January 28

People may doubt what you say, but they'll always believe what you do. (Wise, Action, pg. 9)

In-Flavor: You might promise to do something nice for someone, but only a kind act makes your intention a reality. That is why your actions speak louder than your words or promises.

Inspiration Coffee: Wonder Counselor, help me be a person of actions and not of words or promises, just like you showed your love for me on the Cross, for actions speak louder than words. Thank you, Lord.

Judge not, that you be not judged. For with the judgment you pronounce you will be judged and the measure you give will be the measure you get. (Matthew 7:1) (Religious, Judgment, pg. 282)

Wi-Flavor: People do not hesitate to judge others and condemn their dislike. But you have been warned not to judge others, for that right is reserved for God, who will use the same measure on you.

Wisdom Tea: Wisdom of God, I might like to judge others, but I need to reserve that right for you and be careful about the measures I use on people, for the same measures will be used on me. Thank you, Lord.

January 29

The busy man is troubled with but one devil; the idle man by a thousand. (Spanish proverb) (Wise, Idleness, pg. 75)

In-Flavor: When you keep yourself busy, the only devil you try to resist is laziness. But if you are idle, you might be lured by many things and tempted in all directions. That is why you must avoid idleness.

Inspiration Coffee: Wonder Counselor, help me keep myself busy and avoid idleness, for a busy person has to fight only one devil—namely, laziness—while the idle one, a thousand of them. Thank you, Lord.

Unless we learn the meaning of mercy by exercising it towards others, we will never have any real knowledge of what it means to love Christ. (Thomas Merton, *Life and Holiness*, 1963) (Religious, Mercy, pg. 325)

Wi-Flavor: Most people have not met Christ or God, but have seen other humans who are brothers and sisters. If you claim to love him, you must show your love and mercy to other people first.

Wisdom Tea: Wisdom of God, I might blurt out how much I love you, Lord. But that will not be true unless I have acted mercifully toward others. I need you to help me do that. Thank you, Lord.

January 30

The only place where success comes before work is in the dictionary. (Wise, Success, pg. 127)

In-Flavor: You can only achieve success through hard work. If you do not work, then don't expect any success. That is why work has to come first, before you can see any great success.

Inspiration Coffee: Wonder Counselor, I need to work hard if I want to achieve success in my life, for success cannot come before work. I need you to give me a hand with my work. Thank you, Lord.

Patience is the companion of wisdom. (St. Augustine, *On Patience*, 425 AD) (Religious, Patience, pg. 381)

Wi-Flavor: Everyone wants to have wisdom, but never wonders where it comes from or what it takes to get it. If you wish to have wisdom, know that it takes time, patience, and lifelong experience.

Wisdom Tea: Wisdom of God, I surely want you to be the guide for all the decisions and choices in my life. But I need you to help me realize that wisdom can only come with time and patience. Thank you, Lord.

January 31

The next time Satan reminds you of your past, remind him of your future. (Wit, *Spring & Summer*)

In-Flavor: Satan knows your sins and past habits. He likes to hold you hostage and shame you with your past sins. You need to look ahead and tell him about your bright future. That is how you resist Satan.

Inspiration Coffee: Wonder Counselor, Satan likes to remind me about my past habits and sins. Give me courage to let him know about my new life and bright future. Thank you, Lord.

Prayer is essentially about making the heart strong so that fear cannot penetrate there. (Matthew Fox, *Creation Spirituality*, 1991) (Religious, Prayer, pg. 414)

Wi-Flavor: People come to prayer for various reasons, such as asking for help, searching for guidance, or finding some peace. You could view prayer as a way to make your heart strong and fearless.

Wisdom Tea: Wisdom of God, I might use prayer to ask you for help or get what I want. I should view prayer also as a way to make my heart strong and keep fear away from it. Thank you, Lord.

FEBRUARY

February 1

There are four steps to achievement: Plan purposefully. Prepare prayerfully. Proceed positively. And pursue persistently. Failure is the path of least persistence.
(Practical, Achievement, pg. 2)

In-Flavor: Achievement takes work and persistence. Failure comes when you do not persist. If you want to achieve something, you should follow the four steps above carefully and persistently.

Inspiration Coffee: Wonder Counselor, the stairway to my achievement has four steps: plan purposefully, prepare prayerfully, proceed positively, and pursue persistently. I need to follow them carefully. Thank you, Lord.

Salvation is not putting a man into Heaven, but putting Heaven into man. (Maltbie D. Babcock, *Thoughts for Everyday Living*, 1901) (Religious, Salvation, pg. 502)

Wi-Flavor: Salvation is about helping someone find a new life by putting Heaven into the person. If you want to find salvation, you should not think of it as putting yourself into Heaven, but the other way around.

Wisdom Tea: Wisdom of God, I might view salvation as putting me into Heaven, but it is actually putting Heaven into me. I ask you to help me find that transformation within me and also new life. Thank you, Lord.

February 2

If you can't stand the heat, stay out of the kitchen. (Harry Truman) (Practical, Adversity, pg. 7)

In-Flavor: The kitchen is where all the action is, but it is also the place that produces uncomfortable heat and potential burns. If you fear adversity, you should not enter the kitchen or take on any tough tasks.

Inspiration Coffee: Wonder Counselor, I might not like adversity and its uncomfortable heat. If so, I will have to stay away from tough tasks, but that is where big rewards will be. Help me to embrace adversity. Thank you, Lord.

He who is waiting for something to turn up might start with his own shirtsleeves. (Practical, Action, pg. 4)

Wi-Flavor: Some people hope opportunities or wonderful blessings will simply turn up without doing any work. If you wish any of those things to happen, you must roll up your sleeves and start working.

Wisdom Tea: Wisdom of God, I may hope something spectacular will show up for my good fortune, but you will help me realize that I need to roll up my shirtsleeves and start working. Thank you, Lord.

February 3
How a man plays the game shows something of his character. How he loses shows all of it. (Practical, Character, pg. 28)

In-Flavor: You can figure out a little about someone by the way he/she plays the game. But you know everything about a person by how he/she deals with losses, for losses reveal your true character.

Inspiration Coffee: Wonder Counselor, I can find out something about myself by how I play the game. However, you can help me learn everything about myself by how I handle loses. Thank you, Lord.

For there are six things the Lord hates—no, seven: haughtiness, lying, murdering, plotting evil, eagerness to do wrong, a false witness, sowing discord among brothers. (Proverbs 6:16–19) (Practical, Arrogance, pg. 14)

Wi-Flavor: The Lord hates sins and the seven things mentioned above because they do harm to someone. You might need to add "arrogance" to that list, for it will lead you to defy God.

Wisdom Tea: Wisdom of God, you sure hate the seven things above for all the harm and destruction they might cause. I ask you to help me avoid them every day, especially haughtiness or arrogance. Thank you, Lord.

February 4
Anxious hearts are very heavy, but a word of encouragement does wonders! (Proverbs 12:25) (Practical, Discouragement, pg. 55)

In-Flavor: Your friends might feel anxious about something. You can calm them down with words of encouragement. Likewise, when you feel anxious or discouraged, look for encouragement around you.

Inspiration Coffee: Wonder Counselor, I might feel anxious about something, but you can help me find a word of encouragement around me to calm my anxious heart. Thank you, Lord.

A mirror reflects a man's face, but what he is really like is shown by the kind of friends he chooses. (Proverbs 27:19) (Practical, Character, pg. 27)

Wi-Flavor: A mirror is used to view a person's face, but if you want to find out a person's character, you must look inside of his/her heart by checking out the kind of friends he/she picks.

Wisdom Tea: Wisdom of God, a mirror reflects my face. However, my friendships will show my whole character and personality. Help me attain good character and choose the right friends. Thank you, Lord.

February 5
Faith hears the inaudible, sees the invisible, believes the incredible, and receives the impossible. (Practical, Faith, pg. 72)

In-Flavor: Without your senses, you will be lost in this world. But what about getting the inaudible, the invisible, the incredible, and the impossible? You can only catch those with a sense of faith.

Inspiration Coffee: Wonder Counselor, I might have downplayed the value of faith. However, faith helps me deal with the inaudible, the invisible, the incredible, and the impossible. I need to have faith. Thank you, Lord.

A man who refuses to admit his mistakes can never be successful. But if he confesses and forsakes them, he gets another chance. (Proverbs 28:13) (Practical, Correction, pg. 43)

Wi-Flavor: Most people hate to admit their mistakes or stand corrected. But if you want to be successful, you must be willing to admit your mistakes, correct them, and learn from them.

Wisdom Tea: Wisdom of God, I might be ashamed to admit my mistakes and ask for forgiveness, but help me to know that I will have another chance and be successful if I forsake and correct them. Thank you, Lord.

February 6
It is easier to point a finger than to offer a helping hand. (Practical, Help, pg. 106)

In-Flavor: People love to criticize and point out problems, but they are slow to reach out and offer help. You can act contrary to this public trend by criticizing less and offering more help to others.

Inspiration Coffee: Wonder Counselor, I need to learn to be slow in criticism and quick in offering a helping hand to people in need. That is how I can help create a loving and peaceful world. Thank you, Lord.

Good judgment comes from experience. Experience comes from bad judgment. (Mark Twain) (Practical, Experience, pg. 65)

Wi-Flavor: Bad judgment causes you to make mistakes, but also gives you valuable experiences that help you make good judgment in the future. So, good future judgments indeed come from bad past ones.

Wisdom Tea: Wisdom of God, I might feel embarrassed about my bad past judgments, but help me realize that they bring me valuable experiences to make good judgment in the future. Thank you, Lord.

February 7
Your own soul is nourished when you are kind; it is destroyed when you are cruel.

(Proverbs 11:17) (Practical, Kindness, pg. 126)

In-Flavor: You might not realize your soul/spirit needs care and nourishment, as your body does. Kind acts will strengthen it, and cruel ones will destroy it. You need to do more kind acts every day.

Inspiration Coffee: Wonder Counselor, I may not realize that kindness nourishes my soul, while cruelty or meanness destroys it. I need to speak more kind words and do more kind acts every day. Thank you, Lord.

Real friends are those who, when you've made a fool of yourself, don't feel that you've done a permanent job. (Practical, Friendship, pg. 84)

Wi-Flavor: When you have made a fool of yourself, you might have caused some significant damage to something. But real friends will overlook it, stick around you, and encourage you to try again.

Wisdom Tea: Wisdom of God, I may not see the value of true friendship, but real friends will overlook my foolish moments and stick around to encourage me. I need to cherish those friendships. Thank you, Lord.

February 8
The man who knows right from wrong and has good judgment and common sense is happier than the man who is immensely rich! For such wisdom is far more valuable than precious jewels. Nothing else compares with it.

(Proverbs 3:13–15) (Practical, Man/Husband, pg. 147)

In-Flavor: Being rich with material things does not bring you happiness. Having good moral judgment and common sense will make you content. You need to search for the latter if you want happiness.

Inspiration Coffee: Wonder Counselor, wealth does not give me happiness, for divine wisdom reminds me that good moral judgment and common sense will bring me true peace and happiness. Thank you, Lord.

Wisdom is a tree of life to those who eat her fruit; happy is the man who keeps on eating it. (Proverbs 3:18) (Practical, Happiness, pg. 99)

Wi-Flavor: If you have wisdom, you will make right choices and do the right things. Nothing can make you feel fearful, anxious, or worried. You will have a peaceful, happy, and long life.

Wisdom Tea: Wisdom of God, I need to realize that your wisdom will help me make good decisions and do the right things. By following its guidance, I will find real happiness and contentment. Thank you, Lord.

February 9
Steady plodding brings prosperity; hasty speculation brings poverty. (Proverbs 21:5) (Practical, Persistence, pg. 183)

In-Flavor: You might like to guess and finish things quickly, but that only leads to poverty. The way to prosperity requires steady work and patience. Your persistent work will slowly bring you prosperity.

Inspiration coffee: Wonder Counselor, I need to have steady plan and persistent work to find prosperity, for hasty speculation and impatience will bring me poverty. Thank you, Lord.

Getting wisdom is the most important thing you can do! And with your wisdom, develop common sense and good judgment.
(Proverbs 4:7) (Practical, Intelligence, pg. 118)

Wi-Flavor: Wisdom comes from past mistakes and life experiences that can give you valuable insights for the future. If you have wisdom, it will help you make good judgments and develop common sense.

Wisdom Tea: Wisdom of God, help me see the value of your special gift and try to acquire it over my lifetime. I also need to develop common sense and good judgment to deal with my daily challenges. Thank you, Lord.

February 10
The time to repair the roof is when the sun is shining. (John F. Kennedy) (Practical, Preparation, pg. 194)

In-Flavor: If you want to repair the roof or do something, you need to prepare and do it when it is sunny and in good working condition. So, before doing anything, you should look ahead and prepare for it.

Inspiration Coffee: Wonder Counselor, I need to see the importance of preparation and learn to plan ahead for a project. Otherwise, I might repair the roof when it rains and end up ruining everything. Thank you, Lord.

Even when a marriage is made in heaven, the maintenance work has to be done here on earth. (Practical, Marriage, pg. 150)

Wi-Flavor: Marriage is a sacred bond that God has blessed on a couple. Still, if you want a marriage to last until death, you must do daily maintenance work on it and treat it with tender, loving care.

Wisdom Tea: Wisdom of God, my marriage might be a match made in Heaven. I still need your help and to carry on my daily maintenance work for it with tender, loving care. Thank you, Lord.

February 11

The secret to success is to be like a duck—smooth and unruffled on top, but paddling furiously underneath. (Practical, Success, pg. 212)

In-Flavor: If you want to succeed at something, you should work hard behind the scenes and not ruffle others. That way, you can get good support and a lot done. That is the key to your success.

Inspiration Coffee: Wonder Counselor, I need to be smooth and peaceful with everyone on the surface, while working furiously behind the scenes. That is how I can achieve great success. Thank you, Lord.

The future destiny of the child is always the work of the mother. (Napoleon Bonaparte) (Practical, Mother, pg. 165)

Wi-Flavor: The world might not see the important role of a mother in raising a successful, modeled child. But you must know that the future destiny of a child depends on the important work of the mother.

Wisdom Tea: Wisdom of God, I might not see the important role of the mother in the education and success of a child. But the future destiny of a child depends on the caring work of the mother. Thank you, Lord.

February 12

You can never make your dreams come true by oversleeping. (Practical, Work, pg. 247)

In-Flavor: Like most people, you want your dreams to come true and hopes to be fulfilled. But that takes lots of hard work and persistence. You cannot sleep through life and expect your dreams to come true.

Inspiration Coffee: Wonder Counselor, I cannot oversleep while expecting my dreams come true. Rather, I must toil day and night in spite of all of life's challenges. That is how I can make my hopes a reality. Thank you, Lord.

Life is fragile—handle with prayer. (Practical, Prayer, pg. 188)

Wi-Flavor: Life is sure fragile and full of uncertainties and difficulties. You must handle it with prayer and patience. Otherwise, it might cause you to get frustrated and discouraged when facing challenges.

Wisdom Tea: Wisdom of God, my life is fragile and uncertain. I have to face challenges every day and can feel overwhelmed at times. I need your help to learn to handle it with lots of prayers. Thank you, Lord.

February 13
There is no fire like passion, no shark like hatred, no snare like folly, and no torrent like greed. (*Dhammapada*) Quotations, Emotions, pg. 77)

In-Flavor: There are four tough emotions you need to conquer: passion, hatred, folly, and greed. They are like fire, shark, snare, and torrent, respectively. If you can do that, you will find peace and happiness.

Inspiration Coffee: Wonder Counselor, I need to keep an eye on these emotions: passion, hatred, folly, and greed. Otherwise, they might cause me great harm and destruction. Thank you, Lord.

The man of few words and settled mind is wise; therefore even a fool is thought to be wise when he is risen. It pays him to keep his mouth shut. (Proverbs 17:27–28) (Practical, Quietness, pg. 204)

Wi-Flavor: When people speak, they reveal what is in their heart, and others can see their faults. So, it is wise for you to have only a few words or speak less and keep a settled mind for future decisions.

Wisdom Tea: Wisdom of God, I need to keep quiet and speak less, for when I speak, I might say regrettable things and reveal everything in my heart. I should be wise and careful with my words. Thank you, Lord.

February 14
The best preacher is the heart; the best teacher, time; the best book, the world; the best friend, God. (Hebrew proverb) (Quotations, Ideals, pg. 135)

In-Flavor: What you just see above is the secret of life. If you listen to the heart, let time and the world teach you, and pick God to be your BFF, then you will have a satisfying and meaningful life.

Inspiration Coffee: Wonder Counselor, if I want to have a satisfying and meaningful life, I should listen to the heart, let time and the world educate me, and choose God to be my best friend forever. Thank you, Lord.

He who forgets the language of gratitude can never be on speaking terms with happiness. (Practical, Thankfulness, pg. 222)

Wi-Flavor: People who are grateful will always feel content with their lives and will not have to search constantly for something to make them happy. So, if you want happiness, begin to live in gratitude.

Wisdom Tea: Wisdom of God, help me learn to be grateful for your daily blessings in my life. When I know how to do that, I will stop desiring more things and begin to experience happiness. Thank you, Lord.

February 15

Crises and deadlocks, when they occur, have at least this advantage: that they force us to think. (Jawaharlal Nehru (1889–1964), first prime minister of India) (Quotations, Problems, pg. 217)

In-Flavor: You sure hate crises and problems, for they cause you to worry and feel uneasy. But they also make you think about certain issues and their solutions. You should view problems like that.

Inspiration Coffee: Wonder Counselor, I might not like crises and problems, for they often make me feel anxious and stressful. However, I should see them as opportunities to resolve certain issues. Thank you, Lord.

A hundred men may make an encampment, but it takes a woman to make a home. (Chinese proverb) (Practical, Woman/Wife, pg. 241)

Wi-Flavor: Men can brag about their ability to build huge castles and make a big camp, but you must remember that it takes a woman to turn a castle and a crowd into a home with her tender care.

Wisdom Tea: Wisdom of God, I might be able to make lots of wonderful things, like an encampment. But I need to realize that it takes a caring nature and the gentle touch of a woman to make a home. Thank you, Lord.

February 16

He who is kind and helpful to his neighbors, he will find that God will increase his wealth. (Fakhir al-Din al-Razi (1149-1209), Iranian Sunni Muslim philosopher) (Quotations, Wealth, pg. 303)

In-Flavor: Some people might hesitate to help their neighbors, but you are encouraged today to be kind and help out your neighbors, for God will repay you and increase your wealth a hundredfold.

Inspiration Coffee: Wonder Counselor, I might think it costs me too much to be kind and helpful to my neighbors. However, I need to know that God will repay me a lot more when I do that. Thank you, Lord.

Faith is the belief of the heart in that knowledge which comes from the Unseen. (Mohammad Ibn Khafif (882–982 AD), Arab Sufi poet) (Quotations, Faith, pg. 88)

Wi-Flavor: Most people find it difficult to comprehend the unseen and spiritual world, but if you have faith, your heart will help you see the unseen, hear the inaudible, and make the impossible happen.

Wisdom Tea: Wisdom of God, I might have a hard time understanding the unseen and spiritual world. However, my faith will open my heart to see the unseen, hear the inaudible, and witness the impossible. Thank you, Lord.

February 17

Children, you must remember something. A man without ambition is dead. A man with ambition but no love is dead. A man with ambition and love for his blessings here on earth is ever so alive. (Pearl Bailey, *Talking to Myself*, 1971) (Religious, Ambition, pg. 25)

In-Flavor: Pearl Bailey reminds you to have ambition and dreams. If you do not, or if you have ambition and no love, you will have no desire to live and end up dead. So, have ambition and love in order to stay alive.

Inspiration Coffee: Wonder Counselor, I need to have ambition to keep my desire and hope alive. I also should have love for someone or something to keep my heart beating for it. Otherwise, I will end up dead. Thank you, Lord.

Do not judge others. Be your own judge and you will be truly happy. If you will try to judge others, you are likely to burn your fingers. (Mahatma Gandhi) (Quotations, Judgment, pg. 145)

Wi-Flavor: People often do not hesitate to judge others and criticize things they do not like, but you are advised not to judge others, because your criticism might come back to haunt you.

Wisdom Tea: Wisdom of God, I should judge only myself if I want to be truly happy. I need to be careful about judging others, because my judgment and criticism might backfire on me. Thank you, Lord.

February 18

One thing have I asked of the Lord, that will I seek after; that I may dwell in the house of the Lord all the days of my life, to behold the beauty of the Lord, and to inquire in his temple. (Psalms 27:4) (Religious, Beauty, pg. 43)

In-Flavor: You may wish for lots of things, but one wish you should make is to be in the house of the Lord all the days of your life. That way, you may gaze on the beauty of the Lord and enjoy his company.

Inspiration Coffee: Wonder Counselor, if I am granted one wish, I should use it to ask the Lord to be in his house and enjoy his company all the days of my life. I should do everything I can to make that happen. Thank you, Lord.

Money kills more people than a club. (Igbo (West African proverb) (Quotations, Money, pg. 184)

Wi-Flavor: You might think people mainly use a club to hurt and kill one another. But the truth is that money is the cause of all the fights and conflicts around the world, and kills more people than a club.

Wisdom Tea: Wisdom of God, I might assume money does not kill people, only a club does. I should know that money is the root of all evils, including hurting others. I must not focus on money. Thank you, Lord.

February 19
There is no enlightenment outside of daily life. (Thich Nhat Hanh, *Zen Keys*, 1974) (Religious, Enlightenment, pg. 158)

In-Flavor: Enlightenment is a spiritual, revealing moment. You will get wonderful insights about this life and the next. But a Buddhist monk tells you today that moment cannot happen outside of daily life.

Inspiration Coffee: Wonder Counselor, I look forward to a moment of enlightenment to learn about this life or the next. But I am reminded that it can only happen in the context of my daily life. Thank you, Lord.

Violence never settles anything right: apart from injuring your own soul, it injures the best cause. It lingers on long after the object of hate has disappeared from the scene to plague the lives of those who have employed it against their foes. (Obafemi Awolowo (1909–1987), Nigerian politician) (Quotations, Violence, pg. 294)

Wi-Flavor: Violence has been the object of hate and employed over the years to threaten and intimidate. But you should know that violence only results in injuries and never settles anything.

Wisdom Tea: Wisdom of God, hate drives me to use violence and other evil ways to destroy my enemy. But violence does not settle anything; it only injures others. I must denounce violence and hate. Thank you, Lord.

February 20
God Himself does not speak prose, but communicates with us by hints, omens, inferences and dark resemblances in objects lying all around us. (Ralph Waldo Emerson, *Poetry and Imagination*, 1876) (Religious, Finding God, pg. 189)

In-Flavor: You feel blessed to be near God. But it is difficult to find and meet God every day. Today, you are reminded that God talks with you often by hints, omens, inferences, and other signs.

Inspiration Coffee: Wonder Counselor, God talks to me all day and all night. I might not know it, but God usually does it in hints, omens, inferences, and other signs around me. I must learn to interpret them. Thank you, Lord.

God changes not what is in people, until they change what is in themselves. (Qur'an, sura xiii: 10) (Quotations, Self-Reliance, pg. 258)

Wi-Flavor: Changes are difficult for people to make and accept in their lives, for they are used to the old habits. But if you want God to make some changes in your life, you need to initiate those yourself.

Wisdom Tea: Wisdom of God, I cannot expect God to change me if I do not desire it myself. I need to begin to change myself, and then God can help me finish the rest. Thank you, Lord.

February 21
The joy of a good man is the witness of a good conscience; have a good conscience and thou shalt ever have gladness. (Thomas à Kempis, *Imitation of Christ*, 1441) (Religious, Joy, pg. 276)

In-Flavor: You can experience joy in various ways, but the best way for you to have that experience is to form and maintain a good conscience, for it will free you from all the worries of this life and the next.

Inspiration Coffee: Wonder Counselor, I might search for joy in a lot of places, except my conscience. I need a good conscience to bring me gladness, for it will free me from anxieties about this life and the next. Thank you, Lord.

And Jesus said to them, "... Whoever would be great among you must be your servant, and whoever would be first among you must be slave of all." (Mark 10:42–44) (Religious, Authority, pg. 41)

Wi-Flavor: Humans exercise authority and rule over one another with power and command. But Jesus asks you to be a servant if you want to be great, and the slave of all if you want to be first, as his disciples.

Wisdom Tea: Wisdom of God, I might want to be first or the greatest to exercise authority over others. But I am reminded to be the slave and the servant of all if I want Jesus to consider me the first. Thank you, Lord.

February 22
Love never ends; as for prophesies, they will pass away; as for tongues, they will cease; as for knowledge, it will pass away. (1 Corinthians 13:8) (Religious, Love, pg. 307)

In-Flavor: You might be excited about prophesies, tongues, and knowledge for various reasons. But they will end or pass away. If you choose love and promote it, it will produce great results and never end.

Inspiration Coffee: Wonder Counselor, the gifts of prophecy, tongues, and knowledge are glamorous, but they will all end. I need to focus on the gift of love because it brings about lasting results and never ends. Thank you, Lord.

While we inherit our temperament, we must build our character. (William L. Sullivan, *Worry! Fear! Loneliness!*, 1950) (Religious, Character, pg. 69)

Wi-Flavor: God has created you and blessed you with your temperament at birth. But you can build your character and determine how you would turn out to be by the way you live and treat others.

Wisdom Tea: Wisdom of God, I thank you for giving me my temperament at my birth. However, I can build my unique character by the way I live my life and treat others. Thank you, Lord.

February 23

A hero gives the illusion of surpassing humanity. The saint doesn't surpass it, he assumes it and strives to realize it in the best possible way. (Georges Bernanos, *The Last Essays of Georges Bernanos*, 1955) (Religious, Saints and Sinners, pg. 499)

In-Flavor: Society might make the image of a hero glamorous, but you should focus on the image of sainthood and look up to it because it embraces the whole of humanity and strives to make it better.

Inspiration Coffee: Wonder Counselor, society might want me to be some kind of hero, but I need to look up to the image of sainthood instead, for it embraces the whole of humanity and strives to make it better. Thank you, Lord.

We cannot go to Heaven on beds of down. (Richard Braithwaite, *The English Gentleman*, 1631) (Religious, Comfort, pg. 87)

Wi-Flavor: The right and best way to Heaven requires lots of self-sacrifice and charity work from you. You cannot rest comfortably on the beds of down and expect them to take you there.

Wisdom Tea: Wisdom of God, I certainly want to get to Heaven. But I cannot get there by resting comfortably on the beds of down. I must make lots of sacrifices and do charity work. Thank you, Lord.

February 24

Vision looks inward and becomes duty. Vision looks outward and becomes aspiration. Vision looks upward and becomes faith. (Stephen S. Wise (1847–1949), *Sermons and Addresses*) (Religious, Vision, pg. 597)

In-Flavor: Vision can be inward, outward, and upward. You should have all three visions to guide you every day. That way, you may have a sense of duty, aspiration, and faith to move ahead.

Inspiration Coffee: Wonder Counselor, I must have vision to guide me each day. The three visions of inward, outward, and upward will give me a sense of duty, aspiration, and faith to advance me toward you. Thank you, Lord.

Selfishness is the deepest root of all unhappiness. ... It feeds an insatiable hunger that first eats up everything belonging to others and then causes a creature to devour itself. (Dom Hélder Pessoa Câmara) (Religious, Envy and Jealousy, pg. 158)

Wi-Flavor: Selfishness causes a person to take everything belonging to others and then devour oneself. If you suffer from this problem, it is the deepest root of all unhappiness, and you will never be satisfied.

Wisdom Tea: Wisdom of God, selfishness is the root of envy or jealousy and all unhappiness, for it drives me to take everything belonging to others and then devour myself. I must get rid of selfishness. Thank you, Lord.

February 25

What does man gain by all the toil at which he toils under the sun? A generation goes, and a generation comes, but the earth remains forever. (Ecclesiastes 1:3–4) (Religious, Work, pg. 621)

In-Flavor: You might have ambition and toil every day to achieve it. You need to pause and wonder about the purpose of your work. That way, you might know why you work and find joy in it.

Inspiration Coffee: Wonder Counselor, I must know the purpose for my life and work. That is how I can find joy and blessing for my success. Otherwise, my work will be meaningless. Thank you, Lord.

Human beings judge one another by their external actions. God judges them by their moral choices. (C.S. Lewis, *Christian Behavior*, 1943) (Religious, Judgment, pg. 282)

Wi-Flavor: People judge one another by what they see and criticize certain actions they do not like. But you should know that God judges the world by its moral choices and rewards it for its correct ones.

Wisdom Tea: Wisdom of God, I might judge others by their external actions, but God judges them by their moral choices and rewards them for the right ones. I need to have a good moral life. Thank you, Lord.

February 26

Courage is the ability to "hang in there" five minutes longer. (Wise, Courage, pg. 31)

In-Flavor: People often hesitate to do something different and do not have the patience to wait for something spectacular. You need to have courage to succeed and survive in this challenging world.

Inspiration Coffee: Wonder Counselor, I might not want to stick around a little longer for something wonderful to happen. But I need to have courage to do that and succeed in this challenging world. Thank you, Lord.

Hate is still the main enemy of the human race, the fuel that heats the furnaces of genocide. (I. F. Stone, "When a Two-Party System Becomes a One-Party Rubber Stamp," *in I.F. Stone's Weekly*, September 9, 1968) (Religious, Hatred, pg. 224)

Wi-Flavor: Hate has been the worst enemy of the human race and a dark power that kills lots of people. You need to know how to contain it and hopefully eliminate it for the sake of human survival.

Wisdom Tea: Wisdom of God, hate has been the archenemy of the human race and a powerful fuel that burns away thousands of innocent lives. I need to get rid of it for the sake of human survival. Thank you, Lord.

February 27
A real leader faces the music even when he doesn't like the tune. (Arnold Glasow) (Wise, Leadership, pg. 81)

In-Flavor: You might hear all sorts of tunes every day, from disappointment and frustration to sadness and discouragement. But if you want to be a leader, you must face that reality and work through it.

Inspiration Coffee: Wonder Counselor, I might not like the tunes of my daily life, as I have to deal with disappointments and frustrations. But I need to act as a leader and courageously face that reality. Thank you, Lord.

When in prayer you clasp your hands, God opens his. (German proverb) (Religious, Prayer, pg. 414)

Wi-Flavor: Some people might face problems, but do not like to ask for help. As a believer, you fold your hands before God in prayer to ask for something, and God will open his to pour his blessings on you.

Wisdom Tea: Wisdom of God, when I have a problem, I need to come to you and ask for help. As I clasp my hands together in prayer, you will open yours to outpour your blessings on me. Thank you, Lord.

February 28
Success often comes from taking a misstep in the right direction. (Wise, Success, pg. 127)

In-Flavor: Some might think achievement does not come by accident, but it happens more often than you might think. So, keep yourself in the right direction, and success is just one misstep away for you.

Inspiration Coffee: Wonder Counselor, I might think success does not come by accident, but that does happen a lot. All I have to do is keep myself in the right direction, and success is just one misstep away. Thank you, Lord.

Where there's no shame before men, there's no fear of God. (Yiddish proverb) (Religious, Shame, pg. 516)

Wi-Flavor: Shame serves as a deterrence to keep people from making bad decisions and hurting others. But you might realize that when people feel no shame before others, they will have no fear of God.

Wisdom Tea: Wisdom of God, I need to know shame and embarrassment to keep myself from making bad decisions and hurting others. If I do not, I will also have no fear of God. Thank you, Lord.

February 29

We are not here to see through one another, but to see one another through. (Wit, Spring & Summer)

In-Flavor: People might have various dreams and not hesitate to walk through one another to get them. But you must help them realize that we are here on earth to see one another through.

Inspiration Coffee: Wonder Counselor, I have lots of dreams and desires. But I must not walk through others to grab them or make them come true. Rather, I must learn to see others through and help them. Thank you, Lord.

There is one thing worse than a fool, and that is a man who is conceited. (Proverbs 26:12) (Practical, Conceit, pg. 35)

Wi-Flavor: A fool has little wisdom and common sense, while a con-ceited person has an exaggerated and high opinion of himself. You should avoid them both because you will end up hurting yourself.

Wisdom Tea: Wisdom of God, I need your help to avoid acting like a fool and following foolish ways. I also ask you to keep me from being conceited and arrogant, for both attitudes will end up hurting me. Thank you, Lord.

MARCH

March 1
He who wants to make a place in the sun should expect blisters. (Practical, Achievement, pg. 2)

In-Flavor: All achievements require hard work and lots of sacrifices. If you want to have any achievements, you should expect the same thing—and a few blisters on your hands or feet.

Inspiration Coffee: Wonder Counselor, I want to achieve great success and make a place for myself in the sun. But that can only happen if I work hard and expect some blisters on my body. Thank you, Lord.

A friend is a person who knows all about you and still loves you just the same. (Practical, Friendship, pg. 84)

Wi-Flavor: People look for friendship to bring them companionship, share some fun interests, and so on. But if you find a true friend, that person will support and stand by you after knowing all about you.

Wisdom Tea: Wisdom of God, I might want a friendship to keep me company or share some fun interests. But if I find a true friend, that person will still love and support me after knowing all about me. Thank you, Lord.

March 2
Ability will enable a man to get to the top, but it takes character to keep him there. (Practical, Character, pg. 29)

In-Flavor: You might need special abilities or great skills to get to the top, but if you want to stay there for a while, you must have fine character and good personality to deal with the public.

Inspiration Coffee: Wonder Counselor, I might need special abilities to get to the top and achieve great success. But it takes my fine character and good personality to keep me there. I can do it with your help. Thank you, Lord.

A wise man learns by the experiences of others. An ordinary man learns by his own experience. A fool learns by nobody's experience. (Practical, Experience, pg. 65)

Wi-Flavor: Experience is valuable life knowledge that helps a person deal with daily challenges and succeed. If you are a wise person, you will learn from your own experiences and also the ones of others.

Wisdom Tea: Wisdom of God, help me use my experiences to deal with my daily challenges and succeed. A wise person does it by experiences of others, while a fool uses nobody's experience. Thank you, Lord.

March 3

It doesn't take such a great man to be a Christian; it just takes all there is of him. (Seth Wilson) (Practical, Commitment to God, pg. 34)

In-Flavor: Anyone can be a Christian by fulfilling certain requirements. However, if you choose the Christian way of life, it will demand your whole being and commitment to follow through with it.

Inspiration Coffee: Wonder Counselor, a Christian has to fulfill certain requirements and obey some rules. However, if I really choose the Christian way of life, I have to commit my whole being to it. Thank you, Lord.

A good deal of trouble has been caused in the world by too much intelligence and too little wisdom. (Practical, Intelligence, pg. 119)

Wi-Flavor: Humans have advanced their living standard with the help of intelligence. But you might know that many problems like social justice and politics remain the same, due to lack of wisdom.

Wisdom Tea: Wisdom of God, human intelligence has advanced society and increased living standards. Unfortunately, I have seen very little wisdom to guide this world and resolve many impending problems. Thank you, Lord.

March 4

Most men fail, not through lack of education, but from lack of dogged determination and dauntless will. (Charles Swindoll) (Practical, Discouragement, pg. 56)

In-Flavor: You might have the skills and education to achieve certain dreams. But if you do not have the dogged determination and dauntless will, you might face challenges and fail.

Inspiration Coffee: Wonder Counselor, I might have enough education and great skills to accomplish certain dreams. But if I do not have dogged determination and dauntless will, I may be discouraged and fail. Thank you, Lord.

The good man finds life; the evil man, death. (Proverbs 11:19) (Practical, Life and Death, pg. 141)

Wi-Flavor: It is not easy to tell if a person is good or evil by their appearance. If you want to know about that, you need to examine one's heart and see that the good man finds life, and the evil man, death.

Wisdom Tea: Wisdom of God, I cannot tell if a person is good or evil by their appearance. However, I can figure it out by examining one's heart and seeing that the good man finds life, and the evil man, death. Thank you, Lord.

March 5

Don't be afraid to take a big step if it's required. You can't cross a chasm in two small jumps.
(Practical, Fear, pg. 77)

In-Flavor: Life is full of chasms and valleys. You cannot cross one of those in small jumps. If you want to cross a chasm, you might need to have faith and take a big leap to make it to the other side.

Inspiration Coffee: Wonder Counselor, I might be afraid of taking a big step to go through life. But I must learn to take a big leap of faith to cross a chasm and make it to the other side. Thank you, Lord.

Virtues are learned at Mother's knee—vices at some other joint.
(Practical, Mother, pg. 165)

Wi-Flavor: A mother usually teaches her children to be good and passes on to them many lessons of virtues. So, you have to conclude that they must pick up vices and learn bad things from other places.

Wisdom Tea: Wisdom of God, I must have learned good values and wonderful lessons of virtues at my mother's knees. However, I could have picked up vices and learned bad things at other places. Thank you, Lord.

March 6

A good way to forget your troubles is to help others out of theirs.
(Practical, Help, pg. 106)

In-Flavor: You certainly are not free of life's troubles. You can try to wish them away or forget about them, but a good way for you to deal with them is to reach out and help others with theirs.

Inspiration Coffee: Wonder Counselor, my life is certainly not free of troubles. I cannot wish them away or ignore them. However, I can try to deal with my troubles by helping out others. Thank you, Lord.

Who goes to bed and does not pray, makes two nights to every day. (George Herbert) (Practical, Prayer, pg. 189)

Wi-Flavor: Many people do not pray regularly, but only do it when they need help with something. So, if you do not pray before sleep for safety or thanksgiving, you will get restless and make the night long.

Wisdom Tea: Wisdom of God, I might not be devout with my prayer life. Perhaps I only pray when I want to ask God for something. But if I do not pray before sleep, I will make the night really long. Thank you, Lord.

March 7

Kindness is something you can't give away, since it always comes back. (Practical, Kindness, pg. 127)

<u>In-Flavor</u>: You are encouraged to be kind and generous to others. What you do not know is that you do not give anything away. All your kind and generous acts will always come back to you a hundredfold.

<u>**Inspiration Coffee**</u>: Wonder Counselor, I am encouraged to be kind and generous to others. However, I cannot give away kindness, for it always comes back to me a hundredfold. Thank you, Lord.

Conversation enriches the understanding, but solitude is the school of genius. (Edward Gibbon) (Practical, Quietness, pg. 205)

<u>Wi-Flavor</u>: Most people have to converse with someone to share ideas and seek understanding every day. However, you can be a genius by remaining in solitude and coming up with great insights.

<u>**Wisdom Tea**</u>: Wisdom of God, I might use conversations to exchange ideas and seek understanding. However, I do not realize that a genius remains in solitude and comes up with great insights. Thank you, Lord.

March 8

He who is not afraid to face the music may sometime lead the band. (Practical, Leadership, pg. 138)

<u>In-Flavor</u>: You might have all kinds of fears and problems, and hope that they will disappear. But if you want to lead something in life, you must face your fear of it and resolve that problem.

<u>**Inspiration Coffee**</u>: Wonder Counselor, I might have fears and anxieties about some issues and wish they would vanish. But I need to confront those fears and resolve them if I want to be a leader in the future. Thank you, Lord.

Happiness comes when we stop wailing about the troubles we have, and offer thanks for all the troubles we don't have. (Practical, Thankfulness, pg. 222)

<u>Wi-Flavor</u>: People have searched for happiness since their first moment in the Garden of Eden. However, you should know that the secret to happiness is to have an optimistic and thankful attitude.

<u>**Wisdom Tea**</u>: Wisdom of God, I may have looked for happiness in the wrong places and wished to have it. I should know that the secret to happiness is to have a thankful and hopeful attitude. Thank you, Lord.

March 9
A mistake proves that someone at least tried. (Practical, Mistakes, pg. 156)

In-Flavor: You might be afraid of making a mistake because you feel ashamed and hate to see your fault. But you should keep working hard and learning from your mistakes because it shows you are trying.

Inspiration Coffee: Wonder Counselor, I might not like to make mistakes because they show my weaknesses and hurt my pride. But I should embrace them as a learning experience to help me become wise. Thank you, Lord.

When God wills that an event will occur, He sets the causes that will lead to it. (Babikir Badri (1861–1954), Sudanese scholar, *Memoirs*) (Quotations, Fate, pg. 91)

Wi-Flavor: Some believe in fate or destiny, but it is hard to tell in this challenging and confusing world. As a believer, you should know that God sets causes, leading to an event, if he wills it to happen.

Wisdom Tea: Wisdom of God, I might or might not believe in fate in this uncertain world. However, as a believer, my faith tells me that if God wills an event to happen, he sets causes, leading to it. Thank you, Lord.

March 10
Optimism is a cheerful frame of mind that enables a teakettle to sing though in hot water up to its neck. (Practical, Optimism/Pessimism, pg. 178)

In-Flavor: Your life might be full of troubles, but if you have an optimistic attitude, you will be able to handle any situation with high hopes and a cheerful spirit, no matter how tough it might be.

Inspiration Coffee: Wonder Counselor, I might not see how valuable it is to have an optimistic attitude. But if I do, I will be able to deal with any challenging situation with high hopes and a cheerful spirit. Thank you, Lord.

A gentle answer turns away wrath, but harsh words cause quarrels. (Proverbs 15:1) (Practical, Words, pg. 244)

Wi-Flavor: Words are powerful, and yet most people are not careful in using them in their daily talks. You must know that a gentle answer can turn away wrath, while harsh words might cause quarrels.

Wisdom Tea: Wisdom of God, I may not realize that words are powerful and consequential. If I am not careful about them, my harsh words might cause quarrels. But a gentle answer can quiet wrath. Thank you, Lord.

March 11
By perseverance, the snail reached the ark. (Charles Spurgeon) (Practical, Persistence, pg. 184)

In-Flavor: The snail that wants to get to the ark has to persevere through a rough road. Likewise, if you want to get someplace in life, you must persevere and never let anything keep you from doing it.

Inspiration Coffee: Wonder Counselor, I may not realize that a snail can teach me a great life lesson. If it can reach the ark by persistence, I must follow its example and persevere to get to my mountaintop. Thank you, Lord.

The wise man will not look for the faults of others, nor for what they have done or left undone, but will look rather to his own misdeed. (*Dhammapada*, "Flowers") (Quotations, Fault, pg. 93)

Wi-Flavor: People like to find a scapegoat and blame others when something goes wrong. But if you are a wise person, you would rather look to your own misdeeds, instead of searching for others' faults.

Wisdom Tea: Wisdom of God, I might like to point out the faults of others or blame people when something is wrong. I need to be wise and, rather, look into my own misdeeds to fix them. Thank you, Lord.

March 12
Today's preparation determines tomorrow's achievement. (Practical, Preparation, pg. 194)

In-Flavor: All successful projects need good preparation and hard work. If you want to have lots of achievements in the future, you need to sow their seeds and begin to prepare for them today.

Inspiration Coffee: Wonder Counselor, I might not enjoy preparation work or patiently wait for any future success. However, I need to prepare well today for all my future achievements. Thank you, Lord.

The great man is one who never loses his child's heart. (Mencius (390–305 BC), Chinese philosopher, *Meng-tzu*) (Quotations, Greatness, pg. 118)

Wi-Flavor: A child's heart allows a person to think creatively, speak freely, and dream uninhibitedly. If you want to be a great man, you must always have a child's heart and do everything in that spirit.

Wisdom Tea: Wisdom of God, I might think I will become great by doing everything in the rigid and boring way of an adult's world. But, actually, I can be a great person by continuing to have a child's heart. Thank you, Lord.

March 13

I have learned that success is to be measured not so much by the position one has reached in life as by the obstacles he has overcome while trying to succeed.

(Booker T. Washington (1856–1915), American educator, *Up from Slavery*) (Practical, Success, pg. 212)

In-Flavor: You should not measure success by the positions you have. Rather, you should view it by the obstacles you have overcome, because they have taught you many wonderful life lessons.

Inspiration Coffee: Wonder Counselor, I should not measure my success by all the positions I might have reached in life. Rather, I should look back on all the obstacles I had to overcome to achieve it. Thank you, Lord.

Do not judge your fellowmen until you have stood in his place. (Talmud, Hillel) (Quotations, Judgment, pg. 145)

Wi-Flavor: People like to judge others and are not afraid to give negative comments on things they hate. However, today you are asked to put yourself in someone's place before judging him/her.

Wisdom Tea: Wisdom of God, I might enjoy giving negative comments on something I do not like or cast judgments on others. I need to put myself in his/her place before judging someone. Thank you, Lord.

March 14

If you want to work for God, form a committee. If you want to work with God, form a prayer group. (Practical, Work, pg. 248)

In-Flavor: Working for God means you simply take an order and carry it out. Hence, a committee is good for it. But working *with* God means you listen and let God guide you. Hence, a prayer group suits for it.

Inspiration Coffee: Wonder Counselor, I could form a committee and carry out your orders if I like to work for you. But I could create a prayer group and let you guide me if I want to work *with* you. Thank you, Lord.

To lose patience is to lose the battle. (Mahatma Gandhi) (Quotations, Patience, pg. 199)

Wi-Flavor: Life is full of hurdles and problems. You have to fight and get over those hurdles every day. However, in those fights you must not lose patience. Otherwise, you will lose the whole battle.

Wisdom Tea: Wisdom of God, I have to struggle with lots of problems and overcome all sorts of hurdles every day. However, in those fights I must not lose patience or risk losing the whole battle. Thank you, Lord.

March 15

If your enemy is hungry, give him bread to eat; and if thirsty, give him water to drink. Even if he came to kill you, give him food if he is hungry or water if he is thirsty. (Talmud, Midrash Mishle 27) (Quotations, Enemies, pg. 79)

In-Flavor: Your enemy is the last person you think about. But today, you are asked to treat your enemy compassionately and feed or quench him if he is hungry or thirsty. That is divine forgiveness.

Inspiration Coffee: Wonder Counselor, I might not hold my enemies in high regard. However, I am called to treat them with compassion like my God and give them food and drink if they are hungry and thirsty. Thank you, Lord.

Silence is a fence around wisdom.

(Hebrew proverb) (Quotations, Silence, pg. 260)

Wi-Flavor: People like to be around wisdom, but find it difficult to remain in silence. You should know that only in silence will you be able to search for good insights that will lead to wisdom.

Wisdom Tea: Wisdom of God, I might find it difficult to keep silence, but it will help me find many good insights and not say foolish things. I must know that silence gives good protection around wisdom. Thank you, Lord.

March 16

A ship with two captains sinks.

(Egyptian proverb) (Quotations, Leadership and Leaders, pg. 155)

In-Flavor: A ship heads in one direction at a time, and hence, it can take orders from only one captain. Likewise, you have to make a tough decision for your life and cannot leave it for someone else.

Inspiration Coffee: Wonder Counselor, like a ship that cannot have two captains, I have to be the only captain of my life and make all the tough decisions that affect me and everyone around me. Thank you, Lord.

Five things constitute perfect virtue: gravity, magnanimity, earnestness, sincerity, kindness.

(Confucius, *Analects*) (Quotations, Virtue, pg. 295)

Wi-Flavor: Everyone is encouraged to live a virtuous life and search for new virtues to imitate. If you have not followed a virtuous life yet, the five virtues above are a good beginning.

Wisdom Tea: Wisdom of God, I have been encouraged to take up a life of virtues that will bring me true peace and happiness. I can begin that way of life by following the five things above. Thank you, Lord.

March 17

Creation was not finished at the dawn of this earth, but creation continues, and we have a lot to do to make the world a better place. (George Cadle Price (1919–2011), Belizean politician) (Quotations, Progress, pg. 217)

In-Flavor: God's creation was not done on the sixth day. You are called to continue God's work and make the world a better place. You should take pride in your contribution and do something good.

Inspiration Coffee: Wonder Counselor, I always want to create something and make the world a better place. Now I can do that by continuing the creation and work that God has left behind for me. Thank you, Lord.

Charity knows no race, no creed. (Talmud) (Religious, Charity, pg. 72)

Wi-Flavor: Some religions or past traditions teach people to practice charity only to their own religious group or race. But you are reminded that charity is not bound to a specific race or religious group.

Wisdom Tea: Wisdom of God, some past traditions or beliefs may tell me to be charitable only to my own race or religion. However, I must remember that charity is not limited to certain a race or belief. Thank you, Lord.

March 18

The general of a large army may be defeated, but you cannot defeat the determined mind of a peasant. (Confucius, *Analects*) (Quotations, Will, pg. 304)

In-Flavor: It takes a good plan to defeat a general and his army, but a lot more to win over a determined peasant. So, if you want to succeed, you must have the will of a peasant and stick with your dream.

Inspiration Coffee: Wonder Counselor, I may defeat a general of a large army by having a great plan. However, it sure takes me a lot more to conquer a determined peasant and lead me to great success. Thank you, Lord.

Four things support the world: the learning of the wise, the justice of the great, the prayers of the good, and the valor of the brave. (Muhammad) (Quotations, The World, pg. 314)

Wi-Flavor: God created the world, but humans are assigned to look after it. You need to remember the four things above to keep the world turning every day—namely, knowledge, justice, prayers, and valor.

Wisdom Tea: Wisdom of God, I join with the whole human family in pledging myself to take care of your creation. But I must know that the four things above have supported and kept it turning every day. Thank you, Lord.

March 19
Set your minds on things that are above, not on things that are on earth. (Colossians 3:2) (Religious, Ambition, pg. 26)

In-Flavor: Everything on earth is corruptible and will not last. On the other hand, heavenly things are much desirable and long-lasting. Therefore, you should aim your life on heavenly things.

Inspiration Coffee: Wonder Counselor, I might not know that everything on earth is fragile and not lasting. However, I must set my mind on things above and realize that heavenly things are long-lasting. Thank you, Lord.

Compassion is the chief law of human existence. (Fyodor Dostoyevsky, *The Idiot*, 1869) (Religious, Compassion, pg. 91)

Wi-Flavor: Human society has come up with so many laws to maintain its existence that they have filled hundreds of buildings. You should remember the most important and chief law of all is compassion.

Wisdom Tea: Wisdom of God, I may consider certain sets of rules or religious beliefs to be important in human society. However, help me to see that the chief law of human existence is compassion. Thank you, Lord.

March 20
Conscience is the voice of values long and deeply infused into one's sinew and blood. (Elliot L. Richardson, in *Life* magazine, 1973) (Religious, Conformity, pg. 104)

In-Flavor: Conscience is the inner voice and the moral compass that the Creator has imbedded in all human beings. You should pay attention to it in your daily life, especially in decision time.

Inspiration Coffee: Wonder Counselor, I may take for granted or ignore my conscience, which has been infused into my sinew and blood. I need to listen to this voice of values for guidance and right decisions. Thank you, Lord.

The devil has power to suggest evil, but he was not given the power to compel you against your will. (St. Cyril of Jerusalem, *Catechetical Lectures*) (Religious, Devil, pg. 136)

Wi-Flavor: Temptations are all around you, and the devil never stops suggesting them to you. But they do not have control over your will or make you accept them. You can decide to listen to them or not.

Wisdom Tea: Wisdom of God, help me realize that the devil is real and relentlessly tempts me to do evil things every day. However, he does not have any power to force me to do anything against my will. Thank you, Lord.

March 21

As long as we honestly wish to arrive at truth, we need not fear that we shall be punished for unintentional error. (John Lubbock, *The Pleasures of Life*, 1887) (Religious, Error, pg. 162)

In-Flavor: The road to the truth is full of potholes and errors. You should not let those deter you from searching for the truth. Indeed, the cost for the errors is worth the taste of the truth.

Inspiration Coffee: Wonder Counselor, I may be ashamed of making errors and fearful of the punishment for them. However, I must have courage and keep moving forward to search for the truth. Thank you, Lord.

You shall not covet your neighbor's house; you shall not covet your neighbor's wife, or his manservant, or his maidservant, or his ox, or his ass, or anything that is your neighbor's. (Exodus 20:17) (Religious, Envy and Jealousy, pg. 159)

Wi-Flavor: Envy and jealousy is one of the deadly sins that can totally destroy your relationship with God and your neighbors. When you covet your neighbor's house, it will lead you to lots of evil things.

Wisdom Tea: Wisdom of God, I might downplay the destructive power of envy and jealousy. Open my eyes to see what it can do to my relationship with God and my neighbors if I covet my neighbors. Thank you, Lord.

March 22

The place where man vitally finds God ... is within his own experience of goodness, truth, and beauty, and the truest images of God are therefore to be found in man's spiritual life. (Harry Emerson Fosdick, Adventurous Religion, 1926) (Religious, Finding God, pg. 189)

In-Flavor: You can meet God in a worshipping place or your spiritual life. But the best way for you to have an encounter with God is your experience of goodness, truth, and beauty.

Inspiration Coffee: Wonder Counselor, I am excited to meet God, and the usual place for that to happen is my spiritual life. However, the best way for me find God is my experience of goodness, truth, and beauty. Thank you, Lord.

Faith faces everything that makes the world uncomfortable — pain, fear, loneliness, shame, death — and acts with a compassion by which these things are transformed, even exalted. (Samuel H. Miller, in Look, December 19, 1961) (Religious, Faith, pg. 181)

Wi-Flavor: The world hates to deal with pain, fear, loneliness, shame, and death. But you can help it use faith to face them and act with compassion to transform them to a divine experience.

Wisdom Tea: Wisdom of God, I may not like to deal with pain, fear, loneliness, shame, and death. However, I may rely on faith to face them and act with compassion to transform them to a divine encounter. Thank you, Lord.

March 23

No man truly has joy unless he lives in love. (St. Thomas Aquinas (1225–74), *Summa Theologica*) (Religious, Joy, pg. 276)

In-Flavor: If you have ever been in love, you would know that your heart is always full of joy and nothing else matters to you. So, if you truly want to know a life of joy, then try to live a life of love.

Inspiration Coffee: Wonder Counselor, I may wish to have constant joy in my life but not know where to find it, or look for it in wrong places. I must know that the best way to find lasting joy is to live a life of love. Thank you, Lord.

Money is a good servant but a bad master. (Proverb) (Religious, Money, pg. 338)

Wi-Flavor: People have treated money as a good servant and directed it to serve their needs. However, if you mistakenly make it your master, it will control your life and make you miserable.

Wisdom Tea: Wisdom of God, the world might convince me that money is everything in this life. However, if I make the mistake of turning it into my master, it would make my life sad and miserable. Thank you, Lord.

March 24

Many waters cannot quench love, neither can floods drown it. (Song of Solomon 8:7) (Religious, Love, pg. 307)

In-Flavor: You could aim for many gifts and virtues like knowledge, prophecies, faith, hope, patience, persistence, and so on. But you should desire love because it can endure time and any challenge.

Inspiration Coffee: Wonder Counselor, I may desire and look for virtues like knowledge, prophecies, faith, hope, patience, or persistence. However, I should embrace love which can endure time and challenges. Thank you, Lord.

At the day of judgment it shall not be asked of us what we have read, but what we have done; not how well we have said, but how religiously we have lived. (Thomas à Kempis, *Imitation of Christ*) (Religious, Judgment, pg. 283)

Wi-Flavor: Many people do not think about Judgment Day and prepare for it. But as a believer, you should be ready for it and know that God will ask what you did and how you lived your life.

Wisdom Tea: Wisdom of God, help me to be wise and learn to prepare for Judgment Day while I still can, for you will inquire what I did and how I lived my life, not what I read or how well I spoke. Thank you, Lord.

March 25

The saint ... wants himself to be simply a window through which God's mercy shines on the world. And for this he strives to be holy ... in order that the goodness of God may never be obscured by any selfish act of his. (Thomas Merton, *Life and Holiness*, 1963) (Religious, Saints and Sinners, pg. 500)

In-Flavor: The saints are human and full of sins. But they strive to be holy and become a window for God's mercy to shine onto the world. You should hope to become a saint for that simple reason.

Inspiration Coffee: Wonder Counselor, I should know that the saints might have their own faults, but strive to be holy and become windows for God's mercy to shine onto the world. I must desire to be a saint. Thank you, Lord.

Peacemaking is not an optional commitment. It is a requirement of our faith. ("The Challenge of Peace, God's Promise and Our Response," Bishops' Pastoral Letter, 1983) (Religious, Peace, pg. 383)

Wi-Flavor: War has been a part of human history since the fight and murder of Abel by Cain. If you believe in God, you are required to seek peace and commit to that solution to end all wars.

Wisdom Tea: Wisdom of God, I know that war and fighting have been a part of human history. Help me commit myself as a Christian to search for peace and reconciliation to end all wars. Thank you, Lord.

March 26

There is a feeling of Eternity in Youth, which makes us amend for everything. To be young is to be as one of the immortal gods. (William Hazlitt, "On the Feeling of Immortality in Youth," 1807) (Religious, Youth, pg. 639)

In-Flavor: A youth feels invincible, like an immortal god, and thinks he/she will last forever, despite making many mistakes. You might want to tap into the fountain of youth when feeling discouraged.

Inspiration Coffee: Wonder Counselor, I may not see that a youth feels invincible like an immortal god in spite of making many mistakes. I will come to the fountain of youth when feeling discouraged. Thank you, Lord.

The act of praying centers attention on the higher emotion, unifies the spirit, crystalizes emotions, clarifies the judgments, releases latent powers, reinforces confidence that what needs to be done can be done. (Georgia Harkness, *Prayer and the Common Life*, 1948) (Religious, Prayer, pg. 415)

Wi-Flavor: Prayer can do a lot of things for a person, such as giving peace and comfort, showing guidance, and so on. In case you want to know more about prayer, the list above tells you about it.

Wisdom Tea: Wisdom of God, I often pray to ask for something or to seek guidance and peace in decision time. I need to maximize the power of prayer, and the list above shares with me a lot more about it. Thank you, Lord.

March 27

A man should give a lot of thought before making a sudden decision. (Wise, Decisiveness, pg. 37)

In-Flavor: You make many decisions every day. A hasty decision will result in all kinds of future problems. So, you should take time to consider all the facts and see all the angles before making a decision.

Inspiration Coffee: Wonder Counselor, I might rush and make hasty decisions without considering their consequences. I need to take time for deliberation and consider all the facts before making a decision. Thank you, Lord.

How can you expect God to speak in that gentle and inward voice which melts the soul when you are making so much noise with your rapid reflections? Be silent and God will speak again. (Francois Fenelon, (1651–1715), *Spiritual Letters*, no. XXII) (Religious, Silence, pg. 517)

Wi-Flavor: The Bible tells you that God was found in a whispering wind. The only way for you to hear the soft and gentle voice of God is to force yourself to be silent and stop making so much noise.

Wisdom Tea: Wisdom of God, I want to hear your gentle and sweet voice speaking to me every day. The best way for that to happen is for me to be silent and stop making so much noise in my daily life. Thank you, Lord.

March 28

A man who refuses to admit his mistakes can never be successful. But if he confesses and forsakes them, he gets another chance. (Proverbs 28:13) (Wise, Mistakes, pg. 86)

In-Flavor: It takes humility and courage to learn from mistakes and try again. So, if you want a second chance and to be successful, you must be humble, admit your mistakes, and learn from them.

Inspiration Coffee: Wonder Counselor, I may find it difficult to admit my mistakes. But if I do so with courage and humility, I will have another chance and be able to achieve future success. Thank you, Lord.

What we weave on earth, we'll wear in heaven. (Practical, Action, pg. 5)

Wi-Flavor: People often do not care about their actions on earth and cannot see the connection between earth and Heaven. But truthfully, what you make on earth will be with you in Heaven.

Wisdom Tea: Wisdom of God, I might not pay attention to my actions on earth or see their connection to my life in Heaven. However, I'm reminded that what I do on earth is what I will wear in heaven. Thank you, Lord.

March 29

Cooperation determines the rate of progress. (Wise, Teamwork, pg. 133)

In-Flavor: Nothing happens when people argue and fight over a task, or simply ignore it. So, if you want to make progress on something, you must get everyone to value teamwork and cooperate.

Inspiration Coffee: Wonder Counselor, I like to make good progress on my work and hopefully achieve great success. But that will happen only if I can convince everyone to cooperate and value teamwork. Thank you, Lord.

He who looks down on his neighbors is usually living on a bluff. (Practical, Arrogance, pg. 15)

Wi-Flavor: People who look down on their neighbors usually assume they are superior. So, if you are arrogant, you usually live on a bluff and think you are better than your neighbors.

Wisdom Tea: Wisdom of God, I may have an arrogant attitude and enjoy looking down on my neighbors. I must come down from the bluff and look into my neighbors' eyes to see their joy and worries. Thank you, Lord.

March 30

It is impossible to push yourself ahead while patting yourself on the back. (Wit, Spring & Summer)

In-Flavor: It is important to be acknowledged, but that only keeps a person in one place. If you want to push yourself ahead, you must bend down and strive to move your arms and legs forward.

Inspiration Coffee: Wonder Counselor, I might like to be acknowledged and pat myself on the back. However, I must bend down and try to move my arms and legs forward if I want to push myself ahead. Thank you, Lord.

Conceit is generally assumed as God's gift to little people. (Practical, Conceit, pg. 36)

Wi-Flavor: Conceit usually causes people to overestimate their abilities and overlook everything else. You must avoid conceit by acting humbly and asking God for help in everything you do.

Wisdom Tea: Wisdom of God, little people like to use conceit to overestimate their abilities and overlook other facts of life. I must avoid conceit and humbly ask God for help with all my work. Thank you, Lord.

March 31

That which can't kill us makes us stronger. (Wit, Unknown, pg. 3)

<u>In-Flavor</u>: Like most people, you might not like challenges and mishaps in your daily life. But you should think of them as an effective way to toughen you up and condition you for life's marathon.

<u>Inspiration Coffee</u>: Wonder Counselor, I do not like difficulties and misfortunes in my life, for they can hurt and kill me. But they can also be a great way to condition and toughen me up for life's marathon. Thank you, Lord.

The sturdiest tree is not found in the shelter of the forest but high upon some rocky crag, where its daily battle with the elements shapes it into a thing of beauty. (Practical, Correction, pg. 44)

<u>Wi-Flavor</u>: The strongest tree is found on the mountaintop, where it battles with all sorts of weather conditions. Likewise, if you are the strongest person, you must learn to battle with lots of life challenges.

<u>Wisdom Tea</u>: Wisdom of God, the strongest tree is found on the mountaintop, where it battles with all kinds of weather condition. Like it, I need your help to be strong and battle all my challenges. Thank you, Lord.

APRIL

April 1

Do something. Either lead, follow, or get out of the way. (Ted Turner) (Practical, Action, pg. 5)

In-Flavor: Some people like to criticize, point out the negatives, stand in the way, and do nothing with a problem. If you are a person of action, you need to find a solution for it and then lead or follow.

Inspiration Coffee: Wonder Counselor, I should not be like some people who love to criticize, stand in the way, and do nothing with a problem. I must find a solution for the problem and then lead or follow. Thank you, Lord.

Storms make oaks take deeper roots. (Practical, Correction, pg. 44)

Wi-Flavor: It is hard to tell which tree would last longer in the forest. But storms will separate them and make oaks take deeper roots. Similarly, life challenges will make you strong and deepen your faith.

Wisdom Tea: Wisdom of God, I certainly do not like challenges and problems in my life. However, as storms make oaks take deeper roots, they make me strong and help deepen my faith in God. Thank you, Lord.

April 2

God does not ask about our ability or our inability, but about our availability. (Practical, Commitment to God, pg. 34)

In-Flavor: Some people think they have to be good at something for God to be in contact with them. Truthfully, if you want God to be in touch with you, you just need to make yourself available to God.

Inspiration Coffee: Wonder Counselor, I may think that God requires certain abilities or skills from me to follow God. However, all God needs from me is my availability and willingness to commit to God. Thank you, Lord.

A person becomes wise by observing what happens when he isn't. (Practical, Experience, pg. 68)

Wi-Flavor: Wisdom comes from past experiences and personal mistakes. When you look back on your past experiences and the times you made foolish decisions, you will eventually become wise.

Wisdom Tea: Wisdom of God, I become wise by observing my past mistakes and learning from my personal experiences. Those experiences and mistakes give me knowledge to grow in wisdom. Thank you, Lord.

April 3

It's not the size of the dog in the fight, but the size of the fight in the dog that makes the difference. (Practical, Discouragement, pg. 56)

In-Flavor: You might assume the bigger dog will win the fight. But actually, any dog that has the will to fight will succeed. Likewise, you must have the will and courage to fight if you want to succeed.

Inspiration Coffee: Wonder Counselor, I might think the bigger dog will win the fight. But any dog with fighting spirit will win. Similarly, I have to have courage and the will to fight my challenges in order to succeed. Thank you, Lord.

The reason a dog is a man's best friend is because he does not pretend; he proves it. (Practical, Friendship, pg. 85)

Wi-Flavor: Friendship is a vital part of life on earth. A dog becomes a man's best friend because it proves that friendship in real actions. Likewise, you can tell if someone is your true friend by the way he/she treats you.

Wisdom Tea: Wisdom of God, my dog proves its friendship with me in real actions, and I need lots of friendships like that to survive. So, I can tell if a person is my best friend by the way he/she treats me. Thank you, Lord.

April 4

God gave each of us two ends— one to sit on and one to think with. A person's success or failure depends on the one he uses most. (Practical, Failure, pg. 70)

In-Flavor: People who fail something often sit on their hands and do not spend any time thinking or planning. Similarly, you must use your head all the time if you want to end up in success instead of failure.

Inspiration Coffee: Wonder Counselor, I should use my head frequently to come up with great plans for my success. Otherwise, if I sit on my hands and do nothing, I will certainly end up with failure. Thank you, Lord.

The secret of happiness is to count your blessings while others are adding up their troubles. (Practical, Happiness, pg. 101)

Wi-Flavor: Humans have done research to figure out the secret of happiness, but found nothing. Today, you are told about that secret—namely, remember to count your blessings and not troubles.

Wisdom Tea: Wisdom of God, I should count my blessings every day instead of adding up my troubles. That is the secret of my happiness. The more blessings I can see around me, the happier I will be. Thank you, Lord.

April 5

Fear is the darkroom where the devil takes you to develop your negatives. (Practical, Fear, pg. 77)

In-Flavor: When people become fearful of something, their mind is filled with dark thoughts, and their heart, with negative feelings. You should drive away any fear by entrusting your life to God's hands.

Inspiration Coffee: Wonder Counselor, I might have certain fears that keep me from pursuing my dreams and hopes. I should not let the devil take me to those dark-rooms and develop my negatives. Thank you, Lord.

The man who strays away from common sense will end up dead! (Proverbs 21:16) (Practical, Life and Death, pg. 142)

Wi-Flavor: The earth is full of pitfalls and dangers. So, God equips humans with five senses besides common sense to avoid them. But if you stray away from common sense, you will end up dead.

Wisdom Tea: Wisdom of God, I have been blessed with common sense in addition to my five senses to help me avoid all the dangers in this life. If I do not follow it and use it wisely, I will end up dead. Thank you, Lord.

April 6

A cheerful heart does good like medicine, but a broken spirit makes one sick. (Proverbs 17:22) (Practical, Humor, pg. 113)

In-Flavor: A cheerful heart brings a person joy and good health, while a broken spirit makes one feel sick and depressed. So, you must have a cheerful heart and avoid a broken spirit if you desire a long life.

Inspiration Coffee: Wonder Counselor, I must foster a cheerful heart and keep myself from a broken spirit if I wish to have a long life, for a cheerful heart heals like medicine, while a broken spirit makes me sick. Thank you, Lord.

The most impressive evidence of tolerance is a golden wedding anniversary. (Practical, Marriage, pg. 152)

Wi-Flavor: In marriage, two people have to sacrifice and put up with each other to create a common life. If you see a golden wedding anniversary, it is a great example of tolerance and true love.

Wisdom Tea: Wisdom of God, I have to make sacrifices and bear with my spouse if I want a long-lasting, happy marriage. If I see a golden wedding anniversary, it is good evidence of tolerance. Thank you, Lord.

April 7
The person who sows seed of kindness will have a perpetual harvest. (Practical, Kindness, pg. 128)

In-Flavor: You may choose to live the way you like. But the best way for you to leave behind a great legacy is to live by way of kindness, for your kind acts will continue to influence the future.

Inspiration Coffee: Wonder Counselor, I surely want a perpetual harvest and long-lasting legacy. The best way for me to make that come true is to sow seeds of kindness that will spread like wildfire. Thank you, Lord.

Behind every work of God, you will always find some kneeling form. (Dwight L. Moody) (Practical, Prayer, pg. 191)

Wi-Flavor: People usually kneel to ask for something or show respect to someone. So, if you want God to do something for you, you must find yourself kneeling in prayer and humbly ask God for it.

Wisdom Tea: Wisdom of God, when I want to show respect or ask someone for something, I often kneel. Similarly, if I want God to grant me a miracle or divine help, I need to kneel in prayer and ask for it. Thank you, Lord.

April 8
The lazier a man is, the more he is going to do tomorrow. (Practical, Laziness, pg. 136)

In-Flavor: Laziness is not a virtue or a good way of life. If you choose the way of laziness, you will have a lot to do tomorrow. But if you decide to work hard now, you can enjoy and relax in the future.

Inspiration Coffee: Wonder Counselor, laziness is a bad habit that will leave me with a lot of unfinished work for tomorrow. I need to work hard now to complete all my duties and enjoy a comfortable future. Thank you, Lord.

To everything there is a season, and a time to every purpose under heaven. (Ecclesiastes 3:1) (Practical, Time, pg. 223)

Wi-Flavor: Everything on earth is governed by time and season, for God has planned and destined everything for a purpose. If you wonder about an event, know that God has destined it like that.

Wisdom Tea: Wisdom of God, I may not realize that everything on earth is governed by the order of time and season. I need to trust that God has planned and destined all events in my life for a purpose. Thank you, Lord.

April 9

Most people would learn from their mistakes if they weren't so busy trying to place the blame on someone else. (Practical, Mistakes, pg. 156)

In-Flavor: It is not easy to admit mistakes and try to learn from them. If you want to learn from your mistakes, try to spend less time blaming others and more time learning how to avoid mistakes in the future.

Inspiration Coffee: Wonder Counselor, I need to be humble to admit my mistakes and be willing to learn from them. I could do that if I would spend more time avoiding them and less time blaming others. Thank you, Lord.

The spoken word is like an arrow. You cannot call it back. (Practical, Words, pg. 244)

Wi-Flavor: Most people do not think twice before they speak. But words are powerful and sharper than a knife. Once they leave your mouth, you cannot get them back. So, think carefully before you speak.

Wisdom Tea: Wisdom of God, I must know that spoken words are like arrows that cannot be called back once they leave my mouth. I need to think twice and be careful about everything before I speak. Thank you, Lord.

April 10

The man who removes a mountain begins by carrying away small stones. (Chinese proverb) (Practical, Persistence, pg. 184)

In-Flavor: It takes hard work and resilience to move a mountain. One begins that work by removing small stones. Likewise, if you want to succeed on something, you must do little things persistently.

Inspiration Coffee: Wonder Counselor, I might want to conquer great things, like moving a mountain. I could begin by carrying away small stones one stone at a time and do those little things persistently. Thank you, Lord.

It is easy to see the faults of others, but hard to see one's own. Men point out the faults of others but cover their own as a dishonest gambler hides a losing throw of the dice. (*Dhammapada*, "Defilement") (Quotations, Fault, pg. 93)

Wi-Flavor: People like to criticize and point out others' faults, but find it difficult to see and admit their own. You must be honest with yourself about your faults if you want to conquer great things.

Wisdom Tea: Wisdom of God, I might act like the rest of mankind and enjoy pointing out the faults of others. However, I need to admit my own if I want to conquer and achieve wonderful things. Thank you, Lord.

April 11

He who cannot reach the mission field on his feet can reach it on his knees. (Practical, Prayer, pg. 189)

In-Flavor: It is admirable to see someone risk everything and take on a mission field for a noble cause. But if you cannot be a missionary for some misfortunate, you can at least get there with prayer.

Inspiration Coffee: Wonder Counselor, I may dream of being a missionary in a foreign land and helping out the misfortunate. If that dream cannot come true somehow, I can still reach the mission field with prayers. Thank you, Lord.

We can do no great things—only small things with great love. (St. Mother Teresa, *Life in the Spirit*) (Quotations, Greatness, pg. 118)

Wi-Flavor: People often dream about doing great and wonderful things to achieve some fame. However, you are advised to do small things with great love if you want to achieve great success.

Wisdom Tea: Wisdom of God, I might dream of doing wonderful things and achieving great fame. However, if I want to achieve great success, all I have to do is work on small things with great love. Thank you, Lord.

April 12

A sensible man watches for problems ahead and prepares to meet them. The simpleton never looks and suffers the consequences. (Proverbs 27:12) (Practical, Problems, pg. 197)

In-Flavor: Life is full of problems. You should be a sensible person who anticipates problems and finds solutions for them. Otherwise, you will end up being a simpleton and facing the consequences.

Inspiration Coffee: Wonder Counselor, I must act like a sensible person and prepare to meet problems ahead with good solutions. Otherwise, I will end up like a simpleton and suffer bad consequences. Thank you, Lord.

If you wish to know what justice is, let injustice pursue you. (Eugenio Maria de Hostos (1839–1903), Puerto Rican patriot) (Quotations, Justice, pg. 146)

Wi-Flavor: People might talk about justice, but do not appreciate it until they experience an injustice. So, if you want to know all about justice, put yourself through some unjust situations and find out.

Wisdom Tea: Wisdom of God, I may dream about a world where justice is equally distributed for all. However, the best way for me to know about justice is to put myself in unjust situations and find out. Thank you, Lord.

April 13

Work for the Lord. The pay isn't much, but the retirement plan is out of this world. (Practical, Work, pg. 248)

In-Flavor: You might spend your whole life working for the purposes, benefits, and rewards of this life. But those things only last a short time. If you work for the Lord, your rewards will be eternal.

Inspiration Coffee: Wonder Counselor, I spend my whole life focusing on the work of this life and its rewards that last a short time. I better consider working for the Lord, because that retirement plan is eternal. Thank you, Lord.

Power is of two kinds: one is obtained by the fear of punishment and the other by acts of love. (Mahatma Gandhi) (Quotations, Power, pg. 211)

Wi-Flavor: People use power and influence on each other every day. But you must know that two ways they can obtain it are by fear of punishment and by acts of love. The latter is powerful and long-lasting.

Wisdom Tea: Wisdom of God, I often see leaders exercise power to exert fear of punishment on people. However, I am encouraged to use power that can bring love and admiration out of the people. Thank you, Lord.

April 14

If you shut your door to all errors, truth will be shut out. (Rabindranath Tagore (1861–1941), Indian writer and philosopher, *Stray Birds*) (Quotations, Error, pg. 81)

In-Flavor: To be human is to err. But only in making errors will you be able to find the truth. So, if you wish to find the truth, you must be open to making errors and willing to ask for forgiveness.

Inspiration Coffee: Wonder Counselor, I might like to be around the truth and hate to make errors that might cause me problems. But the only way for me to find the truth is to be open to making errors. Thank you, Lord.

All sins are committed in secrecy. The moment we realize that God witnesses even our thoughts, we shall be free. (Mahatma Gandhi) (Quotations, Sin, pg. 260)

Wi-Flavor: People commit sins in secrecy and then try to hide them. That is how sins can hold them hostage. You can set yourself free from sins by realizing that God witnesses even our thoughts.

Wisdom Tea: Wisdom of God, sins are committed in secrecy and continue to keep me in hiding. However, when I realize that God witnesses even my thoughts, I will be freed from the shackles of sins. Thank you, Lord.

April 15

A noble, courageous man is recognizable by the patience he shows in adversity. (Pachacutec Inca Yupanqui (1438–1471), Incan ruler) (Quotations, Patience, pg. 199)

In-Flavor: People are praised for their noble character and courageous nature in various contexts. If you want to be considered a noble, courageous person, you need to show patience in adversity.

Inspiration Coffee: Wonder Counselor, I may see a noble person or a courageous man being recognized in various occasions. However, a truly noble, courageous person shows patience in adversity. Thank you, Lord.

The superior man thinks always of virtue; the common man thinks of comfort. (Confucius, *Analects*) (Quotations, Virtue, pg. 295)

Wi-Flavor: Common folks spend all their days looking for ways to bring them a comfortable life. But if you are a superior person, you will think of a virtuous life and try to gather as many virtues as possible.

Wisdom Tea: Wisdom of God, I might see the common folks spend most of their time looking for a fun, comfortable life. However, I must try to be the superior person by following a virtuous life. Thank you, Lord.

April 16

Cautious, careful people, always casting about to preserve their reputation and social standing, never can bring about a reform. (Susan B. Anthony (1820–1906), American suffragist) (Quotations, Reform and Reformers, pg. 230)

In-Flavor: People who truly desire reform must be willing to disrupt the status quo and not be concerned about their reputation or social standing. If you are cautious and careful, you cannot be a reformist.

Inspiration Coffee: Wonder Counselor, I may be a cautious, careful person trying to preserve my reputation and social standing. But if I want to be a reformist, I must be willing to disrupt the status quo. Thank you, Lord.

The world exists on three things: truth, justice, and peace. (Talmud, Aboth 1:18) (Quotations, The World, pg. 315)

Wi-Flavor: You might think the world exists because it has water, oxygen, and the sun. But actually, the world would turn chaotic and cease to exist if it did not have three things: truth, justice, and peace.

Wisdom Tea: Wisdom of God, I might think the world survives on water, oxygen, and the sun. But I am reminded that the world would cease to exist if it did not have truth, justice, and peace. Thank you, Lord.

April 17

Those who are prepared to die for any cause are seldom defeated. (Jawaharlal Nehru) (Quotations, Success, pg. 272)

In-Flavor: People have certain causes that motivate them to work hard and die for. So, if you are willing to die for any cause, you are seldom defeated. That is the attitude and recipe for your success.

Inspiration Coffee: Wonder Counselor, I might have certain causes or reasons that motivate me to work hard and die for. However, if I am willing to die for any cause, I will usually succeed in the future. Thank you, Lord.

To believe in God must mean to live in such a manner that life could not possibly be lived if God did not exist. (Jacques Maritain, in *The Review of Politics*, July 1949) (Religious, Belief and Believers, pg. 47)

Wi-Flavor: Everyone claims to believe in God, but they go on to live each day without any need for God. So, if you truly believe in God, you must show that God is an essential part of your daily life.

Wisdom Tea: Wisdom of God, if I believe in God, I must show that my life would not be the same without God, for God helps keep me from bad influences and encourages me to do good things. Thank you, Lord.

April 18

Strength does not come from physical capacity. It comes from an indomitable will. (Mahatma Gandhi) (Quotations, Will, pg. 304)

In-Flavor: Most people often equate strength with physical capacity. They forget about the tremendous strength coming from the willpower. If you have an unbreakable will, your strength is enormous.

Inspiration Coffee: Wonder Counselor, my strength should not come only from my physical capacity but also from my unbreakable will, which I must not forget about in challenging times. Thank you, Lord.

He who gives alms in secret is greater than Moses. (Talmud) (Religious, Charity, pg. 72)

Wi-Flavor: Moses did lots of heroic and charitable acts for the people of God on the way to the Promised Land without expecting anything back. If you give alms in secret, you are definitely greater than him.

Wisdom Tea: Wisdom of God, Moses was one of the most generous and charitable figures in the Bible who always helped out the people of God. If I give alms in secret, I will be greater than Moses. Thank you, Lord.

April 19

Do not neglect to show hospitality to strangers, for thereby some have entertained angels unaware. (Hebrews 13:2) (Religious, Angels, pg. 26)

In-Flavor: Conventional wisdom tells people to focus on families and friends. But today, the wisdom of God calls you to reach out and be hospitable to strangers if you want to meet unexpected angels.

Inspiration Coffee: Wonder Counselor, I may not have had an angel appear to me before. However, if I really want to have that divine experience, all I have to do is to show hospitality to strangers whenever I can. Thank you, Lord.

Kindness has converted more people than zeal, science, or eloquence. (St. Mother Teresa, *Contemplative in the Heart of the World*, 1985) (Religious, Compassion, pg. 92)

Wi-Flavor: Humans have used eloquence, science, and zeal to convince and convert others to their side. Today, you are reminded that kindness and compassion can change more people than all of the above.

Wisdom Tea: Wisdom of God, I may switch people to my side with the help of eloquence, science, and zeal. However, I am told that kindness and compassion can convert more people than those. Thank you, Lord.

April 20

Be strong and of good courage. (Deuteronomy 31:23) (Religious, Courage, pg. 112)

In-Flavor: Your life might be full of challenges and overwhelming. You might feel lost or depressed about your future. But be strong and have courage, because your God will not forget or abandon you.

Inspiration Coffee: Wonder Counselor, I might feel overwhelmed by life pressure, discouraged by daily challenges, or lost by all the distractions around me. The Bible reminds me to be strong and of good courage. Thank you, Lord.

The Evil Will lures man in this world, then testifies against him in the world to come. (Talmud) (Religious, Devil, pg. 136)

Wi-Flavor: Most people do not know the Devil well, but they easily buy into his attractive lures in this world. Today, you are warned that the Devil will use his temptations against you in the next life.

Wisdom Tea: Wisdom of God, I might not realize that the devil is real and never stops luring me in this world. However, he will use those temptations to testify against me in the next world. Thank you, Lord.

April 21

When we deny the evil in ourselves, we dehumanize ourselves, and we deprive ourselves not only of our own destiny but of any possibility of dealing with the evil of others. (J. Robert Oppenheimer, address, New York, March 1963) (Religious, Evil, pg. 169)

In-Flavor: Each person has the ability to act evil and be influenced by darkness. If you do not admit that, you will not see the need for salvation, then you cannot help others deal with their evil either.

Inspiration Coffee: Wonder Counselor, I must know that I have the potential for doing evil things. If I do not realize that, I will not see my need for divine salvation and any possibility of dealing the evil of others. Thank you, Lord.

With God all things are possible. (Matthew 19:26) (Religious, God, pg. 208)

Wi-Flavor: Humans are finite in their abilities and limited in their resources. They often dream big, but cannot make those dreams come true. Today, you are reminded that, with God by your side, all things are possible.

Wisdom Tea: Wisdom of God, I know that I am imperfect and limited in my ability to do anything on my own. But with God's help, I can do everything and achieve anything I want, even the impossible. Thank you, Lord.

April 22

You will seek me and find me; when you seek me with all your heart. (Jeremiah 29:13) (Religious, Finding God, pg. 190)

In-Flavor: God remains elusive for the public. Some deem it difficult to look for God in their lives. But today, the Bible reminds you that you will find God if you earnestly seek God with all your heart.

Inspiration Coffee: Wonder Counselor, God will bring me security, guidance, and many wonderful blessings. The Bible reminds me to seek God earnestly with all my heart, and I will eventually find God. Thank you, Lord.

Faith means being grasped by a power that is greater than we are, a power that shakes us and turns us, and transforms and heals us. Surrender to this power faith. (Paul Tillich, *The New Being*, 1955) (Religious, Faith, pg. 182)

Wi-Flavor: Faith has many definitions. Today, you are told that faith means being grasped by a power that is greater than you are. It shakes you and turns you until you eventually surrender to it.

Wisdom Tea: Wisdom of God, I may define faith in terms of religious denominations. But it is actually about being grasped by a power that is greater than I am and shaking me until I surrender to it. Thank you, Lord.

April 23

Knowledge is the key that first opens the hard heart, enlarges the affections, and opens the way for men into the kingdom of heaven. (Jonathan Edwards (1703–58), *Works*, V, 151) (Religious, Knowledge, pg. 287)

In-Flavor: The best way to convince a doubter is with the help of knowledge. It can move people to admire one another. It also points people to their Creator. So, you need to appreciate knowledge.

Inspiration Coffee: Wonder Counselor, I must realize that knowledge is the key that can help me convince doubters, move people to admire others, and point people to their Creator. I must appreciate it. Thank you, Lord.

To rest in God eternally is the supreme joy of Heaven. Indeed, Heaven has no meaning other than that. (Bede Jarrett, *Meditations for Layfolk*, 1915) (Religious, Heaven and Hell, pg. 228)

Wi-Flavor: When someone dies and goes to Heaven, everyone wishes that person to rest in peace. Today, you are told that the supreme joy for you in Heaven is to rest in God eternally.

Wisdom Tea: Wisdom of God, I may look up to Heaven for other reasons. But the supreme joy for me to be in Heaven is to rest in God's loving arms peacefully and eternally. That is the ultimate goal for me. Thank you, Lord.

April 24

The love we give away is the only love we keep. (Elbert Hubbard (1859–1915), *Notebook*) (Religious, Love, pg. 307)

In-Flavor: People do not like to give away anything. When they give something away, they expect something else back. However, if you give away love, it will come back to you a hundredfold.

Inspiration Coffee: Wonder Counselor, like most people, I do not like to give away anything. But when I give away something like love, it will come back to me more than I can keep or expect. Thank you, Lord.

We were never promised a life free from fear and struggle. We were offered the hope that by committing ourselves to the struggle for a righteous society in solidarity with the wretched of the earth we would discover the secret of life. (Sheila Collins, "Theology in the Politics of Appalachian Women," *Woman spirit Rising*, 1979) (Religious, Justice, pg. 284)

Wi-Flavor: Everyone wishes to have a life free from fear and struggle. But you are reminded that you will find out the secret of life by struggling for a righteous society and the wretched.

Wisdom Tea: Wisdom of God, I wish to have a life free from fear and struggle. However, I have been promised that I will discover the secret of life by fighting for the lowly and a just society. Thank you, Lord.

April 25

One of the chief functions of the saints is to provide us and other Christians with proximate living examples of how Christ would apply His thought and action to the specific circumstances of our own vocations. (John J. Wright, in *The Way*, October 1962) (Religious, Saints and Sinners, pg. 501)

In-Flavor: Saints are Christian heroes who inspire you to be better and also the channel for God's grace to pour into your life. Most importantly, they are the living examples of Christ for you to imitate.

Inspiration Coffee: Wonder Counselor, I might not see much value of the saints in my daily struggles. However, I must know that they give me and other Christians living examples of Christ to imitate. Thank you, Lord.

When money speaks, the truth is silent. (Russian proverb) (Religious, Money, pg. 338)

Wi-Flavor: When people use money as their loudspeakers, they certainly have no interest in the truth. So, if you want to hear the truth, money is not where you should focus your listening ears.

Wisdom Tea: Wisdom of God, I might want to hear the truth and find out all about it. However, whenever money speaks, it usually has its own agenda and keeps me away from knowing the truth. Thank you, Lord.

April 26

The young are looking for living models whom they can imitate and who are capable of rousing their enthusiasm and drawing them to a deeper life. ... They need sure guides to go with them on the paths of liberation that God maps out for them. (Bakole wa Ilunga, *Paths of Liberation*, 1984) (Religious, Youth, pg. 639)

In-Flavor: You make a difference in the life of the young by helping them channel their enthusiasm to a deeper way of life. You should guide them on the right path to their own vocations.

Inspiration Coffee: Wonder Counselor, the young need living models and knowledgeable guides to rouse their enthusiasm and lead them to a deeper kind of life. I could try to act as their guide and model. Thank you, Lord.

Ask not that events should happen as you will, but let your will be that events should happen as they do, and you shall have peace. (Epictetus, *The Enchiridion*, 125 AD) (Religious, Peace, pg. 383)

Wi-Flavor: Everyone wants to have peace, while demanding events happen as they will. But those two cannot exist together. If your will let events happen as they do, then you shall have peace.

Wisdom Tea: Wisdom of God, I might want peace, while expecting everything to happen my way. But the only way I can have peace is to let go of everything and allow my life events to happen as they do. Thank you, Lord.

April 27
No one learns to make right decisions without being free to make wrong ones. (Wise, Decisiveness, pg. 37)

In-Flavor: No one likes to make wrong decisions, because they are painful. But the only way you can get to the right decisions is by knowing that you will possibly make the wrong ones. You will get better with time.

Inspiration Coffee: Wonder Counselor, I might be afraid of making a wrong decision that would cause me pain and sadness. However, I can only learn to make right decisions if I am free to make wrong ones. Thank you, Lord.

Prayer is not bending to my will, but it is bringing of my will into conformity with God's will, so that His works may work in and through me. (E. Stanley Jones, *How to Pray*, 1943) (Religious, Prayer, pg. 417)

Wi-Flavor: People view prayer as a way to bend God's will to theirs and get what they want. But you should see prayer as getting your will into conformity with God's will and letting God work for you.

Wisdom Tea: Wisdom of God, I often think of prayer as making an effort to get God's will to become mine. However, I should look at prayer as the time to bring my will into conformity with God's will. Thank you, Lord.

April 28
If you ever see a turtle on a stump, you know it didn't get there by itself. (Wise, Teamwork, pg. 133)

In-Flavor: A turtle cannot get on a stump on its own. It needs someone to help it get there. Likewise, you cannot succeed in something or get anything done without having some kind of teamwork.

Inspiration Coffee: Wonder Counselor, I know that a turtle could not jump onto a stump by itself. It needs others to bring it there. Similarly, I cannot get to the top and succeed without the help of teamwork. Thank you, Lord.

Our soul is made to be God's dwelling-place; and the dwelling-place of the soul is God, which is unmade. (Juliana of Norwich, *Revelations of Divine Love*, 1670) (Religious, Soul, pg. 531)

Wi-Flavor: Humans have a hard time seeing the soul or God. But today, you learn that your soul is the best human dwelling place for God, while God is the perfectly unmade dwelling place for your soul.

Wisdom Tea: Wisdom of God, I cannot see my soul or God. However, I believe that my soul is made to be God's dwelling place on earth, while God is the perfect dwelling place for my soul in Heaven. Thank you, Lord.

April 29

Lord, when we are wrong, make us willing to change; and when we are right, make us easy to live with. (Wit, Spring & Summer)

In-Flavor: Change does not come easily, but it is much harder to put up with a difficult person every day. So, you need to pray that you can change when you are wrong and be kind when you are right.

Inspiration Coffee: Wonder Counselor, I pray that I might be willing to admit my mistakes and change when I am wrong. Moreover, I hope that I will be easy to live with and be around when I am right. Thank you, Lord.

A conceited person never gets anywhere because he thinks he is already there. (Practical, Conceit, pg. 36)

Wi-Flavor: A conceited person always thinks he knows everything and assumes he is already there. However, you should avoid being that person if you want to get somewhere and achieve something.

Wisdom Tea: Wisdom of God, a conceited person might think he/she is already there, but actually has never gone anywhere. I must not be that person if I want to go somewhere and achieve something. Thank you, Lord.

April 30

Take time to laugh, it's the music of the soul. (Wit, Unknown, pg. 1)

In-Flavor: Life is full of sad and challenging moments. Those moments make your soul ache and shed tears. That is why you need to smile or laugh as much as possible. It is the music of your soul.

Inspiration Coffee: Wonder Counselor, I might not realize how important a laugh is to the soul. I need to take time to laugh, for it is the music of my soul, which is full of sad and challenging moments. Thank you, Lord.

Our wisdom usually comes from our experience, and our experience comes largely from our foolishness. (Practical, Experience, pg. 68)

Wi-Flavor: You should not be afraid of making foolish decisions, for that is the only way for you to gain experience and wisdom. Indeed, wisdom comes from past experience and many foolish choices.

Wisdom Tea: Wisdom of God, I might not like to admit my foolish moments and bad decisions. However, the only way for me to gain some wisdom is from my past experiences and many foolish choices. Thank you, Lord.

May 1
He who is overcautious will accomplish little in life. (Practical, Action, pg. 5)

In-Flavor: Life is full of opportunities, but they do wait until you are good and ready to embrace them. Therefore, you cannot be too cautious and afraid to take chances if you want to accomplish a lot.

Inspiration Coffee: Wonder Counselor, I might want to be cautious and thoughtful about certain life decisions. However, life is full of opportunities, and I need to grab them if I want to achieve great success. Thank you, Lord.

Ill-gotten gain brings no lasting happiness; right living does. (Proverbs 10:2) (Practical, Fulfillment, pg. 87)

Wi-Flavor: Ill-gotten gains are benefits that you might acquire from unethical or illegal ways. Those benefits might bring you a brief moment of joy, but lasting happiness comes from right living.

Wisdom Tea: Wisdom of God, I might acquire ill-gotten gains by an unethical way, but that brings me only brief joy. If I want to have a fulfilling life and lasting happiness, I need to follow right living. Thank you, Lord.

May 2
A good leader inspires men to have confidence in him; a great leader inspires them to have confidence in themselves. (Practical, Confidence, pg. 38)

In-Flavor: A good leader can inspire others to believe and follow him/her. But if you want to be a great leader, you must know how to inspire others to believe in themselves and do the right things.

Inspiration Coffee: Wonder Counselor, I may be able to inspire others to have confidence in me as a good leader. But if I want to be a great leader, I need to inspire people to have confidence in themselves. Thank you, Lord.

The father is the head of the house; the mother is the heart of the house. (Practical, Mother, pg. 164)

Wi-Flavor: The father is often considered the head of the household who makes all the family decisions. However, you must know that it is the mother who is the heart of the family and keeps it alive.

Wisdom Tea: Wisdom of God, I might consider the father as the head of the house, making all the family decisions. But I must realize that it is the mother who is the heart of the house and takes care of it. Thank you, Lord.

May 3

And let us not get tired of doing what is right, for after a while we will reap a harvest of blessing if we don't get discouraged and give up. (Galatians 6:9) (Practical, Discouragement, pg. 56)

In-Flavor: It is not easy to keep on doing the right things while the rest of the world can do whatever it likes. If you do not give up on that mission, you will enjoy a rich harvest of blessings in the end.

Inspiration Coffee: Wonder Counselor, I might not get praise for doing what is right while the world can do whatever it pleases. But I should not get discouraged, because I will reap a harvest of blessings. Thank you, Lord.

Those who chronically suffer injustice have the truest insight into what justice is all about. (Practical, Justice, pg. 125)

Wi-Flavor: Everyone dreams about a good justice system to keep a just and peaceful society. But you must know that only those who suffer injustice will really understand what that system should do.

Wisdom Tea: Wisdom of God, I might hope for a good justice system to maintain a fair and peaceful world. But unless I chronically suffer injustice, I will not know what that system must really do. Thank you, Lord.

May 4

Feed your faith, and your fears will starve to death. (Practical, Fear, pg. 77)

In-Flavor: People fear all sorts of things when they detach themselves from God. But if you feed your faith with prayers and acts of charity, you will be close to God and have nothing to fear or worry.

Inspiration Coffee: Wonder Counselor, I have lots of fears, which can get intensified when I am away from God. I need to feed my faith with prayers and charities to be close to God and drive away my fears. Thank you, Lord.

Hatred stirs old quarrels, but love overlooks insults. (Proverbs 10:12) (Practical, Love, pg. 143)

Wi-Flavor: People who have hatred in their hearts often hold on to past resentment and old quarrels. However, if you have love in your heart, you will overlook all the painful insults and past offenses.

Wisdom Tea: Wisdom of God, I might not know that having hatred in my heart causes me to hold on to old quarrels and hurts. But having love in my heart allows me to overlook past offenses and insults. Thank you, Lord.

May 5

You can win more friends with your ears than with your mouth.

(Practical, Hearing, pg. 104)

In-Flavor: Disagreements and misunderstandings often happen when people talk. So, if you want to win more friends, you need to spend more time listening to others and less time talking in public.

Inspiration Coffee: Wonder Counselor, when I talk, I might cause misunderstandings and disagreements. I need to spend more time listening and less time talking to others if I want to win more friends. Thank you, Lord.

A successful marriage is one in which you fall in love many times, always with the same person. (D. W. McLaughlin) (Practical, Marriage, pg. 152)

Wi-Flavor: Many marriages these days fall apart and end up in divorce or separation. However, you must know that a successful marriage comes about when you fall in love many times with the same person.

Wisdom Tea: Wisdom of God, some marriages might fall apart and end up in divorce because of various reasons. If I want a successful marriage, I need to fall in love many times with the same person. Thank you, Lord.

May 6

A sense of humor is the pole that adds balance to our steps as we walk the tightrope of life.

(William Arthur Ward) (Practical, Humor, pg. 114)

In-Flavor: Life pressures and expectations can make a person tense and unbearable. Therefore, it is very important for you to have a good sense of humor and exchange laughs often to lighten the mood.

Inspiration Coffee: Wonder Counselor, my life can be tense and unbearable due to pressure and expectations. I need to have a good sense of humor and lighten the mood with some laughs and jokes. Thank you, Lord.

We can justify our every deed, but God looks at our motives.

(Proverbs 21:2) (Practical, Motivation, pg. 167)

Wi-Flavor: Humans can come up with excuses for every deed and seldom accept their responsibilities. But you should remember that God knows your heart and sees your motives behind every deed.

Wisdom Tea: Wisdom of God, I might have justifications and excuses for every deed. However, I need to accept my responsibility and remember that God looks at my heart and knows my motives. Thank you, Lord.

May 7

One kind word can warm three winter months. (Japanese proverb) (Practical, Kindness, pg. 128)

In-Flavor: The harsh conditions of the winter and its frigid temperatures can depress the human spirit. But if you can hear one kind word, it helps lift up your spirit and keep you warm for the winter months.

Inspiration Coffee: Wonder Counselor, the cold temperatures and harsh conditions of the winter can make me feel depressed. But a kind word can help lift up my spirit and keep me warm in the winter. Thank you, Lord.

Proud men end in shame, but the meek become wise.

(Proverbs 11:2) (Practical, Pride, pg. 195)

Wi-Flavor: The proud assume they are in charge, but God is, and they will end up in shame. However, you will learn that the meek become wise because they act humbly and realize that God is in charge.

Wisdom Tea: Wisdom of God, I might assume that I am in charge, like the proud, and end up in shame. However, if I act like the meek and realize that God is in charge, then I will be humble and become wise. Thank you, Lord.

May 8

Laughter is the brush that sweeps away the cobwebs of the heart. (Mort Walker) (Practical, Laughter, pg. 133)

In-Flavor: Your heart might collect dust balls and cobwebs as the result of sad events and difficult encounters in your life. But you can brush those away with laughter and cheerful spirit.

Inspiration Coffee: Wonder Counselor, my heart can collect cobwebs and worries because of problems and challenges every day. However, I can use laughter and a cheerful spirit to wipe those away. Thank you, Lord.

If you must choose, take a good name rather than great riches; for to be held in loving esteem is better than silver and gold. (Proverbs 22:1) (Practical, Reputation, pg. 206)

Wi-Flavor: Most people these days are not concerned about reputation or shame, but focus on great riches. If you must choose, you should take a good name and loving esteem instead of silver and gold.

Wisdom Tea: Wisdom of God, I might focus on great riches and be less concerned about my name and reputation. If I must choose, I should take a good name and warm admiration instead of wealth. Thank you, Lord.

May 9

Coaches who can outline plays on a blackboard are a dime a dozen. The ones who win get inside their players and motivate. (Vince Lombardi) (Practical, Motivation, pg. 168)

In-Flavor: A typical coach can outline a good game plan and all the trick plays on a blackboard. But if you want to be a winning coach, you need to know how to get inside your players and motivate them.

Inspiration Coffee: Wonder Counselor, I can be a typical coach or teacher and know how to outline plays or lessons on a board. But a winning coach can get inside the players or students and motivate them. Thank you, Lord.

Most of our troubles stem from too much time on our hands and not enough on our knees. (Practical, Time, pg. 225)

Wi-Flavor: When people have too much time on their hands, they often squander it on bad habits. So, if you want to reduce your troubles, you must spend more time on your knees, praying instead.

Wisdom Tea: Wisdom of God, I may have too much time on my hands and squander it on bad habits and wrong choices. I can reduce my troubles and spend more time on my knees, praying instead. Thank you, Lord.

May 10

We should make plans—counting on God to direct us. (Practical, Plans, pg. 185)

In-Flavor: It is wise for you to make plans and try to figure out how to deal with your future and life problems. But you should also count on God to lead you and show you the way forward.

Inspiration Coffee: Wonder Counselor, I must be wise and try to make plans for how to deal with my future and potential problems. I should also learn to count on God to direct me and show me the way. Thank you, Lord.

A wise man adapts himself to circumstances as water shapes itself to the vessel that contains it. (Chinese proverb) (Quotations, Adaptability, pg. 4)

Wi-Flavor: Most people do not like changes or to adapt themselves to new circumstances. However, if you are a wise person, you should learn to adapt yourself to circumstances and go with the flow.

Wisdom Tea: Wisdom of God, water retains so much power because it knows how to shape and adapt itself to the surroundings. I can be wise and learn to adapt and change to new circumstances. Thank you, Lord.

May 11
He who has not prepared for the trip should not begin his journey.
(Practical, Preparation, pg. 194)

In-Flavor: Before you go on a trip, you should take time to prepare for it. Otherwise, you might end up in disaster and hurt yourself. Life is a journey, and you better make careful preparation for it.

Inspiration Coffee: Wonder Counselor, my life is a long, tough journey. Before any trip, I should make careful preparation for it. Otherwise, I might hurt myself or get stranded on the side of the road. Thank you, Lord.

The fool is thirsty in the midst of water.
(Ethiopian proverb) (Quotations, Fools and Foolishness, pg. 99)

Wi-Flavor: Some people are foolish and continue to inquire for other things amidst their current blessings. You should avoid being a fool and try to give thanks for everything you have right now.

Wisdom Tea: Wisdom of God, I must stop acting like a fool who keeps on inquiring for other things amidst all the current blessings. I need to learn to be grateful for everything I have right now. Thank you, Lord.

May 12
Our problems should make us better, not bitter.
(Practical, Problems, pg. 198)

In-Flavor: People often find themselves bitter at life because of the problems they have encountered along the way. You should view problems as God's way of molding you into a better person.

Inspiration Coffee: Wonder Counselor, my life is full of problems that can make me bitter and angry. However, I should welcome and look at them as the subtle ways God uses to make me a better person. Thank you, Lord.

Nothing destroys one's respect in the hearts of others more than greed.
(Muhammad Taqi (811–835), Arab religious leader) (Quotations, Greed, pg. 119)

Wi-Flavor: Greed makes people care only about themselves and show little respect and concern for others. You should avoid greed if you want people to have their respect and care for you.

Wisdom Tea: Wisdom of God, I might not see the destructive power of greed to my life. I need your help to avoid greed and learn to show respect and concern for others and their needs. Thank you, Lord.

May 13
Don't you know that this good man, though you trip him up seven times, will each time rise again? (Proverbs 24:16) (Practical, Tenacity, pg. 218)

In-Flavor: Life has a way to trip you up with various hurdles. Some wicked folks also do the same to you. However, if you have been tripped up, you must rise again and continue on with your mission.

Inspiration Coffee: Wonder Counselor, life hurdles and wicked people might try to trip me up and keep me from moving ahead. However, whenever I get tripped up and fall, I must rise again and keep going. Thank you, Lord.

Cooking is impossible without fire, and liberation is impossible without knowledge. (Shankara (788–820), Indian Hindu philosopher) (Quotations, Knowledge, pg. 149)

Wi-Flavor: You need to start a fire and keep it burning if you want to cook something. Similarly, you need knowledge and the desire for it if you want to start a liberation movement and keep it going.

Wisdom Tea: Wisdom of God, I cannot cook something without making a fire and keeping it burning. Likewise, I cannot begin a liberation movement without having knowledge and desire for it. Thank you, Lord.

May 14
Duty without enthusiasm becomes laborious; duty with enthusiasm becomes glorious. (William Arthur Ward) (Practical, Zeal, pg. 251)

In-Flavor: Imagine doing something you do not like. That task becomes laborious, and its time seems endless. However, if you carry out a duty with enthusiasm, it becomes glorious and goes by fast.

Inspiration Coffee: Wonder Counselor, I must learn to carry out my daily duties with enthusiasm and find them as a glorious and enjoyable time. Otherwise, they become laborious and overbearing for me. Thank you, Lord.

Harmony between two individuals is never granted—it has to be conquered indefinitely. (Simone de Beauvoir (1908–1986), French writer and philosopher, *Le Force de l'Age*) (Quotations, Relationships, pg. 232)

Wi-Flavor: Humans wish to have harmony in all their relationships. But this great blessing was never granted at creation. If you want harmony around you, you must keep working on it every day.

Wisdom Tea: Wisdom of God, I might dream about harmony among mankind. However, God never granted that blessing at creation. I must work hard to achieve it in all my relationships. Thank you, Lord.

May 15
Failure is nothing but the kiss of Jesus. (St. Mother Teresa, *Life in the Spirit*) (Quotations, Failure, pg. 87)

In-Flavor: When you fail at something, you feel devastated and want to give up on everything. Today, you are reminded to view failure as the encouraging kiss of Jesus and a call on you to keep on going.

Inspiration Coffee: Wonder Counselor, I will certainly encounter many failures in my life and want to give up on everything. However, I am encouraged to see those as the kisses of Jesus and keep trying again. Thank you, Lord.

Once you have spoken, even the swiftest horses cannot retract your words. (Chinese proverb) (Quotations, Speech, pg. 266)

Wi-Flavor: Words are powerful and have deadly consequences, like arrows. You have to be careful with words because they can heal or hurt a person. Once they leave the mouth, they cannot be retracted.

Wisdom Tea: Wisdom of God, I usually do not pay much attention to the words I speak every day. I must be careful with them because they cannot be retracted and can heal or hurt someone. Thank you, Lord.

May 16
Heroes are made in the hour of defeat. Success is, therefore, well described as a series of glorious defeats. (Mahatma Gandhi) (Quotations, Success, pg. 271)

In-Flavor: You cannot succeed without having to face a series of painful defeats. But it is in those dark hours of defeat that heroes are made. If you want to succeed and be a hero, you have to face defeat.

Inspiration Coffee: Wonder Counselor, I want to be a hero and celebrate successes. But I should remember that a hero is made in the dark hours of defeat, and I have to face those before seeing successes. Thank you, Lord.

Men should beware of coveting riches; when riches come through covetousness, Heaven's calamities follow. (Chinese proverb) (Quotations, Wealth, pg. 302)

Wi-Flavor: Covetous riches do not come from hard work and discovery. They come from illegal and sinful ways. You must not acquire riches by coveting, because Heaven's calamities will follow you.

Wisdom Tea: Wisdom of God, coveting riches comes from illegal and sinful ways, not by hard work. I must be careful about acquiring riches by coveting, for Heaven's calamities often follow it. Thank you, Lord.

May 17

If we develop a force of will, we shall find that we do not need the force of arms. (Mahatma Gandhi) (Quotations, Will, pg. 304)

In-Flavor: People often count on the force of arms and guns as the way to give them an upper hand. But Gandhi calls on you to develop a force of will as the alternative and better way to win out in the end.

Inspiration Coffee: Wonder Counselor, humans like to use the force of arms and guns to get what they want. I have been suggested to develop the force of will as another way to find a solution for a problem. Thank you, Lord.

And this I do believe above all, especially in times of greater discouragement; I must BELIEVE in my fellow men, in myself, and in God if life is to have any meaning. (Margaret Chase Smith, for the series "This I Believe," 1954) (Religious, Belief and Believers, pg. 49)

Wi-Flavor: It is hard for you to believe in an uncertain world or in discouraging times. But if your life is to have any meaning, you must learn to believe in yourself, your fellow men, and your God.

Wisdom Tea: Wisdom of God, I live in a world that gradually turns secular, and I find it difficult to believe during times of discouragement. But I must try to believe in myself, my fellow men, and my God. Thank you, Lord.

May 18

No one eats better food than that which he eats from the work of his hands. (Muhammad, *Hadith*) (Quotations, Work, pg. 314)

In-Flavor: Most people prefer home food over restaurant food because it is made out of love and hard work. Similarly, when you toil and sweat for your success, its fruits will taste sweeter and more fulfilling.

Inspiration Coffee: Wonder Counselor, I may prefer homemade stuffs over mass-produced products because they were created out of love and sweat. When I toil for my success, its fruits will taste sweeter. Thank you, Lord.

[A] society that puts the needs of its children dead last is a society "progressing" rapidly toward moral ruin. (Jean Bethke Elshtain, "Just War and American Politics," *The Christian Century*, January 15, 1992) (Religious, Children, pg. 74)

Wi-Flavor: Children are the livelihood and future of a society. If you see a society that puts the needs of its children dead last, it is not concerned about its future and heading rapidly toward moral ruin.

Wisdom Tea: Wisdom of God, I can tell if a society is concerned about its future or heading rapidly toward moral ruin by the way it puts the needs of its children dead last, for they are its hope and future. Thank you, Lord.

May 19

We do not realize that, as Chesterton reminded us, the angels fly because they take themselves so lightly. (Alan Watts, *The Way of Liberation*, 1983) (Religious, Angels, pg. 27)

In-Flavor: You might need to take your work seriously and get the result you like. However, you should imitate the angels and take yourself lightly if you want to fly gently like them.

Inspiration Coffee: Wonder Counselor, I may not realize how angels can fly. It is because they take themselves so lightly. I should imitate them and take myself lightly if I hope to fly high like them. Thank you, Lord.

Our lack of compassion, our ruthlessness towards other men, is an impenetrable curtain between ourselves and God. (Alexander Yelchaninov (1881–1934), *Fragments of a Diary*) (Religious, Compassion, pg. 93)

Wi-Flavor: Everyone wants to see God and be close to God all the time. That will happen if you can take down the impenetrable curtain between you and God by showing more compassion toward others.

Wisdom Tea: Wisdom of God, I wish to meet God and be close to God. The best way for that to happen is if I can take down the curtain between me and God by showing compassion toward others. Thank you, Lord.

May 20

Courage is never to let your actions be influenced by your fears. (Arthur Koestler, *Arrow in the Blue*, 1951) (Religious, Courage, pg. 113)

In-Flavor: Most people have some kind of fear that makes them worry and keeps them from doing certain things. But if you have courage, you will not let your actions be influenced by any fear.

Inspiration Coffee: Wonder Counselor, I might have fears that make me anxious and keep me from living up to my potential. I pray for courage and not letting my actions be influenced by any fear. Thank you, Lord.

Resist the devil and he will flee from you. (James 4:7) (Religious, Devil, pg. 137)

Wi-Flavor: The devil usually tempts and charms people to follow his wicked plans. People are flattered by his charm offensive and let him hang around. To drive him away, you must resist the devil's temptations.

Wisdom Tea: Wisdom of God, I should not underestimate the devil's temptations and charm offensive. With your help, I will try hard to resist his temptations and keep him far away from me. Thank you, Lord.

May 21

To be human is to be challenged to be more divine. Not even to try to meet such a challenge is the biggest defeat imaginable.

(Maya Angelou, 1993) (Religious, Failure and Defeat, pg. 175)

In-Flavor: If you are human, you will have imperfections and commit errors. You will pray for divine assistance and wish to be strong and perfect like the divine. That is the challenge you cannot fail.

Inspiration Coffee: Wonder Counselor, I may be regrettably full of human imperfections and errors. However, I have been challenged to be more divine and work on my thoughts and actions to be perfect. Thank you, Lord.

In a consumer society there are inevitably two kinds of slaves: the prisoners of addiction and the prisoners of envy. (Ivan Illich, *Tools for Conviviality*, 1973) (Religious, Envy and Jealousy, pg. 159)

Wi-Flavor: Addiction turns people into slaves of a bad habit and keeps them in that prison for years. Envy is another prison that you should avoid, because it will make you its slave for a long time.

Wisdom Tea: Wisdom of God, I am not surprised that addiction is a prison holding slaves of a bad habit for years. But I should be concerned about another prison that keeps slaves of envy indefinitely. Thank you, Lord.

May 22

God only comes to those who ask him to come; and he cannot refuse to come to those who implore him long, often and ardently.

(Simone Weil, *Waiting for God*, 1951) (Religious, Finding God, pg. 191)

In-Flavor: People sometimes complain that they cannot find God, especially in difficult times. But the truth is that if you implore God long, often, and ardently, God cannot refuse to come to see you.

Inspiration Coffee: Wonder Counselor, I might feel God is not around for me in difficult times. However, if I implore and search for God long, often, and ardently, God cannot refuse to come to see me. Thank you, Lord.

From the loving example of one family, a whole state becomes loving. (Confucius, *The Great Learning*, 500 BC) (Religious, Family, pg. 185)

Wi-Flavor: Family is the cornerstone of a society or nation. If you can get a family to be loving and kind to each other, you will be able to help a society or nation to do the same to one another.

Wisdom Tea: Wisdom of God, I might not know that family is the cornerstone of a society or nation. If I can help a family to be loving to one another, I will be able to get a society or nation to do the same. Thank you, Lord.

May 23
The fear of the Lord is the beginning of knowledge; but fools despise wisdom and instruction.
(Proverbs 1:7) (Religious, Knowledge, pg. 288)

In-Flavor: Knowledge is power and the key to the heart of God, and fear of the Lord is the beginning of it. If you are not a fool, you will learn to fear the Lord and absorb as much knowledge as possible.

Inspiration Coffee: Wonder Counselor, I may not realize that knowledge is the key to the heart of God, and fear of the Lord is its beginning. I should not be a fool and learn to absorb as much knowledge as possible. Thank you, Lord.

God ... is not a transcendent being living in a distant heaven whence from time to time he intervenes in the affairs of the earth. He is an ever-present spirit bringing all that happens to a wise and holy end. (David Hume, *Dialogues Concerning Natural Religion*, 1779) (Religious, God, pg. 209)

Wi-Flavor: In the Old Testament, God was a transcendent being living in a distant Heaven. Then, as you might know, God has come down to earth in Jesus and become an ever-present spirit with his people.

Wisdom Tea: Wisdom of God, you are no longer a transcendent being living in the distant Heaven mentioned in the Old Testament. I know you have come down to earth and become an ever-present spirit. Thank you, Lord.

May 24
Not many men may be willing to die for love these days. But you can't escape the fact that millions are dying daily for the very lack of it. (John E. Large, *The Small Needle of Doctor Large*, 1962) (Religious, Love, pg. 308)

In-Flavor: People tend to focus on themselves and are not willing to share God's love with a broken world. If you have a caring heart, you can commit yourself to fill the world with kindness and love.

Inspiration Coffee: Wonder Counselor, many people are not willing to share God's love with others these days. But if I have a caring heart, I will try to fill the world with as much kindness and love as possible. Thank you, Lord.

Hell has three doors: lust, rage, and greed. (Bhagavad-Gita) (Religious, Hell, pg. 229)

Wi-Flavor: Nobody likes to end up in Hell. But three sure ways that might get you there are lust, rage, and greed. Those are called deadly sins, which will destroy your relationship with God and others.

Wisdom Tea: Wisdom of God, I might not wish to end up in Hell after this life. However, I must be careful and avoid three things that will lead me right to the doors of Hell, namely, lust, rage, and greed. Thank you, Lord.

May 25

Nothing great in the world has been accomplished without passion.

(G. W. F. Hegel (1770–1831), *Philosophy of History*) (Religious, Passion, pg. 379)

In-Flavor: Passion drives people to go out of their way to do something and make great sacrifices for it. If you want to succeed at something, you must first have a passion for it and then follow it through.

Inspiration Coffee: Wonder Counselor, passion drives me out of my comfort zone and pushes me to do new things. If I want to achieve something, I must first have a passion for it and then follow through with it. Thank you, Lord.

You shall not bear false witness against your neighbor.

(Exodus 20:16) (Religious, Liars and Lies, pg. 294)

Wi-Flavor: The Bible praises people who treat their neighbors with care and respect, but condemns anyone hurting others with lies or false witness. So, you should not tell lies against your neighbors.

Wisdom Tea: Wisdom of God, I might not like people who lie to me and try to hurt me that way. However, people can hurt me the same way by bearing false witness against me. I need to avoid doing that. Thank you, Lord.

May 26

Be patient with everyone, but above all with thyself. I mean, do not be disheartened by your imperfections, but always rise up with fresh courage.

(St. Francis De Sales (1567–1622), in Jean-Pierre Camus's *The Spirit of St. Francis De Sales*) (Religious, Patience, pg. 382)

In-Flavor: You might need lots of patience in dealing with people every day. But you need more than patience in dealing with your imperfections. You need courage and fresh vision to rise up again.

Inspiration Coffee: Wonder Counselor, I need a lot of patience in handling people every day, especially myself. But I also need courage and fresh vision to rise up again from my imperfections and failures. Thank you, Lord.

Music is well said to be the speech of angels.

(Thomas Carlyle, *Essays: The Opera*, 1857) (Religious, Music, pg. 348)

Wi-Flavor: Angels are the most interested heavenly creature for humans besides God. They spoke the most at Christmas with their glorious singing. So, music is the closest speech of angels you can hear.

Wisdom Tea: Wisdom of God, I hear the angels spoke the loudest at Christmas. In fact, they were singing the Gloria on that holy night. Now I know that music is the speech of angels spoken on earth. Thank you, Lord.

May 27

A serene spirit accepts pleasure and pain with an even mind, and is unmoved by either. He alone is worthy of immortality. (Bhagavad-Gita) (Religious, Serenity, pg. 509)

In-Flavor: Life can be overwhelming because it is full of sadness and pain. Furthermore, it is chaotic and unpredictable. What you need to pray for is a serene spirit to handle all that pressure with grace.

Inspiration Coffee: Wonder Counselor, my life is a mixture of pleasure and pain, and I can feel overwhelmed sometimes. I need a serene spirit to accept all those emotions and moments with an even mind. Thank you, Lord.

It is absurd to seek peace while rejecting God. For where God is left out, justice is left out; and where justice is lacking, there can be no hope of peace. (Pius X, "E Supremi," October 4, 1903) (Religious, Peace, pg. 385)

Wi-Flavor: Everyone wants peace and justice for the world, but keeps God out of that discussion. So, if you want peace at home or in the world, you must first seek God, who will guide you on how to get it.

Wisdom Tea: Wisdom of God, the world wants peace and justice, but tries to keep you out of that conversation. If I want those gifts, I first need to seek you, who will show me how to get them. Thank you, Lord.

May 28

No wind is favorable for the sailor who doesn't know where he is going. (Wise, Direction, pg. 41)

In-Flavor: A gentle wind is favorable to a sailor if he knows where he is going. Otherwise, it is useless. Similarly, if you know the purpose of your life, then an opportunity of a lifetime would matter to you.

Inspiration Coffee: Wonder Counselor, a sailor who does not know his destination does not care about the favorable wind. Also, I need to know the purpose of my life if I can appreciate a lifetime opportunity. Thank you, Lord.

[Prejudice is] our method of transferring our own sickness to others. It is our ruse for disliking others rather than ourselves. (Ben Hecht, *A Guide for the Bedeviled*, 1944) (Religious, Prejudice, pg. 429)

Wi-Flavor: The world is full of prejudices and often assumes ignorance and hatred are at their root. You are called to get rid of your prejudice, which is a ruse of transferring your own sickness to others.

Wisdom Tea: Wisdom of God, I might not realize that prejudice is my method of transferring my own sickness to others. I need to eliminate my prejudices and stop my ruse for disliking others. Thank you, Lord.

May 29

Learn from the mistakes of others; you can't live long enough to make them all yourself. (Wise, Mistakes, pg. 87)

In-Flavor: Life on earth is short and full of challenges. You want to avoid those painful moments by learning from the mistakes of others. That way, you can make the best of your life and enjoy it.

Inspiration Coffee: Wonder Counselor, my life on earth is short and full of challenges. I need to avoid those difficult moments by trying to learn from the mistakes of others and enjoying much of it. Thank you, Lord.

Time cures sorrows and squabbles because we all change and are no longer the same persons. Neither the offender nor the offended is the same. (Blaise Pascal, *Pensées*, 1670) (Religious, Time, pg. 563)

Wi-Flavor: People come to medicine and traditional methods to find healing for their sorrow and other problems. Today, you are revealed a secret of time, which can cure sorrow and many life problems.

Wisdom Tea: Wisdom of God, I might have learned about Western medicine and Eastern methods that can heal my problems. Today, I am told about a secret of time that can cure sorrows and squabbles. Thank you, Lord.

May 30

Winning isn't everything, but wanting to win is. (Vince Lombardi, in *Esquire* magazine, November 1962) (Wise, Winning/ Losing, pg. 145)

In-Flavor: Everybody wants to win something in life. When that moment comes, it also goes by very fast. But it takes everything you have to prepare for that triumphant moment. That makes winning exciting.

Inspiration Coffee: Wonder Counselor, I might want to win really bad and think winning is everything. But actually, *wanting* to win is everything because I would have to prepare a long time for that moment. Thank you, Lord.

Confidence is keeping your chin up; overconfidence is sticking your neck out. (Practical, Confidence, pg. 38)

Wi-Flavor: Overconfidence can make a person cocky and stumble. That is not the attitude you should have in carrying out your duty. Instead, you need to pray for confidence and courage to complete it.

Wisdom Tea: Wisdom of God, I should not be overconfident and have a cocky attitude about doing my task. Rather, I could use some confidence and lots of courage to keep my chin up and finish my task. Thank you, Lord.

May 31
Don't look down on people unless you are helping them up. (Wit, Unknown, pg. 1)

In-Flavor: When people look down on others, they often think they are better and show little respect and concern to them. So, if you have ever looked down on others, it would better be to help them up.

Inspiration Coffee: Wonder Counselor, the world might not emphasize the importance of showing respect and care for others. However, I must try to help people up and not look down on them. Thank you, Lord.

Making decisions is simple: Get the facts; seek God's guidance; form a judgment; act on it; worry no more. (Charles E. Bennett) (Practical, Decision Making, pg. 50)

Wi-Flavor: You have to make many decisions every day. Some of them might carry major consequences. But if you know how to make a decision correctly (as shown above), you have nothing to worry about.

Wisdom Tea: Wisdom of God, I sure make lots of decisions every day and do not often think carefully about them. Today, I am reminded to deliberate every decision by the process above and rest easy. Thank you, Lord.

JUNE

June 1

God brings men into deep waters, not to drown them, but to cleanse them. (Practical, Adversity, pg. 7)

In-Flavor: You might hate adversity, for it is painful and makes you wonder if God is letting you drown in the deep waters. But truthfully, God just wants to buff you up for the future glorious moment.

Inspiration Coffee: Wonder Counselor, I might not like adversity or deep waters in my life. But I must realize that God brings me into deep water not to drown me, but to buff me up for future glory. Thank you, Lord.

The wise man saves for the future, but the foolish man spends whatever he gets.
(Proverbs 21:20) (Practical, Future, pg. 89)

Wi-Flavor: Foolish people do not think about the future and squander whatever they get right now. But if you are a wise person, you should work hard now and try to save some for the future.

Wisdom Tea: Wisdom of God, I should not be a foolish person and spend everything I get now. I should be a wise person and try to save for the future some of my hard-earned income. Thank you, Lord.

June 2

Crooks are jealous of each other's loot, while good men long to help each other. (Proverbs 12:12) (Practical, Cooperation, pg. 41)

In-Flavor: Crooked and wicked people often get jealous and fight over what others might have. But if you are a good and virtuous person, you will always share your blessings and help out others.

Inspiration Coffee: Wonder Counselor, crooked and wicked people get jealous of each other's loot and fight over it. However, as a good and virtuous person, I will learn to share my blessings and help others. Thank you, Lord.

The Lord hates cheating and delights in honesty.
(Proverbs 11:1) (Practical, Honesty, pg. 107)

Wi-Flavor: Everyone hates cheating people and likes honest ones. The Lord feels the same way. You must avoid all the cheating acts and embrace an honest attitude if you want the Lord to love you.

Wisdom Tea: Wisdom of God, you hate cheating and delight in honesty like everyone else. I must avoid all the acts of cheating and make an honest attitude an important part of my life to win your love. Thank you, Lord.

June 3

They that wait upon the Lord shall renew their strength. They shall mount up with wings like eagles; they shall run and not be weary; they shall walk and not faint. (Isaiah 40:31) (Practical, Endurance, pg. 62)

In-Flavor: Waiting for the day of the Lord and his salvation is an enduring test. But if you can make it, you will have an amazing power to soar like an eagle and incredible strength to run without becoming weary.

Inspiration Coffee: Wonder Counselor, I should wait for you and the day of your salvation. If I can endure that, I shall be blessed with the power to soar like an eagle and the strength to run without becoming weary. Thank you, Lord.

If a cause is just, it will eventually triumph in spite of all the propaganda issued against it. (Practical, Justice, pg. 125)

Wi-Flavor: For any cause, you will see people line up on both sides to create a lively discussion. But if the cause is just, you should rest assured that it will eventually triumph, despite opposition against it.

Wisdom Tea: Wisdom of God, people line up on both sides of a cause to debate it. However, if a cause is just, I can be sure that it will eventually triumph, despite all the propaganda issued against it. Thank you, Lord.

June 4

We make our future by the best use of the present. (Practical, Future, pg. 91)

In-Flavor: Like most people, you have been given a limited amount of resources and gifts. The kind of future you create for yourself depends on how you make good use of those resources and gifts.

Inspiration Coffee: Wonder Counselor, I am grateful for all the blessings and gifts you have given me so far. I should make good use of those present resources to achieve wonderful things in the future. Thank you, Lord.

Love forgets mistakes; nagging about them parts the best of friends. (Proverbs 17:9) (Practical, Love, pg. 143)

Wi-Flavor: Your friendships will last a long time if your love for each other can overlook the mistakes. But if you keep nagging about every mistake, that negative attitude will part even best friends.

Wisdom Tea: Wisdom of God, love can do wonders and change lives. Today, I am reminded that love can also forget mistakes and build up lasting friendships. But nagging destroys even best friends. Thank you, Lord.

June 5

A sense of humor reduces people and problems to their proper proportions. (Practical, Humor, pg. 115)

In-Flavor: A good sense of humor helps you put things in perspective and not take yourself too seriously or make a big deal out of a situation. That way you can laugh at yourself or a problem easily.

Inspiration Coffee: Wonder Counselor, my life is full of problems and worries that can make me so tense and overwhelmed. Perhaps humor can loosen me up and reduce my problems to their proper proportions. Thank you, Lord.

Among the attributes of God, although they are all equal, mercy shines with even more brilliance than justice. (Practical, Mercy, pg. 154)

Wi-Flavor: It is difficult for you to find justice on earth. Hence, you may desire divine justice for the Last Day. But you should pray for divine mercy, because it shines even more brilliantly than divine justice.

Wisdom Tea: Wisdom of God, you have many attributes that I really admire. Your divine justice is what many people wish to happen on earth. But it is your shining mercy that I appreciate the most. Thank you, Lord.

June 6

Be kind to everybody. You never know who might show up on the jury at your trial. (Practical, Kindness, pg. 128)

In-Flavor: People often view relationships in terms of a transaction. They are kind to someone only if they can get something. You should be kind to everyone as if they would be on the jury at your trial.

Inspiration Coffee: Wonder Counselor, I might be kind to people only if they give me the same treatment or if I get something out of it. But I should do so because they might be on the jury at my trial. Thank you, Lord.

Motivation is what gets you started. Habit is what keeps you going. (Jim Ryun) (Practical, Motivation, pg. 168)

Wi-Flavor: You should have good motivation and purpose for your life to get started on various dreams. But you should also have good habits and discipline to keep you going on the right path to success.

Wisdom Tea: Wisdom of God, I need your help to motivate me to do the right things and dream big. However, I know that I must have good habits to keep me going on that right path to my success. Thank you, Lord.

June 7
You have to know the ropes in order to pull the strings. (Practical, Knowledge, pg. 131)

In-Flavor: You need to educate yourself in life and have as much knowledge about various issues as possible. That way, if you have to make a decision on an issue, you will know it well beforehand.

Inspiration Coffee: Wonder Counselor, I need to educate myself and have as much knowledge about various issues as possible. That will help me know an issue well and make a good, informed decision. Thank you, Lord.

A sure cure for conceit and pride is a visit to the cemetery, where eggheads and boneheads get equal billing. (Practical, Pride, pg. 196)

Wi-Flavor: It is not easy to get a proud person to be humble. However, you are promised that the sure cure for conceit and pride is a visit to the cemetery to help you see that everyone will end up the same.

Wisdom Tea: Wisdom of God, conceit and pride can cause me a lot of troubles. But the sure cure for it is a visit to the cemetery, where everyone will end up the same. I must learn to avoid being prideful. Thank you, Lord.

June 8
Laughter is the sun that drives winter from the human face. (Victor Hugo) (Practical, Laughter, pg. 133)

In-Flavor: Daily life can pull you down or make you feel like a cold and cloudy winter day. But laughter can brighten up your spirit like the glorious sun and make you forget all the troubles of your day.

Inspiration Coffee: Wonder Counselor, my life might have quite a few cold and cloudy winter days that can dampen my spirit. However, laughter is the sun that can brighten it up and drive the winter away. Thank you, Lord.

Associate yourself with men of good quality if you esteem your own reputation, for it is better alone than in bad company. (George Washington) (Practical, Reputation, pg. 207)

Wi-Flavor: You might not realize how important it is to hang around people of good quality and charac-ters. But if you want to protect your good reputation, you should avoid bad company.

Wisdom Tea: Wisdom of God, if I care about my reputation, I want to be with people of good quality and fine character. Otherwise, I am better off being alone than in bad company. Thank you, Lord.

June 9

Opportunity is missed by most people because it is dressed in overalls and looks like work.

(Thomas Edison) (Practical, Opportunity, pg. 174)

In-Flavor: You might not recognize an opportunity when it appears before you. It is usually well hidden as work and high-risk gamble. So, pay attention and grab it, for opportunity does not come by often.

Inspiration Coffee: Wonder Counselor, I might not recognize opportunity every day because it is usually well hidden as work or high-risk gambling. But I need to identify it and grab every opportunity as I can. Thank you, Lord.

Time is a great healer, but a poor beautician.

(Lucille S. Harper) (Practical, Time, pg. 225)

Wi-Flavor: You may not know all the secrets about time. Today, you are reminded that time will help you heal when you are hurt, but time will not make you look good as you have to wrestle with life's challenges.

Wisdom Tea: Wisdom of God, time can heal all wounds and has a lot of secrets for me to yet discover. However, it will not help me look good, as I have to wrestle with many life challenges every day. Thank you, Lord.

June 10

He who lays no plans for the future will have an empty old age.

(Practical, Plans, pg. 186)

In-Flavor: The future is full of uncertainties and challenges. You need to prepare thoughtful and detailed plans to help you handle it gracefully. Otherwise, you will face a chaotic and empty old age.

Inspiration Coffee: Wonder Counselor, it would be foolish for me to have no plans for my future and face an empty, chaotic old age. I must be wise and prepare careful plans to deal with my future challenges. Thank you, Lord.

Beware of him who gives thee advice according to his own interests.

(Talmud, Sanhedrin 76a) (Quotations, Advice, pg. 7)

Wi-Flavor: You will need advice and help from others throughout your life. But you should beware of people who admonish you with their own agendas, for they do not have your interests at heart.

Wisdom Tea: Wisdom of God, I might need advice and help from others every day. However, I should be careful about taking advice from people with their own agendas, for they do not have my interests. Thank you, Lord.

June 11
God delights in those who keep their promises and abhors those who don't. (Proverbs 12:22) (Practical, Promises, pg. 199)

In-Flavor: It is easy for someone to make all kinds of promises without any intention of fulfilling them. But if you want God not to abhor and delight in you, you better follow through with your promises.

Inspiration Coffee: Wonder Counselor, I rejoice and delight in those who keep their promises, like you do. But I abhor and detest people who do not. So, I will stick to my promises and follow them through. Thank you, Lord.

The biggest fool is he who has learned much, taught much, and is still discontented. (Thiruvalluvar, Indian Tamil writer, *Kural*) (Quotations, Fools and foolishness, pg. 100)

Wi-Flavor: You are encouraged to learn more about life and share your knowledge with the world while keeping a thankful spirit. However, you will be the biggest fool if you are still discontent in the process.

Wisdom Tea: Wisdom of God, I am admonished to learn more about life and share my knowledge with others. But I will be the biggest fool if I am still discontent and not grateful with that process. Thank you, Lord.

June 12
The difference between the impossible and the possible lies in a man's determination. (Tommy Lasorda) (Practical, Tenacity, pg. 219)

In-Flavor: Success never comes easy, for there are always hurdles standing in the way. You can look at those difficulties and give up, or you can be determined to make the impossible a reality.

Inspiration Coffee: Wonder Counselor, I might have a wonderful dream, but many hurdles stand between it and its success. However, I can turn that impossible dream to possible success by my tenacity. Thank you, Lord.

He who is guilty is the one that has much to say. (Ashanti (West African) proverb) (Quotations, Guilt, pg. 120)

Wi-Flavor: It can be difficult for you to discern who is guilty and who is innocent at a hearing. Today, you are given a great insight on finding out who might be guilty—namely, the one who has much to say.

Wisdom Tea: Wisdom of God, I might find it difficult to figure out who is guilty without peering into his/her heart. Now I am told that anyone who has much to say is the guilty one because of all the excuses. Thank you, Lord.

June 13
The person who has no fire in himself cannot ignite others.
(Practical, Zeal, pg. 251)

In-Flavor: A good leader knows how to motivate his followers to believe in a mission and get it done. But if you do not have that fire of motivation in you, you cannot ignite and get it burning in others.

Inspiration Coffee: Wonder Counselor, if I want to be a leader, I need to know how to motivate others to believe in a task and complete it. But I need to have that fire in me first before I can ignite it in others. Thank you, Lord.

Give a man a fish and you feed him for a day. Teach a man to fish and you feed him for a lifetime.
(Chinese proverb) (Quotations, Learning and Education, pg. 159)

Wi-Flavor: You are encouraged to help people in need and also teach them to take care of themselves. If you give them a fish, it lasts only a day. But if you teach them how to fish, that lesson will last them a lifetime.

Wisdom Tea: Wisdom of God, I am always encouraged to help the needy by giving them something. However, the best way for me to help them is to teach them how to earn a living to last a lifetime. Thank you, Lord.

June 14
You gain strength, courage, and confidence by every experience in which you really stop to look fear in the face.
(Eleanor Roosevelt (1884–1962), American humanitarian and First Lady) (Quotations, Fear, pg. 93)

In-Flavor: Fear makes a person weak, discouraged, and doubtful to do anything. The best way for you to gain strength, courage, and confidence to complete a task is to look fear in the face and just do it.

Inspiration Coffee: Wonder Counselor, I might be fearful and feel weak, discouraged, and doubtful to do anything. But I can gain back my strength, courage, and confidence by looking fear in the face. Thank you, Lord.

The most important thing in any relationship is not what you get, but what you give.
(Eleanor Roosevelt) (Quotations, Relationships, pg. 232)

Wi-Flavor: People often expect to get something out of a relationship. You should keep in mind that the most important thing in any of your relationships is what you give to them, not what you get out of them.

Wisdom Tea: Wisdom of God, I often see people try to exploit a relationship and get something out of it. However, the most important thing in any relationship is what I will give to it. Thank you, Lord.

June 15

The small man is one who throws away his opportunities, whereas great deeds are accomplished through utilizing the mistakes [of others] and inflexibly following them up. (Li Ssu (280–208 BC), Chinese official and writer) (Quotations, Success, pg. 272)

In-Flavor: A fool throws away an opportunity and accomplishes nothing. But if you are a wise person, you learn from the mistakes of others and make good use of the opportunities to get to your success.

Inspiration Coffee: Wonder Counselor, a foolish person throws away his opportunities and gets nothing. But I can be a wise person who learns from the mistakes of others and uses my opportunities to succeed. Thank you, Lord.

Men see only the present; Heaven sees the future. (Chinese proverb) (Quotations, Time, pg. 277)

Wi-Flavor: Humans can only see things in the present time and find it difficult to comprehend anything happening in the future. You need to rely on heavenly knowledge to help you see the future.

Wisdom Tea: Wisdom of God, as a human I can only see things in the present time. But if I want to understand and see anything happening in the future, I need to count on heavenly knowledge. Thank you, Lord.

June 16

Nothing ever comes to one that is worth having, except as a result of hard work. (Booker T. Washington, *Up from Slavery*) (Quotations, Work, pg. 314)

In-Flavor: You might inherit a fortune or win a jackpot, but that huge treasure will not mean a lot to you. However, if you work hard to earn a living, that little income is worth more to you than anything.

Inspiration Coffee: Wonder Counselor, I might have acquired a huge fortune by an inheritance or winning the lottery. But that does not mean a lot to me compared to something I have worked hard to acquire. Thank you, Lord.

Riches are not from an abundance of worldly goods, but from a contented mind. (Muhammad) (Quotations, Wealth, pg. 303)

Wi-Flavor: People think wealth is about acquiring an abundance of worldly goods, and hence, they do everything possible to achieve it. But true wealth for you must come from your contented mind.

Wisdom Tea: Wisdom of God, I may assume that wealth is all about accumulating an abundance of worldly goods and would do anything to get it. But true wealth really comes from a contented mind. Thank you, Lord.

June 17

Have no anxiety about anything, but in everything by prayer and supplication with thanksgiving let your requests be made known to God. And the peace of God, which passes all understanding, will keep your hearts and minds in Christ Jesus. (Philippians 4:6–7) (Religious, Anxiety and Fear, pg. 30)

In-Flavor: Anxiety and fear are a couple of problems you might face every day. But today, you are called to put all your problems and prayer requests to God so that the peace of God may be with you.

Inspiration Coffee: Wonder Counselor, I might face anxiety and fear every day. However, I am encouraged to put those problems and my prayer requests to God if I want the peace of God in my heart. Thank you, Lord.

Love one another with brotherly affection; outdo one another in showing honor. (Romans 12:10) (Religious, Agape, pg. 20)

Wi-Flavor: What might help the current world to stop hatred and bring it healing is love and respect. Indeed, you can help transform this world by showing love and giving respect to people around you.

Wisdom Tea: Wisdom of God, the world is full of hatred and vengeance. I can stop those acts and change the current world by learning to show love and give respect to people around me every day. Thank you, Lord.

June 18

Give to him who begs from you, and do not refuse him who would borrow from you. (Matthew 5:42) (Religious, Conduct and Behavior, pg. 95)

In-Flavor: Lending and sharing is not inherent in human nature. But today, you are asked to lend to anyone who wants to borrow from you and give to anyone who begs from you.

Inspiration Coffee: Wonder Counselor, it may not be in my human nature to lend and share God's blessings with others. But today, I am asked to lend to those who want to borrow and give to those who beg me. Thank you, Lord.

The Bible, the greatest medicine chest of humanity. (Heinrich Heine, *Ludwig Marcus*, 1844) (Religious, Bible, pg. 53)

Wi-Flavor: The Bible is considered the inspiring words of God and Jesus, and written tradition in the life of the people of God. Today, you are told that it is also the greatest source of healing for humanity.

Wisdom Tea: Wisdom of God, I know the Bible is the inspiring words of God and Jesus, and written tradition for the people of God. Today, I am informed that it is also the greatest source of healing for humanity. Thank you, Lord.

June 19

Repay evil with good and, lo, between whom and you there was enmity will become your warm friend. (Koran) (Religious, Evil, pg. 168)

In-Flavor: You might have heard the saying, "An eye for an eye, and a tooth for a tooth." However, today you are called to follow a new way of living and repay evil with good to help turn enmity to friendship.

Inspiration Coffee: Wonder Counselor, I might have been told, "An eye for an eye, and a tooth for a tooth." But today, I am called to embrace a new thinking and repay evil with good to turn enmity to friendship. Thank you, Lord.

True contentment is a real, even an active virtue—not only affirmative but creative. It is the power of getting out of any situation all there is in it. (G. K. Chesterton, *A Miscellany of Men*, 1912) (Religious, Contentment, pg. 109)

Wi-Flavor: Most people talk about personal happiness and how to maximize it. But nobody can define what it is. Today, you are focused on the virtue of true contentment that will bring you real happiness.

Wisdom Tea: Wisdom of God, I might have heard about personal happiness and how everyone has searched long and hard for it. But today, I am called to find true contentment as the way to real happiness. Thank you, Lord.

June 20

No man can become a saint in his sleep. (Henry Drummond, *The Greatest Thing in the World*, 1890) (Religious, Deeds, pg. 128)

In-Flavor: Like any achievement, sainthood demands commitment, sacrifice, and hard work. If you want to be a saint, you must make great sacrifices, do extraordinary work, and commit yourself to it.

Inspiration Coffee: Wonder Counselor, I might want to be a sports hero, a tycoon, a movie star, or a glamorous figure. Perhaps I can try to become a saint by making sacrifices and doing extraordinary work. Thank you, Lord.

Train up a child in the way he should go, and when he is old he will not depart from it. (Proverbs 22:6) (Religious, Children, pg. 74)

Wi-Flavor: Humans are creatures of habit. If you want children to grow old with a good habit and not depart from it, you must teach them that habit and train them early in their childhood.

Wisdom Tea: Wisdom of God, children are like sponges who can absorb good habits and bad ones. The earlier I am trained in good habits, the better person I will become later on in life. Thank you, Lord.

June 21

The important thing is to begin again, humbly and courageously, after every fall. (Dom Hélder Câmara (1909–1999)) (Religious, Failure and Defeat, pg. 175)

In-Flavor: It is always difficult to get up after a fall. Therefore, the most important thing you must do after every failure or defeat is to begin again humbly and courageously amidst other challenges.

Inspiration Coffee: Wonder Counselor, I will surely stumble and fall throughout my life. However, I need to get up and begin again humbly and courageously after every failure or defeat to face more challenges. Thank you, Lord.

A jealous person is doubly unhappy—over what he has, which is judged inferior, and over what he has not, which is judged superior. Such a person is doubly removed from knowing the true blessings of creation. (Desmond Tutu, 1988) (Religious, Envy and Jealousy, pg. 160)

Wi-Flavor: Jealousy is one of the deadly sins that can seriously hurt a person. Today, you are warned that a jealous person is doubly unhappy and doubly removed from seeing the true blessings of life itself.

Wisdom Tea: Wisdom of God, I might not realize how harmful jealousy can be. Today, I am cautioned that jealousy can make me doubly unhappy and doubly removed from seeing my true blessings. Thank you, Lord.

June 22

The greatest power God gave us is the power to choose. We have the opportunity to choose whether we're going to act or procrastinate, believe or doubt, pray or curse, help or heal, to be happy or sad. (Lou Holtz, Gonzaga University commencement, *Christian Science Monitor*, June 12, 1989) (Religious, Free Will, pg. 199)

In-Flavor: Like freedom, free will is a powerful gift that the Creator has entrusted to all human beings, and it can bring serious, long-term results. You must use it carefully to make wise choices.

Inspiration Coffee: Wonder Counselor, free will is an awesome gift that I have received from my Creator. It is a wonderful opportunity for me to choose anything from the list above. I must use it wisely. Thank you, Lord.

The Devil's cleverest wile is to make men believe that he does not exist. (Gerald C. Treacy, *The Devil!*, 1952) (Religious, Devil, pg. 138)

Wi-Flavor: The Devil has a big bag of tricks to deploy against humans and pull them away from God. You must know that his cleverest wile is to make you believe that he does not exist, to hide his ugly work.

Wisdom Tea: Wisdom of God, the Devil has a lot of tricks to lure me away from God and keep me on his side. But his cleverest wile is to convince me to believe that he does not exist, to continue his work. Thank you, Lord.

June 23

Knowledge is the food of the soul. (Socrates, "Protagoras," in Plato's *Dialogues*, 399 BC) (Religious, Knowledge, pg. 289)

In-Flavor: Your body needs food and water to give it nutrition to survive. Likewise, you should provide your soul or spirit with knowledge for its refreshment and help it make the right decisions and choices.

Inspiration Coffee: Wonder Counselor, I need food and water for my physical body to survive. Similarly, my soul or spirit should have enough knowledge to help it make the right decisions and be refreshed. Thank you, Lord.

We don't have choices about who our parents are and how they treated us, but we have a choice about whether we forgive our parents and heal ourselves. (Bernie Siegel, in *New Age Journal*, May/June 1989) (Religious, Family, pg. 186)

Wi-Flavor: You might not be blessed with a loving family and a good beginning. But you now have a choice of letting the past hurt imprison you or learning to forgive your offenders and heal yourself.

Wisdom Tea: Wisdom of God, my parents or family might have mistreated me. However, I have a choice on whether I will forgive them and get myself healed or let past hurts continue to imprison me. Thank you, Lord.

June 24

The well of life is love, and he who dwells not in love is dead. (John Tauler (1300–1361), sermon for Thursday in Easter Week) (Religious, Love, pg. 311)

In-Flavor: Love brings joy to daily routines and makes life worth living. It has an incredible power to energize and rejuvenate a person. If you do not remain in love, you will dry up and die from loneliness.

Inspiration Coffee: Wonder Counselor, love can do a lot of wonderful things for me. But what I appreciate the most about love is the well of life it brings me. I need to remain in love or else end up dead. Thank you, Lord.

Covetousness is the greatest of monsters, as well as the root of all evil. (William Penn, *Some Fruits of Solitude*, 1693) (Religious, Greed, pg. 218)

Wi-Flavor: A monster is a scary creature that can harm people and cause collateral damage. Today, you are cautioned that greed can turn you into an evil monster that covets and devours the resources of others.

Wisdom Tea: Wisdom of God, greed makes me forget about my life's blessings and stirs up the endless desire to devour my neighbors' possessions. I need to watch out for this covetousness monster. Thank you, Lord.

June 25

Serenity comes not alone by removing the outward causes and occasions of fear, but by the discovery of inward reservoirs to draw upon. (Rufus M. Jones, *The Testimony of the Soul,* 1936) (Religious, Serenity, pg. 510)

In-Flavor: Life can be stressful and unbearable. But you cannot find serenity by simply removing the external causes. Serenity can only be achieved by your discovery of inner reservoirs to draw upon.

Inspiration Coffee: Wonder Counselor, my life is full of pressures and stresses. I cannot find serenity by simply removing the outward causes of fears. I also need to find inward reservoirs to draw my strength. Thank you, Lord.

Heaven has a road, but no one travels it; Hell has no gate but men will bore through to get there. (Chinese proverb) (Religious, Hell, pg. 229)

Wi-Flavor: The road to Heaven is filled with tears and heavy crosses, while the way to Hell is paved with empty promises and fleeting joy. Today, you are advised to choose the road to Heaven and avoid Hell.

Wisdom Tea: Wisdom of God, Hell has no gate, but people keep digging their way to get there. I need to avoid it and stay on the road to Heaven, where tears and heavy crosses fill it, but no one travels it. Thank you, Lord.

June 26

Unless you try to do something beyond what you have already mastered, you will never grow. (Ronald E. Osborn) (Wise, Dreams, pg. 45)

In-Flavor: Most people like their daily routines and become complacent with their growth. You need to challenge yourself to grow and maximize your potential by creating new dreams and hopes.

Inspiration Coffee: Wonder Counselor, I should not settle for what I have already mastered. Rather, I need to challenge myself to grow every day and maximize my potential with new dreams and hopes. Thank you, Lord.

False words are not only evil in themselves, but they infect the soul with evil. (Socrates, "Apology," in Plato's *Dialogues,* 399 BC) (Religious, Liars and Lies, pg. 294)

Wi-Flavor: False words make a mockery of the truth and mislead the public about the current issue. But what you should be concerned about is that they could infect the soul with their evil power.

Wisdom Tea: Wisdom of God, false words and sins are evil in themselves and can lead me away from the right path to God, the truth. But they can also infect my soul with evil viruses and destroy it forever. Thank you, Lord.

June 27
He who rolls up his sleeves seldom loses his shirt. (Wise, Laziness, pg. 79)

In-Flavor: When you roll up your sleeves, you usually work hard to earn a living. In that case, you cannot become poor and lose your shirt. However, if you are lazy, you will eventually lose your shirt.

Inspiration Coffee: Wonder Counselor, if I work hard to earn a living, I would have to roll up my sleeves and seldom lose my shirt. However, if I am lazy and do not toil under the sun, I would soon lose my shirt. Thank you, Lord.

All men desire peace, but few desire the things that make for peace. (Thomas à Kempis, *Imitation of Christ*, 1441) (Religious, Peace, pg. 385)

Wi-Flavor: Humans desire peace, among other things. But you will see that they do not always move beyond thoughts and make it a reality. Otherwise, they would come to God to find ways to peace.

Wisdom Tea: Wisdom Tea: Wisdom of God, I might desire peace inside of me and all around me. However, if I truly want that dream to come true, I would need to come to God to find out how I can achieve it. Thank you, Lord.

June 28
Wicked men obey from fear; good men, from love. (Aristotle) (Wise, Obedience, pg. 93)

In-Flavor: Wicked people will stop their evil deeds only when they become fearful or feel threatened. But if you are a good person, you will obey and do right things out of love and respect.

Inspiration Coffee: Wonder Counselor, I must not obey out of fear and the threat of punishment, like wicked people do. Rather, I should learn obedience and follow the rules because of love and respect. Thank you, Lord.

Tolerance implies a respect for another person, not because he is wrong or even because he is right, but because he is human. (John Cogley, in *Commonweal*, April 24, 1959) (Religious, Tolerance, pg. 565)

Wi-Flavor: Tolerance is considered a dirty word these days, for no one wants to compromise. But you are asked to show tolerance every day by giving respect to someone because he/she is human.

Wisdom Tea: Wisdom of God, the word I hear a lot is to "fight" for my rights, which often causes hatred and disrespect. I need to instead learn to tolerate and show respect for others, for the sake of humanity. Thank you, Lord.

June 29

Winners are people who aren't afraid to take a chance now and then. Losers sit around and wait for the odds to improve. (Wise, Winning/Losing, pg. 145)

In-Flavor: Many people do not like to gamble and prefer to wait around for their odds to improve. But that is the attitude of a loser. If you want to be a winner, you should take a chance now and then.

Inspiration Coffee: Wonder Counselor, I might continue my old, losing way and wait for my odds to improve. Or I might take a chance now and then, and do something different to help myself be a winner. Thank you, Lord.

Little drops of water wear down big stones. (Russian proverb) (Practical, Adversity, pg. 7)

Wi-Flavor: Nobody would think that little drops of water might wear down a boulder. But that will be possible with time. Likewise, you will be able to overcome any adversity by your persistence over time.

Wisdom Tea: Wisdom of God, today I am assured that little drops of water can wear down big stones over time. Likewise, my persistence and patient endurance can overcome all adversities over time. Thank you, Lord.

June 30

In order to succeed, we must first believe that we can. (Wit, Unknown, pg. 1)

In-Flavor: Most people who succeeded did not get there by doubting their ability to overcome the challenges and complete the task. If you hope to succeed, you must first believe you can do it.

Inspiration Coffee: Wonder Counselor, living in an uncertain world and with daily challenges, I continue to doubt my ability to achieve something. But with your help, I believe that I can succeed at all my dreams. Thank you, Lord.

A relaxed attitude lengthens a man's life; jealousy rots it away. (Proverbs 14:30) (Practical, Attitude, pg. 17)

Wi-Flavor: Everyone loves to have a relaxed attitude, but the internal battle with vices like jealousy will cause chaos. You will see that jealousy also shortens your life, while a relaxed attitude lengthens it.

Wisdom Tea: Wisdom of God, I dream of a relaxed attitude, but vices like jealousy causes me an internal battle. But I am reminded that a relaxed attitude lengthens my life, while jealousy rots it away. Thank you, Lord.

July 1

Admonish your friends privately, but praise them openly.

(Cyrus the Younger, Persian prince)
(Practical, Advice, pg. 9)

In-Flavor: It is not easy to deal with family and friends. The best way for you to handle them is to admonish them privately and praise them openly in public. Doing the opposite would be problematic.

Inspiration Coffee: Wonder Counselor, I might find it difficult to deal with my family and friends. Today, it is suggested that I admonish them privately, but praise them publically. Any other way is problematic. Thank you, Lord.

A man's conscience is the Lord's search light exposing his hidden motives. (Proverbs 20:27) (Practical, Conscience, pg. 39)

Wi-Flavor: It is difficult to see what is in a human heart. That is where a person can hide wicked desires and bad intentions. But you know that God uses your conscience to search and expose those motives.

Wisdom Tea: Wisdom of God, I might try to hide my motives and wicked desires in my heart. But you can use my conscience like your search light to peer into my heart and expose those motives. Thank you, Lord.

July 2

Coming together is a beginning; staying together is progress; working together is success.

(Practical, Cooperation, pg. 42)

In-Flavor: If you are a group leader, it is a good beginning for its members to come together, a wonderful progress for you to get them to stay together, and a great success to convince them to work together.

Inspiration Coffee: Wonder Counselor, I can be a leader if I know how to bring people together and make them stay together. I will be a successful leader if I can get them to work together. Thank you, Lord.

A vital faith gives us the courage to face the present with confidence and the future with expectancy. (Practical, Future, pg. 91)

Wi-Flavor: Nonbelievers do not know how important it is for a person to have faith in this life. But you know that your faith can help you face the present with confidence and see the future with hope.

Wisdom Tea: Wisdom of God, I may not realize how vital my faith can be for me in this life. But it helps me face the present challenges with confidence and the future uncertainties with hope. Thank you, Lord.

July 3

Today's mighty oak is just yesterday's nut that held its ground.

(Practical, Endurance, pg. 63)

In-Flavor: All wonderful things usually have a humble start and, over time, become the tested reality. Likewise, your current success was a little idea of yesterday that endured lots of tests and survived.

Inspiration Coffee: Wonder Counselor, I must know that the mighty oak is just yesterday's nut that survived the tough tests. Likewise, if my little idea can endure the tests of time, it will bring me a great success. Thank you, Lord.

Lies will get any man into trouble, but honesty is its own defense. (Proverbs 12:13) (Practical, Honesty, pg. 107)

Wi-Flavor: Lies lead people down the path of deception and get them into all sorts of troubles. Honesty is the best policy for you to follow and the great virtue that brings you honor and respect from others.

Wisdom Tea: Wisdom of God, I must know that lies can get me into lots of troubles and lead down the path of deception. But honesty brings me admiration from others and is the best policy for me to live by. Thank you, Lord.

July 4

It is possible to give away and become richer! It is also possible to hold on too tightly and lose everything. Yes, the liberal man shall be rich! By watering others, he waters himself.

(Proverbs 11:24–25) (Practical, Giving, pg. 95)

In-Flavor: It is human nature to hold on tight to all possessions. But you can act contrary to that nature and help out others by giving away some of your possessions, for they might repay you more.

Inspiration Coffee: Wonder Counselor, it may not be my nature to share my blessings with others. However, I will become richer and happier if I learn to give away some of my possessions and help out others. Thank you, Lord.

Justice delayed is justice denied.

(William Gladstone) (Practical, Justice, pg. 125)

Wi-Flavor: When justice is delayed, it tells the world that something else is more important than itself. If you believe in justice, you must not delay or hide it. Rather, you must let it prevail and promote it.

Wisdom Tea: Wisdom of God, I must remember that justice is the important value that holds society together. If it is delayed or hidden somehow, it tells me something else is more important than itself. Thank you, Lord.

July 5

The thing that counts the most in the pursuit of happiness is choosing the right traveling companion. (Practical, Happiness, pg. 101)

In-Flavor: In the pursuit of happiness, you might find certain things to make you feel satisfied. But what matters the most is for you to pick the right traveling companion who shares your sense of adventure.

Inspiration Coffee: Wonder Counselor, I might be in search of happiness like the rest of the world. But I need to know that what matters the most in that pursuit is to choose the right traveling companion. Thank you, Lord.

A wise youth makes hay while the sun shines, but what a shame to see a lad who sleeps away his hour of opportunity. (Proverbs 10:5) (Practical, Laziness, pg. 135)

Wi-Flavor: Lazy people sleep away when they have good opportunities and great working conditions. But if you are a wise person, you will take advantage of God's blessings and make good use of them.

Wisdom Tea: Wisdom of God, a lazy person sleeps away when he has great opportunities and good working conditions. However, if I am a wise person, I will make good use of those blessings for my success. Thank you, Lord.

July 6

An idea is a funny little thing that won't work unless you do. (Practical, Ideas, pg. 117)

In-Flavor: It is always wonderful to have an awesome idea for a future project. But if you do not turn it into action and work on it, it is just a nice thought that has no great impact on your life or others.

Inspiration Coffee: Wonder Counselor, I am excited to have a great idea about something. However, if I do not work on it and make it a reality, it is simply a nice thought that has no real value or impact in life. Thank you, Lord.

Love God completely; love others compassionately; love yourself correctly. (Practical, Love, pg. 144)

Wi-Flavor: Humans have dreamed, talked, and sung about love since creation. But they do not know what to do with it. Today, you are advised on how to love yourself, others, and God.

Wisdom Tea: Wisdom of God, love is a nice gift God gives me in this life. I need to learn to love myself correctly, love others compassionately, and love God completely. That is how I should handle love. Thank you, Lord.

July 7

Money will buy a fine dog, but only kindness will make him wag his tail. (Practical, Kindness, pg. 127)

In-Flavor: Money can buy you lots of things, even a smart dog that can do tricks. But only your kind treatment will get the dog to wag its tail, for kindness is a language everyone can understand.

Inspiration Coffee: Wonder Counselor, I might think money is everything. Money might even buy me a smart dog, but it is my kind treatment of that dog that will make it wag its tail. I need to think and act kindly every day. Thank you, Lord.

He that does good for God's sake seeks neither praise nor reward; he is sure of both in the end. (William Penn) (Practical, Motivation, pg. 168)

Wi-Flavor: Most people do good things for all kinds of reasons, but usually for praises or rewards. If you do something good for God's sake, your motivation is neither praise nor reward; it is because of God.

Wisdom Tea: Wisdom of God, I might have different motivations to do good things while the world often does them for praises or rewards. I am encouraged today to do something good for your sake instead. Thank you, Lord.

July 8

Four things never come back—the spoken word, the sped arrow, the past life, and the neglected opportunity. (Arab proverb) (Practical, Opportunity, pg. 174)

In-Flavor: Among things that never come back, you will find the spoken word and neglected opportunity. You ought to be careful with your spoken words and not miss an opportunity God gives you.

Inspiration Coffee: Wonder Counselor, the list above tells me four things that I cannot call back once I have let them go. I need to be careful with my spoken words and the opportunities God has given me. Thank you, Lord.

A good reputation is more valuable than the most expensive perfume. (Ecclesiastes 7:1) (Practical, Reputation, pg. 207)

Wi-Flavor: People use perfume to impress and get others to like them. But you must know that your good reputation can get people to like you. It is more valuable than the most expensive perfume.

Wisdom Tea: Wisdom of God, I might use perfume and jewelries to make myself smell and look good in public. But I am told that a good reputation will last longer than the most expensive perfume. Thank you, Lord.

July 9

When you're dying of thirst, it's too late to think about digging a well. (Japanese proverb) (Practical, Plans, pg. 186)

In-Flavor: It is always wise for you to plan ahead and prepare for your future. You should not wait until there is an emergency before doing something about it. Otherwise, it might be too late.

Inspiration Coffee: Wonder Counselor, I should plan ahead and prepare for an emergency the best I can. If I wait for an emergency, like dying of thirst, to do something about it, it is too late to dig a well. Thank you, Lord.

Anger is the foundation of every evil. (Muhammad Husan Askari (1919–1978), Pakistani writer) (Quotations, Anger, pg. 16)

Wi-Flavor: Anger is one of the deadly sins that destroys your relationship with God and others. Anger causes you to say hurtful things and do destructive acts. You must avoid this root of every evil.

Wisdom Tea: Wisdom of God, anger is the root of every evil and can cause me to say and do harmful things to others. I need to avoid this deadly sin that can destroy my relationship with God and others. Thank you, Lord.

July 10

Reputation is made in a moment; character is built in a lifetime. (Practical, Reputation, pg. 207)

In-Flavor: You may like to be famous and have a good reputation, which can be acquired in a short time. But if you want to have a fine character, you might need to spend a whole lifetime to achieve it.

Inspiration Coffee: Wonder Counselor, the world is often interested in a good reputation, which is made in a short moment. However, if I want to have a good character, I might need a whole lifetime to build it. Thank you, Lord.

He who forgives ends the quarrel. (African proverb) (Quotations, Forgiveness, pg. 100)

Wi-Flavor: Quarrels happen all around you every day. They do not end the moment two sides walk away. But you can end a quarrel if you can forgive the other side and forget all about it.

Wisdom Tea: Wisdom of God, I may see or get involved in a quarrel in my daily life that does not end when the two sides walk away. The best way for me to end it is if I can forgive the other person. Thank you, Lord.

July 11

If you don't stand for something, you'll fall for anything. (Practical, Tenacity, pg. 219)

In-Flavor: It is risky and scary to take a stand on something, for you might meet opposition and hostility. But if you are not tenacious and do not stand up for something, you will be whimsical and fall for anything.

Inspiration Coffee: Wonder Counselor, I might not like to take a stand on an issue, because I am afraid people might hate me. But if I do not have the tenacity to stand for something, I will fall for anything. Thank you, Lord.

There can be no education without leisure; and without leisure, education is worthless. (Sarah Josepha Hale (1788–1879), American writer and editor) (Quotations, Learning and Education, pg. 159)

Wi-Flavor: Most creatures learn by playing; humans are no exception. If you want to learn about life, you need to leisurely explore it. But your education is worthless if you do not have fun with it.

Wisdom Tea: Wisdom of God, if I want to learn more about life, I need to leisurely explore it and play with it. But I should keep in mind that my education is useless if I do not have fun with it. Thank you, Lord.

July 12

Take time to work, it is the price of success. Take time to think, it is the source of power. Take time to play, it is the secret of youth. Take time to read, it is the foundation of knowledge. Take time to laugh, it is the music of the soul. Take time to be courteous, it is the work of a gentleman. Take time to pray, it is the Christian's vital breath. (Practical, Time, pg. 226)

In-Flavor: Time is something most people do not have. But you need to take time to work, think, play, read, laugh, be courteous, and pray, because each of those moments brings you a special blessing.

Inspiration Coffee: Wonder Counselor, I may not have time in a day to do everything on that list. However, if I take time to work, think, play, read, laugh, be courteous, and pray, I will find lots of blessings. Thank you, Lord.

Be happy. It's one way of being wise. (Colette (1873–1954), French writer) (Quotations, Happiness, pg. 121)

Wi-Flavor: Some people define wisdom in terms of knowledge; others, of life experience. You can define wisdom in a new way by calling people who try to achieve happiness "wise people."

Wisdom Tea: Wisdom of God, I may consider knowledge and life experience as the basis of wisdom. However, today I am reminded that if I search for true happiness, I am truly wise. Thank you, Lord.

July 13

Truth stands the test of time; lies are soon exposed. (Proverbs 12:19) (Practical, Truth, pg. 231)

In-Flavor: Most people hate lies and love truth because they do not want to be hurt or come out looking like a fool. But you should love truth because it will stand the test of time, while lies will soon be exposed.

Inspiration Coffee: Wonder Counselor, I might be indifferent to truth and lies. But lies often hurt and cause a lot of problems. I should avoid lies and stick with the truth, which stands the test of time. Thank you, Lord.

Religion is not what is grasped by the brain, but a heart grasp. (Mahatma Gandhi) (Quotations, Religion, pg. 232)

Wi-Flavor: People often discuss religion in terms of knowledge of the faith or the thinking side of the brain. But you should know that religion is actually welcomed and embraced by the heart.

Wisdom Tea: Wisdom of God, I might talk about religion in terms of the Bible's knowledge or the proofs of your existence. However, the truth is that my heart, not my brain, leads me to religion. Thank you, Lord.

July 14

God gives nothing to those who keep their arms crossed. (Bambara (West African) proverb) (Quotations, Action, pg. 2)

In-Flavor: When you have your arms crossed, you are basically saying that you do not need any help from God or anyone. But if you want God to give you something, you should open up your hands to Heaven.

Inspiration Coffee: Wonder Counselor, I cross my arms when I do not need any help from God or anyone. However, if I want God to help me with something, I should open up my hands to Heaven and pray. Thank you, Lord.

We must use time creatively, and forever realize that the time is always ripe to do right. (Martin Luther King Jr., "Letter from a Birmingham Jail") (Quotations, Time, pg. 278)

Wi-Flavor: People often squander their free time and use it to achieve wrongful things. You must use your time wisely and creatively by committing yourself to doing right and honorable things.

Wisdom Tea: Wisdom of God, I might find myself misusing my time or squandering it on wrongful things. Today, I am reminded to use my time wisely and creatively to do good and honorable things. Thank you, Lord.

July 15

Hatred does not cease by hatred; hatred ceases only by love. This is the eternal law. (Dhammapada, "The Twin Verses") (Quotations, Hate, pg. 122)

In-Flavor: Hatred is a dark energy and bad influence that has caused constant fighting and endless wars around the world. The only way you can put an end to hatred is by way of love and acts of kindness.

Inspiration Coffee: Wonder Counselor, I can see the world is filled with hatred and vengeance. I cannot drive away that negative influence by more acts of hatred, but by more acts of love and compassion. Thank you, Lord.

When you are rich, people come to meet you and people see you to your door; when you are penniless, you may go out early and come home late, and nobody cares a hoot. (Vietnamese proverb) (Quotations, Wealth, pg. 304)

Wi-Flavor: People often say, "Money talks." Today, you learn that if you are rich, people will treat you like a royal person. But if you are poor, you might work hard all day and nobody will care about you.

Wisdom Tea: Wisdom of God, I may hear that money talks. Today, I am reminded that if I am rich, I am sure to get the royal treatment. But if I am poor, I might work diligently and nobody will care about it. Thank you, Lord.

July 16

A man can make what he wants of himself if he truly believes that he must be ready for hard work and many heartbreaks along the way. (Thurgood Marshall (1908–1993), American jurist) (Quotations, Success, pg. 272)

In-Flavor: Success is never handed to you. If you want to achieve something in your life, you must believe in it, be prepared for hard work, and be not afraid of many heartbreaks along the way.

Inspiration Coffee: Wonder Counselor, if I want to accomplish something wonderful with my life, I must truly believe in it, be ready for hard work, and be not fearful of many heartbreaks along the way. Thank you, Lord.

So faith, hope, love abide, these three; but the greatest of these is love. (1 Corinthians 13:13) (Religious, Agape, pg. 21)

Wi-Flavor: The three greatest virtues a person can find in the Bible are faith, hope, and love. Yet, you will learn that the greatest of these is love because it makes you real and helps you endure anything.

Wisdom Tea: Wisdom of God, I know that the three greatest virtues in the Bible are faith, hope, and love. Each can do marvelous things in my life, but love is the greatest of all because it endures to the end. Thank you, Lord.

July 17
Work is the medicine for poverty.
(Yoruba (West African) proverb)
(Quotations, Work, pg. 314)
In-Flavor: You might end up in poverty for various reasons. But that living condition is not something you want to be around a day longer. The only way you can get out of it and find a new life is through work.
Inspiration Coffee: Wonder Counselor, poverty is the living condition that I do not want my life to end up in forever. However, the best way for me to bring it healing and find a new life is through work. Thank you, Lord.

If there is anything in this life which sustains a wise man and induces him to maintain his serenity amidst the tribulations and adversities of the world, it is the meditation and knowledge of the Scriptures. (St. Jerome, in Ephesios, 400 AD) (Religious, Bible, pg. 54)
Wi-Flavor: Many people these days get their knowledge from the internet and find peace by taking drugs. You are admonished to seek wisdom by learning the Scriptures and find serenity by meditating on it.
Wisdom Tea: Wisdom of God, I see people deal with their tribulations and adversities by relying on alcohol and drugs. But I am advised to find wisdom from Scriptures and serenity by meditating on it. Thank you, Lord.

July 18
If our conscience tells us that we ought to perform a particular act, it is our moral duty to perform it.
(Frederick Copleston, *Aquinas*, 1955)
(Religious, Actions, pg. 16)
In-Flavor: Your conscience is the moral compass the Creator has entrusted to you to help guide you through your daily life and make the right choices. If it tells you to act a certain way, you better do it.
Inspiration Coffee: Wonder Counselor, I have been blessed with the great gift of my conscience to guide me and help me make the right choices. If my conscience tells me to act a certain way, I must do it. Thank you, Lord.

The goal of the Christian life is not to save your soul but to transcend yourself, to vindicate the human struggle of which all of us are a part, to keep hope advancing. (William Sloane Coffin, *Living the Truth in a World of Illusions*, 1985) (Religious, Christianity, pg. 77)
Wi-Flavor: Some people believe that the goal of a Christian is to have his/her soul saved. But you are told that your Christian goal is to exceed your limitations, justify your struggle, and remain hopeful.
Wisdom Tea: Wisdom of God, I might think the goal of a Christian is to save one's soul. However, I am reminded that my Christian goal is to transcend myself, vindicate my struggle, and advance my hope. Thank you, Lord.

July 19

No Christian escapes a taste of the wilderness on the way to the Promised Land. (Evelyn Underhill, *The Fruits of the Spirit*, 1942) (Religious, Adversity, pg. 20)

In-Flavor: Like the people of God in the Bible, you dream to get to the Promised Land. But the only way for you to get there is to cross the wilderness, which is full of adversities and temptations.

Inspiration Coffee: Wonder Counselor, I wish to get to the Promised Land like the people of God do. However, the only way for that dream to come true for me is to cross the wilderness, which is full of adversities. Thank you, Lord.

No man is condemned for anything he has done; he is condemned for continuing to do wrong. (George MacDonald, *Unspoken Sermons, Series III*, 1887) (Religious, Damnation, pg. 119)

Wi-Flavor: Humans always make mistakes. You are not criticized for anything you might have done. However, you will be condemned for continuing to do wrong and failing to change.

Wisdom Tea: Wisdom of God, I make mistakes, like all humans do. Still, I am not criticized for anything I might have done. But I will be condemned for continuing to do wrong and failing to avoid it. Thank you, Lord.

July 20

Yea, though I walk through the valley of the shadow of death, I will fear no evil: for thou art with me; thy rod and thy staff they comfort me. (Psalms 23:4) (Religious, Anxiety and Fear pg. 30)

In-Flavor: You might feel anxious about your future or fearful about death and evil. But you should not feel that way, for God will be with you to protect and comfort you along your faith journey.

Inspiration Coffee: Wonder Counselor, I feel worried about the future and fearful about the surrounding dangers. But I should not feel like that anymore, for you are with me to protect and comfort me. Thank you, Lord.

Self-discipline never means giving up anything—for giving up is a loss. Our Lord did not ask us to give up the things of earth, but to exchange them for better things. (Fulton J. Sheen, *Lift Up Your Hearts*, 1950) (Religious, Discipline, pg. 140)

Wi-Flavor: Some believers think they have to give up earthly things for the eternal life. But you are told that Christians are called to follow a self-disciplined life and simply exchange those earthly things for better things.

Wisdom Tea: Wisdom of God, I might believe that I have to give up earthly things for the eternal life. However, I am called as a Christian to follow a self-disciplined life and exchange those for better things. Thank you, Lord.

July 21
Good deeds are the best prayer.
(Serbian proverb) (Religious, Deeds, pg. 129)

In-Flavor: People pray to show devotion to their God or help them live up to their faith. But today, you are reminded that good deeds are the best prayer because they help you avoid being a hypocrite.

Inspiration Coffee: Wonder Counselor, I pray to show my faith in God or ask God to do something for me. But today, I am told that good deeds are the best prayer because they show God my honest intention. Thank you, Lord.

Eternal life is not a life for the future. By charity we start eternity right here below. (Henri de Lubac, *Paradoxes*, 1948) (Religious, Eternity, pg. 164)

Wi-Flavor: People might think eternal life begins after the present one is done. However, you are admonished that you can begin that future right now and make it a reality by a life of love.

Wisdom Tea: Wisdom of God, I look forward to the eternal life and assume it comes after this life. However, I can start eternity right here below and make it a reality by a life of love. Thank you, Lord.

July 22
It is often much more difficult to learn from victory than from defeat. In defeat, questions are asked about what went wrong, so that those mistakes will not be made in the future. But victory seldom creates the need to inquire as to its sources. (Gary Hart, in the *Washington Post*, May 5, 1991) (Religious, Failure and Defeat, pg. 175)

In-Flavor: Everyone loves victory more than defeat. But it is in moments of defeat or failure that you want to know what went wrong and try to learn from your mistakes. You seldom learn from victory.

Inspiration Coffee: Wonder Counselor, like most people, I surely prefer victory to defeat. However, in moments of defeat or failure, I will try to figure out what went wrong. I seldom learn anything from victory. Thank you, Lord.

An ounce of parent is worth a pound of the clergy. (Spanish proverb) (Religious, Family, pg. 186)

Wi-Flavor: People come to the clergy to find moral guidance and learn how to be good. You will not have to make your children do that if you would try to be a good parent and teach them the right way.

Wisdom Tea: Wisdom of God, I might count on the clergy for moral guidance and examples of fine character. But my children will not need that if I would be a good parent and teach them how to be good. Thank you, Lord.

July 23

Give humanity hope and it will dare and suffer joyfully, not counting the cost – hope with laughter on her banner and on her face the fresh beauty of morning. (John Elof Boodin, God: A Cosmic Philosophy of Religion, 1934) (Religious, Hope, pg. 234)

In-Flavor: Hope is a unique virtue that will dare you to do the impossible and suffer joyfully in the face of hardship. If you do not have hope, you will not have the strength and desire to live one more day.

Inspiration Coffee: Wonder Counselor, if I do not have hope, I will not have the courage and desire to live any more. Hope dares me to think the impossible and suffer joyfully in the midst of daily challenges. Thank you, Lord.

No one truly knows happiness who has not suffered, and the redeemed are happier than the elect. (Henri Amiel, *Amiel's Journal*, 1882) (Religious, Happiness, pg. 221)

Wi-Flavor: Everyone searches for happiness and understands its blessings in their lives. But you know that the people who appreciate it the most are the ones who have endured much suffering.

Wisdom Tea: Wisdom of God, I might like happiness and see its blessings in my life, like everyone else does. However, I would appreciate it the most if I have endured much suffering and been redeemed. Thank you, Lord.

July 24

Let us have love and more love; a love that melts all opposition, conquers all foes, sweeps away all barriers, abounds in charity, a large-heartedness, tolerance, forgiveness, and noble striving; a love that triumphs over all obstacles. (Abdul Baha (1844–1921), in *I Heard Him Say*) (Religious, Love, pg. 303)

In-Flavor: Love is not just the magic that happens between two people; it also has power to help you tolerate, trust, hope, endure, forgive, and much more. You should find it and share it generously.

Inspiration Coffee: Wonder Counselor, love can do a lot of wonderful things for me. Most importantly, it helps me learn to tolerate, trust, hope, endure, forgive, and a lot more. I should have it and then share it. Thank you, Lord.

A holy person is one who is sanctified by the presence and action of God within him. (Thomas Merton, *Life and Holiness*, 1963) (Religious, Holiness, pg. 232)

Wi-Flavor: Holiness is not the quality many people wish to have. In fact, the world often makes fun of it. If you want to be a holy person, know that God sanctifies you and makes his presence within you.

Wisdom Tea: Wisdom of God, the world might not wish to embrace holiness, but if I want to be a holy person, the transformation happens as God sanctifies me and makes his presence within me. Thank you, Lord.

July 25

An apology is a good way to have the last word. (Wit, Unknown, pg. 1)

In-Flavor: In an argument or real life, everyone likes to have the last word, for it makes them feel superior and totally in control. But the best last word you should always say is an apology.

Inspiration Coffee: Wonder Counselor, I might like to have the last word in an argument, to make me feel superior. But I am admonished that the best last word I should say is an apology to restore peace. Thank you, Lord.

Loneliness and the feeling of being unwanted is the most terrible poverty. (St. Mother Teresa, in *Time* magazine, 1975) (Religious, Loneliness, pg. 302)

Wi-Flavor: Some people have to endure loneliness, while others are not wanted by society. If you feel lonely, come to God and ask him to be your friend. Then you can reach out to the outcasts of society.

Wisdom Tea: Wisdom of God, the most terrible form of poverty is loneliness and rejection. If I feel lonely, I just need to come to God to seek his friendship. Then I can reach out to the outcasts of society. Thank you, Lord.

July 26

Let each one remember that he will make progress in all spiritual things only insofar as he rids himself of self-love, self-will and self-interest. (St. Ignatius of Loyola, *Spiritual Exercises*, 1548) (Religious, Spirituality, pg. 535)

In-Flavor: The public might down-play the importance of good spirituality, but when your spiritual life is in good order and you could get rid of all selfish things, it will radiate to every aspect of your life.

Inspiration Coffee: Wonder Counselor, I might not see the value of good spirituality. However, when my spiritual life is strong and healthy, I will be able to get rid of all selfish things and show my generosity. Thank you, Lord.

There is nothing beautiful or sweet or great in life that is not mysterious. (François-René de Chateaubriand, The Genius of Christianity, 1802) (Religious, Mysteries, pg. 350)

Wi-Flavor: Humans are fascinated by all the mysteries of life. Today, you are reminded that anything that is beautiful or sweet or great in life is always mysterious and fascinating to comprehend.

Wisdom Tea: Wisdom of God, my life is fascinating and full of mysteries. I am also told that any beautiful, sweet, and great thing in life is mysterious for me to understand. Help me appreciate all mysteries. Thank you, Lord.

July 27

Climb high, climb far; your aim the sky, your goal the star. (Wise, Goals, pg. 63)

In-Flavor: You need to aim high with your life and focus on achievable goals for it. You also have to remind yourself to keep climbing high and walking far to accomplish those, despite challenges.

Inspiration Coffee: Wonder Counselor, I need to aim high for my life and concentrate on some goals. I should also remind myself to keep climbing high and running far to achieve those, in spite of challenges. Thank you, Lord.

Lasting peace of mind is impossible apart from peace with God; yet enduring peace with God comes only when a man is ready to surrender his own peace of mind. (A. Roy Eckardt, in *The Christian Century*, November 17, 1954) (Religious, Peace of Mind, pg. 386)

Wi-Flavor: You cannot have lasting peace of mind without being at peace with God. However, you cannot have enduring peace with God if you do not learn to surrender your peace of mind.

Wisdom Tea: Wisdom of God, I cannot have lasting peace of mind if I do not make peace with God. But my peace with God is achieved only if I am willing to surrender my peace of mind to God. Thank you, Lord.

July 28

Long-range goals keep you from being frustrated by short-term failures. (Wise, Goals, pg. 63)

In-Flavor: You should have long-range and short-range goals for your life. The short-range goals help you feel successful, while the long-range ones keep you from getting frustrated by life's failures.

Inspiration Coffee: Wonder Counselor, I must have short-term goals to help me see the achievable successes. Meanwhile, long-term goals help me avoid getting frustrated by short-term failures. Thank you, Lord.

Do not despise others because, as it seems to you, they do not possess the virtues you thought they had; they may be pleasing to God for other reasons which you cannot discover. (St. John of the Cross (1542–1591), *The Living Flame of Love*) (Religious, Tolerance, pg. 566)

Wi-Flavor: Some people do not hesitate to judge and despise others who do not share certain virtues. However, you should know that they may be pleasing to God for other unknown reasons.

Wisdom Tea: Wisdom of God, I might mistakenly judge and despise others who do not possess the same virtues as me. I should know that they may be pleasing to God for other unknown reasons. Thank you, Lord.

July 29
Opportunity knocks, but it has never been known to turn the knob and walk in. (Wise, Opportunity, pg. 95)

In-Flavor: Opportunity does not come by a lot and is not easily recognized in real life. You must be attentive to realize it and embrace it wholeheartedly as an important part of your life's success.

Inspiration Coffee: Wonder Counselor, I might not see opportunity knock and call on me to invite it in. I must recognize it in my life and welcome it to be a part of my life's journey to bring me great success. Thank you, Lord.

After crosses and losses, men grow humbler and wiser.
(Benjamin Franklin) (Practical, Adversity, pg. 7)

Wi-Flavor: Crosses make you stronger and more resilient, while losses help you become humble and wise. If you want to grow humbler and wiser, you need to face your daily crosses and life losses.

Wisdom Tea: Wisdom of God, I might not like adversities and failures because they bring me worries and problems. However, crosses make me stronger, while losses help me grow humbler and wiser. Thank you, Lord.

July 30
Failure is the path of least persistence. (Wise, Winning/Losing, pg. 145)

In-Flavor: No one likes to fail, because it hurts. But failure is certainly a part of life. You will see it a lot if you do not work hard and persist in your mission, in spite of many life challenges along the way.

Inspiration Coffee: Wonder Counselor, failure is a part of life, but I do not like it, because it hurts. If I do not work hard and persist with my task amidst my daily challenges, I will run into it a lot and feel sad. Thank you, Lord.

Life is a grindstone. But whether it grinds us down or polishes us up depends on us.
(L. Thomas Holdcroft) (Practical, Attitude, pg. 18)

Wi-Flavor: Life is full of difficult moments and can be seen as a grindstone. You can let it grind you down or polish you up, but that depends on your attitude and the way you deal with life challenges.

Wisdom Tea: Wisdom of God, life can be like a grindstone, with all of its difficulties. I can let it grind me down and feel bitter or polish me up, depending on how I deal with challenges in my life. Thank you, Lord.

July 31

You must act in your friend's interest whether it pleases him or not; the object of love is to serve, not to win. (Woodrow Wilson, address, Princeton, May 9, 1907) (Religious, Love, pg. 312)

In-Flavor: Most people watch out for their interests and find it difficult to serve others. But if you truly love and care about a friend, you must act in his/her interest no matter how he/she feels about it.

Inspiration Coffee: Wonder Counselor, I might find it difficult to watch out for others' interests. However, if I really love and care for a friend, I must act in his/her interest whether it pleases him/her or not. Thank you, Lord.

A good conscience is a continual Christmas. (Benjamin Franklin) (Practical, Conscience, pg. 40)

Wi-Flavor: Christmas is a joyful time for the people of God to celebrate the coming of God into their world. So, a good conscience is a continual Christmas because it always rejoices in God's presence.

Wisdom Tea: Wisdom of God, Christmas is a joyful time for me to celebrate the appearance of God on earth. A good conscience is a continual Christmas because it constantly rejoices in God's presence. Thank you, Lord.

August 1
Aim high, but stay on the level.
(Practical, Aim, pg. 11)

In-Flavor: You should aim high and come up with lots of wonderful dreams to have a hopeful life. But you need to keep those reasonable and achievable. Otherwise, they remain simply abstract ideas.

Inspiration Coffee: Wonder Counselor, I should aim high and never stop dreaming big. However, I should keep those dreams reasonable and achievable. Otherwise, they are simply ideas in my head. Thank you, Lord.

Diplomacy is the ability to give the other guy a shot in the arm without letting him feel the needle. (Practical, Diplomacy, pg. 52)

Wi-Flavor: Part of the challenge for you to learn in the adult world is to be diplomatic with others. Diplomacy means that you need to address a tough issue with others in a tactful, gentle way.

Wisdom Tea: Wisdom of God, diplomacy is a skill that I need to use daily to address a tough issue in a tactful way. I need your help to make good use of it and bring the world tolerance and courtesy. Thank you, Lord.

August 2
Don't be afraid to go out on a limb. That's where the fruit is.
(Practical, Courage, pg. 46)

In-Flavor: Some people are very cautious and hesitate to go out on a limb to accomplish something. You should not be afraid to take risks sometimes to achieve your dreams or succeed in something.

Inspiration Coffee: Wonder Counselor, I might hesitate to go out on a limb to accomplish something. I should not be afraid to take risks to achieve my dreams, because the fruit is often found on a limb. Thank you, Lord.

A wise man thinks ahead; a fool doesn't and even brags about it! (Proverbs 13:16) (Practical, Fools and Foolishness, pg. 79)

Wi-Flavor: It would be foolish for you not to plan anything or be prepared for the future. Unfortunately, some fools even brag about it. But if you are wise, you will think ahead and plan for your future.

Wisdom Tea: Wisdom of God, I would be foolish not to plan or be prepared for the future and even brag about it. But if I am wise, I will think ahead and plan for the future as much as I can. Thank you, Lord.

August 3
Those who fear the future are likely to fumble the present.
(Practical, Future, pg. 91)

In-Flavor: An uncertain future can cause you to feel overwhelmed and develop lots of current problems. You should entrust your future to God and ask him to help with the present challenges.

Inspiration Coffee: Wonder Counselor, an uncertain future can cause me to feel overwhelmed and have all kinds of problems. I should entrust my future to God and ask for help with current challenges. Thank you, Lord.

If you've mortgaged the future to buy present pleasure, don't complain when the foreclosure comes.
(Practical, Future, pg. 91)

Wi-Flavor: Some people like to enjoy a life of pleasure at all costs. But you are warned to avoid mortgaging your future to buy present pleasure, because unexpected foreclosure might come.

Wisdom Tea: Wisdom of God, I am warned to avoid mortgaging my future to buy the present pleasure and enjoy it without any concern, for the unexpected foreclosure might close in on me any time. Thank you, Lord.

August 4
We make a living by what we get, but we make a life by what we give.
(Practical, Giving, pg. 96)

In-Flavor: It is not in human nature to share God's blessings with others. So, while trying to make a living, you also need to make a life and legacy by giving generously of yourself to the world.

Inspiration Coffee: Wonder Counselor, I might be busy making a living and trying to acquire as much as possible. I have to remember to make a life and legacy by giving generously of myself to the world. Thank you, Lord.

Wisdom and good judgment live together, for wisdom knows where to discover knowledge and understanding.
(Proverbs 8:12)
(Practical, Knowledge, pg. 130)

Wi-Flavor: If you want to have good judgment, you must have full knowledge and understanding of an issue. But wisdom knows all about that. So, good judgment and wisdom are good, old neighbors.

Wisdom Tea: Wisdom of God, I cannot have good judgment without having full knowledge and understanding of an issue. Your wisdom gives me all of that, and it lives together with good judgment. Thank you, Lord.

August 5
Deceit fills hearts that are plotting for evil; joy fills hearts that are planning for good!
(Proverbs 12:20) (Practical, Joy, pg. 120)

In-Flavor: Nobody wants to be around people whose hearts are filled with deceit and plotting for evil. But you should learn to be a joyful person because joyful people love to plan for good, and everyone likes that.

Inspiration Coffee: Wonder Counselor, I must not have a heart that is filled with deceit and plotting for evil. Rather, I should have a heart that is full of joy and planning for good. Thank you, Lord.

Money can build a house, but it takes love to make it a home.
(Practical, Love, pg. 144)

Wi-Flavor: Many people like to build a big, fancy house and throw a lot of money into it. But you must know that it takes love and tender care to turn a house into a home for you and your family.

Wisdom Tea: Wisdom of God, I might have lots of money and wish to use it to build a huge, fancy house. However, I should know that it takes love and tender care for me to turn it into a home. Thank you, Lord.

August 6
Never tire of loyalty and kindness. Hold these virtues tightly. Write them deep within your heart.
(Proverbs 3:3) (Practical, Kindness, pg. 126)

In-Flavor: When people treat you kindly, you will remember and be loyal to them. Similarly, when people are loyal to you, you will be grateful and kind to them. So, remember well these virtues.

Inspiration Coffee: Wonder Counselor, I should be loyal to people who are kind to me. I should also be kind to people who are loyal to me. I must hold tightly to these two virtues and write them in my heart. Thank you, Lord.

Trust in your money and down you go! Trust in God and flourish as a tree.
(Proverbs 11:28) (Practical, Money, pg. 157)

Wi-Flavor: Despite the message "In God we trust" on the currency, people still put their trust in money and then get disappointed. But you must trust in God if you want all the right resources to flourish.

Wisdom Tea: Wisdom of God, I see that people who put their trust in money often end up with a disappointing life. However, if I want my life to flourish and be happy, I just need to put my trust in God. Thank you, Lord.

August 7
The bee that makes the honey doesn't hang around the hive.
(Practical, Laziness, pg. 136)

In-Flavor: Worker bees are always on the move to search for ways to bring home the ingredients to make sweet honey. If you keep hanging around the hive, you will not find any work or produce any income for your family.

Inspiration Coffee: Wonder Counselor, like a worker bee, I need to be out of the house in search of the ingredients to make sweet honey. If I keep hanging around the house, I will not find any work to earn a living for my family. Thank you, Lord.

A fool gets into constant fights. His mouth is his undoing! His words endanger him. (Practical, Mouth/Speech, pg. 169)

Wi-Flavor: A fool constantly gets into fights with his/her loose tongue and bad mouth. You must avoid being a fool by thinking about every word before speaking and being careful with your mouth.

Wisdom Tea: Wisdom of God, I should not act like a fool and get into constant fights with others. Rather, I should think carefully before speaking and choose the right words to express my thoughts. Thank you, Lord.

August 8
I'll study and get ready and be prepared for my opportunity when it comes. (Abraham Lincoln)
(Practical, Opportunity, pg. 174)

In-Flavor: Opportunity does not come by a lot. President Lincoln was wise to get himself prepared to welcome it. Likewise, you should study and train yourself well to spot an opportunity and embrace it.

Inspiration Coffee: Wonder Counselor, opportunity does not show up in my life a lot. I need to study hard and prepare myself well to recognize it and make good use of it to bring me great success. Thank you, Lord.

A wise man controls his temper. He knows that anger causes mistakes. (Proverbs 14:29) (Practical, Self-Control, pg. 208)

Wi-Flavor: A wise person is often known for his/her knowledge and life experience. Today, you have another reason to be wise. You know how to control your temper because anger causes mistakes.

Wisdom Tea: Wisdom of God, anger might cause me to make mistakes and lead me to other problems. Today, I am encouraged to be a wise person and do my best to control my temper. Thank you, Lord.

August 9

The Lord is far from the wicked, but he hears the prayers of the righteous. (Proverbs 15:29)
(Practical, Prayer, pg. 187)

In-Flavor: The Lord is often far from the wicked because they do not obey his commandments. However, if you are righteous and follow his teachings, he will definitely hear your prayers in times of need.

Inspiration Coffee: Wonder Counselor, if I am wicked and do not follow the Lord's commandments, he will be far from me. However, if I am righteous and obey his teachings, he will surely hear my prayer. Thank you, Lord.

One of the worst things about retirement is that you have to drink coffee on your own time.
(Practical, Time, pg. 226)

Wi-Flavor: Everyone looks forward to retirement and all its perks. What you must know is that you will have no break time on your retirement. You have to drink coffee and do everything on your own time.

Wisdom Tea: Wisdom of God, I might look forward to retirement and enjoy its benefits. But what I may not realize is that I will no longer have my break time and have to drink coffee on my own time. Thank you, Lord.

August 10

Reputation is what men say about you on your tombstone; character is what angels say about you before the throne of God. (William Hersey Davis)
(Practical, Reputation, pg. 207)

In-Flavor: Most people spend their whole life building up reputation, which is remembered on their tombstone. You should instead build up your character, which is what angels will say about you before God.

Inspiration Coffee: Wonder Counselor, I might be interested in creating my good reputation, which is remembered only on my tombstone. But if I try to build up my character, angels will report it before God. Thank you, Lord.

He who hath compassion upon others receives compassion from Heaven. (Talmud, Shabbat 151)
(Quotations, Compassion, pg. 45)

Wi-Flavor: People of this world deal with one another on the principle "Quid pro quo." So, you are reminded that if you show compassion to others in this life, you will receive the same thing in Heaven.

Wisdom Tea: Wisdom of God, I might not care about treating people kindly and mercifully. However, I am told that if I have compassion for others in this life, I will receive the same treatment in Heaven. Thank you, Lord.

August 11
Never put off till tomorrow what you can do the day after tomorrow. (Mark Twain) (Practical, Tomorrow/Today/Yesterday, pg. 228)

In-Flavor: Some people like to procrastinate and delay their work till tomorrow. But that creates a long backlog. You should take care of this day's work today because tomorrow has troubles of its own.

Inspiration Coffee: Wonder Counselor, I might like to procrastinate and push back my work until later. However, I am encouraged to take care of my work today and not to push it off till tomorrow. Thank you, Lord.

Forgiving the unrepentant is like drawing pictures on water.
(Japanese proverb) (Quotations, Forgiveness, pg. 100)

Wi-Flavor: The Bible shares many stories about sinners and forgiveness. But you will see that forgiveness can only happen if sinners truly repent. Otherwise, it is like drawing pictures on water.

Wisdom Tea: Wisdom of God, forgiveness is an important topic in the Bible. But my forgiveness is only meaningful if an offender truly repents. Otherwise, it will be like drawing pictures on water. Thank you, Lord.

August 12
Men of principle are always bold, but bold men are not always men of principle. (Confucius, *Analects*) (Quotations, Boldness, pg. 26)

In-Flavor: People of principle always try to do the right things, regardless of personal costs, and take a bold stand on any issue. But the opposite is not always true. You should be a person of principle.

Inspiration Coffee: Wonder Counselor, bold people are just obnoxious and not fearful of anything. However, people of principle try to take a bold stand and do the right thing, regardless of personal costs. Thank you, Lord.

The greatest happiness is to transform one's feelings into actions. (Madame de Staël (1766–1817), French writer) (Quotations, Happiness, pg. 121)

Wi-Flavor: Happiness has many definitions depending on the viewpoint. Today, you will learn that the greatest happiness for you might be to turn your feelings on an issue into real actions.

Wisdom Tea: Wisdom of God, I can come up with many definitions of happiness. However, today I find out that the greatest happiness is for me to turn my feelings about something into real actions. Thank you, Lord.

August 13

He who has help has hope, and he who has hope has everything.
(Arab proverb) (Quotations, Hope, pg. 127)

In-Flavor: If you feel you always have help from a divine source, you will never run out of hope, and if you have hope, you have everything, because you can dream of anything you want.

Inspiration Coffee: Wonder Counselor, I will always have hope if I can get constant help from a permanent source like God. And if I have hope in my life, I will have everything, because I can dream about anything. Thank you, Lord.

To honor an old man is showing respect to God. (Muhammad)
(Quotations, Respect, pg. 238)

Wi-Flavor: God the Father has been described as an old, wise man with white, long hair and a beard. If you show honor to an old man who is made in the image of God, you actually give God the respect.

Wisdom Tea: Wisdom of God, you are often pictured as an old, wise man, while a typical old man is believed to be made in your image. So, if I give honor to an old man, I really show *you* the respect. Thank you, Lord.

August 14

Success often comes to those who dare and act; it seldom goes to the timid who are ever afraid of the consequences. (Jawaharlal Nehru) (Quotations, Success, pg. 272)

In-Flavor: If you want to see success, you must dare to dream the impossible and act on it to make it a reality. If you are timid to dream or afraid to take on consequences, you will not experience success.

Inspiration Coffee: Wonder Counselor, if I want to experience success, I must dare to dream the impossible and make it a reality. But if I am timid to dream or afraid of the consequences, I will not see success. Thank you, Lord.

One falsehood spoils a thousand truths. (Ashanti (West African) proverb) (Quotations, Lies, pg. 162)

Wi-Flavor: It is not easy to get people to trust you. You might have to do a thousand of truthful things for people to trust you. But it only takes one false thing for people to stop trusting you.

Wisdom Tea: Wisdom of God, trust is the basis of all relationships. I might need to complete over a thousand truths to get people to trust me. But it just takes one falsehood for people to stop trusting me. Thank you, Lord.

August 15

Whatever a man sows, that he will also reap. (Galatians 6:7) (Religious, Actions pg. 16)

In-Flavor: One thing Nature can assure us is that the type of seed you sow will produce the same fruit. Likewise, if you sow kindness and mercy, you will receive the same thing back at harvest time.

Inspiration Coffee: Wonder Counselor, Nature tells me that the kind of seed I sow will produce the exact fruit. Similarly, if I sow good deeds, I will get a good harvest. If I sow bad ones, I will have a bad harvest. Thank you, Lord.

The highest result of education is tolerance. (Helen Keller (1880–1968), American writer and lecturer) (Quotations, Tolerance, pg. 279)

Wi-Flavor: The system of education passes on knowledge and other life lessons to help humans survive. However, you must know that the highest result of education is to teach you how to tolerate others.

Wisdom Tea: Wisdom of God, I get education to gain knowledge and other life lessons to help me survive on earth. But I believe that the highest result of education is to teach me to tolerate others. Thank you, Lord.

August 16

O, do not pray for easy lives. Pray to be stronger men. Do not pray for tasks equal to your powers. Pray for powers equal to your tasks. (Phillips Brooks, "Going Up to Jerusalem," in *Twenty Sermons*, 1886) (Religious, Adversity, pg. 18)

In-Flavor: People usually pray for God to take away all their troubles and make their lives easy. But you should pray to be strong and powerful enough to match your adversity and challenges.

Inspiration Coffee: Wonder Counselor, I like to pray to be free of all daily problems and have an easy life. However, I should pray to be strong and powerful enough to handle my daily tasks and life adversity. Thank you, Lord.

If one extends knowledge to the utmost, one will have wisdom. Having wisdom, one can then make choices. (Cheng Yi (1033–1108), Chinese scholar, *I-shu*) (Quotations, Wisdom, pg. 305)

Wi-Flavor: Wisdom is the result of comprehending all the knowledge in this world over time. Once you have wisdom, you will be able to make the right decisions and pick the wise choices in your life.

Wisdom Tea: Wisdom of God, I gain wisdom by embracing all the knowledge of this world over the years. Then wisdom will help me make wise decisions and pick the right choices in my life. Thank you, Lord.

August 17

Most souls are afraid of God precisely because of His Goodness. ... Our greatest fear is not that God may not love us enough but that He may love us too much. (Fulton J. Sheen, *Peace of Soul*, 1949) (Religious, Anxiety and Fear, pg. 32)

In-Flavor: The world is often afraid of people who might threaten it with death and hatred. But you should be fearful of God's goodness and abundant love for you, even though you do not deserve it.

Inspiration Coffee: Wonder Counselor, I might be afraid of anyone who threatens me with hate and bodily harm. But I should be fearful of God's goodness and abundant love for me in spite of my sinfulness. Thank you, Lord.

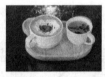

You have heard that it was said, "An eye for an eye and a tooth for a tooth." But I say to you, "Do not resist one who is evil. But if anyone strikes you on the right cheek, turn to him the other also." (Ezekiel 7:23) (Religious, Aggression and Violence pg. 22)

Wi-Flavor: Most religions teach their believers to follow the rule "An eye for an eye, and a tooth for a tooth." Christianity goes further by asking you to be peaceful and turn the other cheek if struck.

Wisdom Tea: Wisdom of God, I may have been told about the rule "An eye for an eye, and a tooth for a tooth." But Christianity asks me to be different and turn the other cheek when struck. Thank you, Lord.

August 18

Our visions begin with our desires. (Audre Lorde, in Claudia Tate's *Black Women Writers at Work*, 1983) (Religious, Desire, pg. 131)

In-Flavor: Your vision will lead to your success. But you do not have any vision if you do not have any desire or dream. So, if you want great success, you need to have a desire that brings you its vision.

Inspiration Coffee: Wonder Counselor, when I want success, I need to have a great desire that will produce a good vision. That vision will make me turn it into actions and eventually bring me a huge success. Thank you, Lord.

You can learn more about human nature by reading the Bible than living in New York. (William Lyon Phelps, radio speech, 1933) (Religious, Bible, pg. 55)

Wi-Flavor: New York is a crowded city with lots of people who can tell you much about human nature. However, you can learn more on that by reading the Bible, which is a collection of human tradition.

Wisdom Tea: Wisdom of God, I can watch people in a crowded city like New York to figure out the human nature. But I can also learn more about it by reading the human history in the Bible. Thank you, Lord.

August 19

We are never defeated unless we give up on God. (Ronald Reagan, 1984) (Religious, Failure and Defeat, pg. 176)

In-Flavor: The world is always at war with one another. The battle between good and evil is already under way. Life might beat you down, but you will never be defeated unless you give up on God.

Inspiration Coffee: Wonder Counselor, I might have to face daily challenges while the world is in constant turmoil. I must know that I will never be defeated in my daily struggle unless I give up on you. Thank you, Lord.

Conscience is an instinct to judge ourselves in the light of moral laws. It is not a mere faculty; it is an instinct. (Immanuel Kant, Lecture at Konigsberg, 1775) (Religious, Conformity, pg. 101)

Wi-Flavor: Humans depend on moral laws and social rules to guide them and help them make the right decisions. God has entrusted conscience to you to judge yourself and pick the right choices in life.

Wisdom Tea: Wisdom of God, I need moral laws and social rules to guide me on the right path of life. You have also given me conscience to judge and hold myself accountable for my choices and actions. Thank you, Lord.

August 20

Hope ... is one of the ways in which what is merely future and potential is made vividly present and actual to us. Hope is the positive, as anxiety is the negative, mode of awaiting the future. (Emil Brunner, *Eternal Hope*, 1954) (Religious, Hope, pg. 235)

In-Flavor: Hope helps you look into the future with great expectation and turn its potential into a reality. It is also a positive energy that can help you deal with an uncertain future and its challenges.

Inspiration Coffee: Wonder Counselor, hope makes what is merely future and potential vividly present and actual to me. Unlike anxiety, it is also a positive power to help me face my future challenges. Thank you, Lord.

You can do very little with faith, but you can do nothing without it. (Samuel Butler, *The Note-Books of Samuel Butler*, 1912, (Religious, Faith, pg. 177)

Wi-Flavor: Faith requires you to put everything in God's hands, and hence, you cannot do much with it. But you cannot go through this life and do everything well without having some faith in God.

Wisdom Tea: Wisdom of God, faith requires me to put my life and future in your hands. I really can do very little with faith, but I cannot go through this life and expect to do everything well without its help. Thank you, Lord.

August 21

The happy man is he who lives of love, not for the honors it may bring, but for the life itself.
(R. J. Baughan, *Undiscovered Country*, 1946) (Religious, Love, pg. 303)

In-Flavor: Love has great potential and can bring about all sorts of great blessings and spectacular miracles for you. If you live for love, you will find not only happiness but also purpose for your life.

Inspiration Coffee: Wonder Counselor, love can bring me all kinds of wonderful blessings and great miracles. If I live for love, I will find not only happiness but also the real purpose for my life. Thank you, Lord.

The family's survival depends on the shared sensibility of its members. (Elizabeth Stone, *Black Sheep and Kissing Cousins*, 1988) (Religious, Family, pg. 186)

Wi-Flavor: A family has many members, and each of them has his/her own role. If you want your family to survive the challenges of this life, each and every member must share his/her responsibility.

Wisdom Tea: Wisdom of God, a family has lots of members, and each of them has a role. If I want my family to survive the challenges of this life, each and every member should share his/her responsibility. Thank you, Lord.

August 22

The pearl of great price always begins as a pain in the oyster's stomach! (John E. Large, *The Small Needle of Doctor Large*, 1962) (Religious, Pain, pg. 378)

In-Flavor: An oyster has to carry great pain in its stomach before a pearl of great price may come about. Like that fine pearl, your achievement will always begin with lots of pain and sweat.

Inspiration Coffee: Wonder Counselor, an oyster has to endure great pain in its stomach before a pearl of great value can come about. Similarly, my achievement will always begin with great pain and sacrifice. Thank you, Lord.

True happiness flows from the possession of wisdom and virtue and not from the possession of external goods. (Aristotle (384–322 BC), *Politics* (Book VII) (Religious, Happiness, pg. 221)

Wi-Flavor: Many people who mistakenly identify their happiness with possession of external goods only get disappointed later. But your true happiness comes from the possession of wisdom and virtues.

Wisdom Tea: Wisdom of God, I must realize that true happiness does not come from possession of external goods and earthly pleasures. Rather, it comes from the possession of wisdom and virtues. Thank you, Lord.

August 23

Suffering which produces the kind of character we admire and love is not only not regrettable but precious. (Martin C. D'Arcy, *Problem of Evil*, 1928) (Religious, Suffering, pg. 539)

In-Flavor: You might admire and love certain people because of their fine characters. But it took them lots of suffering and sacrifice to get there. So, if you want to build your character, suffering is the way.

Inspiration Coffee: Wonder Counselor, I might admire certain people and their wonderful characters. However, I must know that it has taken them lots of suffering and great sacrifice to achieve that. Thank you, Lord.

The present world crisis ... is a crisis of man's spirit. It is a great religious and moral upheaval of the human race, and we do not really know half the causes of this upheaval. (Thomas Merton, in *The Way*, June 1963) (Religious, Human Spirit, pg. 252)

Wi-Flavor: The human race has had to deal with lots of crises. You should know that its current crisis is the starvation of the human spirit, which has resulted in a great religious and moral upheaval for the people.

Wisdom Tea: Wisdom of God, I should realize that among the world crises, its current one is the starvation of the human spirit, which has resulted in a great religious and moral upheaval for the people. Thank you, Lord.

August 24

Progress always involves risk; you can't steal second base and keep your foot on first. (Frederick Wilcox) (Wise, Accomplishment, pg. 7)

In-Flavor: If you want to get to second base, you have to take a risk and leave first base. Similarly, if you want to make progress on a task or accomplish something, you must take a risk and not be afraid of it.

Inspiration Coffee: Wonder Counselor, if I want to steal second base, I have to take a risk and leave first base. Likewise, if I want to make progress and accomplish something, I must not be afraid to take a risk. Thank you, Lord.

The goal in marriage is not to think alike, but to think together. (Robert C. Dodds, *Two Together*, 1959) (Religious, Marriage and Divorce, pg. 316)

Wi-Flavor: Couples often brag about how much they have in common as the reason for their marriage. You must remember that the main goal in marriage is to think *together* and not to think the *same*.

Wisdom Tea: Wisdom of God, I might think that couples must have a lot in common if they want to get married. Today, I am told that the main goal in marriage is to think *together* and not *alike*. Thank you, Lord.

August 25

Roadside sign in Kentucky: "Pray for a good harvest, but keep on hoeing!" (Wise, Action, pg. 9)

In-Flavor: A good harvest requires lots of planning, tilling, sweat, toil, and fair weather. So, you might pray for a good harvest, but you should keep on hoeing, plowing, and working hard for that time.

Inspiration Coffee: Wonder Counselor, I should ask for divine help in all my work, including a good harvest. However, I must also remember that I need to keep on hoeing, plowing, and working hard for that time. Thank you, Lord.

Everything that is unconscious in ourselves we discover in our neighbor, and so treat him accordingly... What we combat in him is usually our inferior side. (C. G. Jung, *Modern Man in Search of a Soul*, 1932) (Religious, Neighbor, pg. 361)

Wi-Flavor: Each person has his/her own weaknesses, but they often get projected onto his/her neighbors. You must examine your inferior side and be careful about seeing the negatives in others.

Wisdom Tea: Wisdom of God, I must know that I have own weaknesses, but often unconsciously project them onto my neighbors. I must treat them accordingly and take good care of my inferior side. Thank you, Lord.

August 26

What a shame—yes, how stupid—it is to decide before knowing the facts! (Proverbs 18:13) (Wise, Decisiveness, pg. 36)

In-Flavor: A sound and informed decision requires a person to know all the facts. If you want to make a good decision and avoid errors, you should get all the facts and study them well beforehand.

Inspiration Coffee: Wonder Counselor, a good and sound decision requires me to know all the facts. Therefore, I need to get all the facts and study them well before confidently making a good decision. Thank you, Lord.

It is God, in silence and wisdom, who uses the Church's enemies to perfect His saints and purify His religion. (Thomas Merton, *The Waters of Siloe*, 1949) (Religious, Persecution, pg. 391)

Wi-Flavor: Humans often hate criticism and persecution. But you could view an attack on your faith as God's secret way of using the Church's enemies to perfect his saints and purify his religion.

Wisdom Tea: Wisdom of God, I often view criticism and persecution of the Church as an attack of the world. I should see it as God using the Church's enemies to perfect his saints and purify his religion. Thank you, Lord.

August 27

In everything you do, put God first, and he will direct you and crown your efforts with success.
(Proverbs 3:6) (Wise, Direction, pg. 41)

In-Flavor: Some people mistakenly assume *they* are in control of their lives and not God. But that is how they could fail. If you want to succeed, you need to put God first and let him direct your work.

Inspiration Coffee: Wonder Counselor, if I want to experience success, I need to put God first and let him direct me and my work. I should not assume that I am in charge of my life and then end up in failure. Thank you, Lord.

Religion is the hunger of the soul for the impossible, the unattainable, the inconceivable. ... This is its essence and this is its glory. This is what religion means. Anything which is less than this is not religion. (W. T. Stace, *Time and Eternity*, 1952) (Religious, Religion, pg. 474)

Wi-Flavor: People seek out religion for various reasons. Today, you are reminded of three more reasons—namely, the hunger of your soul for the impossible, the unattainable, and the inconceivable.

Wisdom Tea: Wisdom of God, I assume I know why religion exists. Today, I am given three more reasons for it—namely, the hunger of the soul for the impossible, the unattainable, and the inconceivable. Thank you, Lord.

August 28

Obstacles are those frightful things you see when you take your eyes off the goal. (Hannah Moore) (Wise, Goals, pg. 63)

In-Flavor: The road to your goal and success is full of obstacles that can frighten and discourage you. If you keep your eyes off your goal, you will see lots of obstacles that might scare you from getting there.

Inspiration Coffee: Wonder Counselor, I should not take my eyes off my goal and final rewards. Otherwise, I will see only the obstacles that might frighten and discourage me from making it there. Thank you, Lord.

A fool thinks he needs no advice, but a wise man listens to others.
(Proverbs 12:15) (Practical, Advice, pg. 8)

Wi-Flavor: A fool does a lot of silly things, and one of them is taking no advice. If you are a wise person, you will make good decisions and do a lot of right things—most importantly, listening to others.

Wisdom Tea: Wisdom of God, if I am a fool, I will do a lot of foolish things and refuse to take advice. However, I can try to be a wise person who makes good choices and learns to listen to others. Thank you, Lord.

August 29
He who kills time buries opportunities. (Wise, Opportunity, pg. 95)

In-Flavor: Some feel they have too much time on their hands and want to get rid of it. But if you want lots of opportunities, you should not kill time, for opportunities are embedded in time.

Inspiration Coffee: Wonder Counselor, I might want a lot of opportunities, but do not see the value of time. Today, I am reminded that the more time I have, the more opportunities I might encounter. Thank you, Lord.

When we turn to each other, and not on each other, that's victory. When we build each other and not destroy each other, that's victory. Red, yellow, brown, black, and white—we're all precious in God's sight. Everybody is somebody. (Jesse L. Jackson, in the *Los Angeles Times*, April 2, 1988) (Religious, Unity, pg. 582)

Wi-Flavor: People often turn on each other and destroy each other over the years. You need to help them turn *to* each other and build up each other to make this world a more unified and better place.

Wisdom Tea: Wisdom of God, I see people turn on each other and destroy each other every day. I need to help them turn *to* each other and build up each other to create a loving and peaceful world. Thank you, Lord.

August 30
The harder you work, the luckier you get. (Gary Player) (Wise, Work, pg. 151)

In-Flavor: Many people feel they should work less and yet hope to get more luck. Today, you are reminded that you should work harder, for when you do that, you will get much luckier.

Inspiration Coffee: Wonder Counselor, I might not see that hard work equals luck. Today, I am told that if I work harder every day, I will get luckier in achieving my success. I cannot work less and expect more luck. Thank you, Lord.

With good men in authority, the people rejoice; but with the wicked in power, they groan. (Proverbs 29:2) (Practical, Authority, pg. 19)

Wi-Flavor: If wicked folks are in power, they will create mayhem for the people. However, you will appreciate it when good folks are in authority, for they will care more about the people's well-being.

Wisdom Tea: Wisdom of God, I groan if wicked folks are in power because of the mayhem the people might get. But I rejoice if good folks are in power because the people's well-being is greatly honored. Thank you, Lord.

August 31

In life what sometimes appears to be the end is really a new beginning. (Wit, Unknown, pg. 1)

<u>In-Flavor</u>: Besides work, no one likes to see the end of something in life, for it often brings tears and sadness. But when you face the end of something, sometimes it is a new beginning for you.

<u>Inspiration Coffee</u>: Wonder Counselor, I do not like the end of something, because it brings me tears and sadness. But I am reminded that in life what some-times appears to be the end is truly a new beginning. Thank you, Lord.

There's no pillow so soft as a clear conscience. (French proverb) (Practical, Conscience, pg. 40)

<u>Wi-Flavor</u>: People like a soft pillow to give them a good night's sleep after a long, hard day at work. But the best pillow to help you rest easy, regardless of your daily challenges, is a clear conscience.

<u>Wisdom Tea</u>: Wisdom of God, I might want to have many soft pil-lows to give me a good night's sleep after a long workday. But the best pillow I can rest easy on, despite my challenges, is a clear conscience. Thank you, Lord.

SEPTEMBER

September 1

If at first you don't succeed, try a little ardor. (Practical, Ambition, pg. 13)

In-Flavor: It is always difficult for someone to experience failure, for the person will often give up after that. But if you did not succeed after the first trial, you need to try again with passion.

Inspiration Coffee: Wonder Counselor, if I did not succeed after the first trial, I should try again and again with passion until I achieve success. I should not feel discouraged and give up after experiencing failure. Thank you, Lord.

If you don't know where you're going, you will wind up somewhere else. (Yogi Berra) (Practical, Direction, pg. 54)

Wi-Flavor: When you leave home without knowing your destination, you will wind up somewhere else. Likewise, if you do not know your life direction, you will sure be lost and end up in wrong places.

Wisdom Tea: Wisdom of God, I have to know my destination before leaving home, or I will end up somewhere else. Likewise, if I do not know what to do with my life, I will be lost and wind up in wrong places. Thank you, Lord.

September 2

Getting a new idea should be like sitting on a tack; it should make you get up and do something about it. (Practical, Creativity, pg. 48)

In-Flavor: It is always exciting to come up with a new idea. But that idea does not mean much if you do not do anything with it. So, if you get a new idea, you should get up and do something about it.

Inspiration Coffee: Wonder Counselor, I rejoice when I come up with a new idea and the possibility of a huge reward. But I should get up and do something with it, or that idea will not mean much at all. Thank you, Lord.

Fool me once, shame on you! Fool me twice, shame on me! (Practical, Fools and Foolishness, pg. 81)

Wi-Flavor: This basically tells you not to make the same mistake twice. If someone fools you once, shame on that person. But if you let that same person fool you twice, you should be ashamed of yourself.

Wisdom Tea: Wisdom of God, I should not make the same mistake twice. If I let someone fool me once, shame on that person. But if I let that person fool me again, shame on me for mistaking twice. Thank you, Lord.

September 3
The train of failure usually runs on the track of laziness. (Practical, Failure, pg. 70)

In-Flavor: Failure is a fact of life. But if you get lazy, you will encounter more failures than you might expect. So, you must work hard and stay away from the track of laziness to avoid the train of failure.

Inspiration Coffee: Wonder Counselor, I will encounter failures in my life. But if I get lazy, I will see more failures. So, I must work hard to stay away from the track of laziness and avoid the train of failure. Thank you, Lord.

We may not know what the future holds, but we know who holds the future. (Practical, Future, pg. 92)

Wi-Flavor: The future is uncertain and full of surprises. That is why most people are afraid of it. But you must know that you hold the key to your future if you work hard and rely on God for the rest of it.

Wisdom Tea: Wisdom of God, my future is uncertain and full of surprises that make me discouraged. But if I work hard and rely on God for the rest of it, I hold the key to my future and its successes. Thank you, Lord.

September 4
Don't fear tomorrow; God is already there. (Practical, Fear, pg. 77)

In-Flavor: One of the reasons why many people fear tomorrow is because it looks overwhelming and is totally unknown. If you are fearful of tomorrow, know that God is already there to help you.

Inspiration Coffee: Wonder Counselor, I might look at my future and feel overwhelmed by its mystery and uncertainty. If I am fearful about tomorrow, I should know that God is already there to help me. Thank you, Lord.

Knowing without doing is like plowing without sowing. (Practical, Knowledge, pg. 131)

Wi-Flavor: Knowledge is the key to a successful future. That is why you should do anything to seek more knowledge. But if you do not use that knowledge for anything, it will be like plowing without sowing.

Wisdom Tea: Wisdom of God, I must not stop seeking knowledge, because it is the key to my future success. But if I have all the knowledge without using it, it will be like plowing without sowing. Thank you, Lord.

September 5
The secret of happy living is not to do what you like but to like what you do. (Practical, Happiness, pg. 100)

In-Flavor: Everyone likes to have a happy life. But the way to it is not to find and do what you like. Rather, you must learn to like what you do every day, for that is the secret of happy living.

Inspiration Coffee: Wonder Counselor, I might want to have a happy life and do only what I like. However, the secret of happy living is for me to change my attitude and learn to like what I do every day. Thank you, Lord.

Love is the glue that cements friendship; jealousy keeps it from sticking. (Practical, Love, pg. 144)

Wi-Flavor: Friendship is an important part of human survival. If your friendship with someone is broken, jealousy cannot heal it. But love will bring you back with that friend and heal your friendship.

Wisdom Tea: Wisdom of God, friendship is certainly an important part of my life. Jealousy keeps those relationships from sticking. However, love is the glue that cements and heals them for me. Thank you, Lord.

September 6
Friendship doubles our joy and divides our grief. (Practical, Joy, pg. 121)

In-Flavor: Most human beings crave for a relationship to provide them companionship and bring them joy and comfort. If you want to end your grief and double your joy, you should search for a friendship.

Inspiration Coffee: Wonder Counselor, I sure cherish a good friendship, because it brings me laughs and comfort. However, I should remember that a good friendship will also double my joy and end my grief. Thank you, Lord.

Money can't buy you friends, but it can bring you a better class of enemies. (Practical, Money, pg. 158)

Wi-Flavor: Money is the root of all evil. It has caused many fights and wicked intentions. It might not get you any friends, but it can bring you a new group of enemies who might happen to be rich and famous.

Wisdom Tea: Wisdom of God, money might not buy me long-lasting friends. However, I must know that it can do a lot of things, including bringing me a better class of enemies who are rich and famous. Thank you, Lord.

September 7
Evil men don't understand the importance of justice, but those who follow the Lord are much concerned about it.
(Proverbs 28:5) (Practical, Justice, pg. 124)

In-Flavor: Justice is what everyone searches for in this life and the next. Unfortunately, evil people cannot see the importance of it. But you who follow the Lord are much concerned about it.

Inspiration Coffee: Wonder Counselor, everyone often talks about justice. But I should know that people who follow the Lord are much concerned about it, while evil people do not see the importance of it. Thank you, Lord.

Don't put a promise in my ear; put it in my hand. (Russian proverb) (Practical, Promises, pg. 201)

Wi-Flavor: People make promises to each other every day, but do not really intend to fulfill them. Today, you want to tell those people to stop putting promises in your ear and instead make them real in your hand.

Wisdom Tea: Wisdom of God, I hear promises made every day, but most of them are not fulfilled. I am reminded to keep my promises by putting them in others' hands and stop putting them in their ears. Thank you, Lord.

September 8
Laziness travels slowly and is soon overtaken by poverty.
(Practical, Laziness, pg. 136)

In-Flavor: People who adopt laziness as their way of life will not strive to make their lives productive and gain awesome rewards. If you follow that way of life, you will soon experience poverty.

Inspiration Coffee: Wonder Counselor, people who take up laziness as their way of life will not make use of their gifts and gain success. But I must know that if I follow that way of life, I will end up in poverty. Thank you, Lord.

Self-expression is good; self-control is better. (Practical, Self-Control, pg. 209)

Wi-Flavor: Everyone is so focused on expressing themselves these days that they do not know how to control themselves sometimes. So, you should learn more about self-control before self-expression.

Wisdom Tea: Wisdom of God, I know that people put more emphasis these days on expressing themselves than controlling themselves. I must learn more about self-control than self-expression. Thank you, Lord.

September 9
An optimist is a person who is a hope addict. (Practical, Optimism/Pessimism, pg. 176)

In-Flavor: An optimist is always upbeat and can see the positive in the most difficult situation. If you choose to be an optimist, you will search for hope everywhere and enjoy being a "hope addict."

Inspiration Coffee: Wonder Counselor, an optimist can see the positive in every situation, even the toughest one. I should learn to be an optimist and search for hope every day as a "hope addict." Thank you, Lord.

Teach us to number our days and recognize how few they are; help us to spend them as we should. (Psalm 90:12) (Practical, Tomorrow/Today/Yesterday, pg. 227)

Wi-Flavor: Some people think they will live forever on earth and therefore squander their days on regrettable things. You should know that your days are few and numbered. So, you should use them wisely.

Wisdom Tea: Wisdom of God, the world might convince me that I will live forever and I can squander my days. I need to realize that my days are numbered, and I should spend them wisely. Thank you, Lord.

September 10
If your day is hemmed with prayer, it is less likely to unravel. (Practical, Prayer, pg. 189)

In-Flavor: Your day is usually filled with challenges and surprises. You need to know how to handle them before it unravels and turns chaotic. The best way for you to do that is with prayer and divine help.

Inspiration Coffee: Wonder Counselor, my day might be filled with challenges and surprises. The best way for me to hold it together before it turns chaotic and unravels wildly is with prayer and divine help. Thank you, Lord.

A tiger cannot beat a crowd of monkeys. (Chinese proverb) (Quotations, Competition, pg. 45)

Wi-Flavor: A tiger is a powerful creature of the jungle, but it cannot beat a crowd of monkeys, due to their number. Similarly, if you want strength and power, those often come in number and crowd size.

Wisdom Tea: Wisdom of God, if a tiger, a powerful creature of the jungle, cannot beat a crowd of monkeys, then the power of the competition must be in its number. Likewise, if I look for power, it is in the crowd size. Thank you, Lord.

September 11
Live in such a way that when death comes, the mourners will outnumber the cheering section.
(Practical, Reputation, pg. 207)

In-Flavor: Most people want a good reputation and will do everything to build it up amidst their critics. You should live in such a way that when death comes, the mourners will outnumber your critics.

Inspiration Coffee: Wonder Counselor, I wish to have a good reputation. But what I need to remember is that I should live in such a way that when death comes, my mourners will outnumber my critics. Thank you, Lord.

A kind speech and forgiveness is better than alms followed by injury. (Qur'an) (Quotations, Forgiveness, pg. 100)

Wi-Flavor: People hurt and injure one another every day. They then try to make up for it with alms and gifts. However, you are admonished to repay it best with kind speech and forgiveness.

Wisdom Tea: Wisdom of God, I might hurt and injure people every day. I could make up for it with alms and gifts. But today, I am told that the best way to mend it is with kind speech and forgiveness. Thank you, Lord.

September 12
The truth will set you free—but first it will make you mad.
(Practical, Truth, pg. 232)

In-Flavor: Everyone desires the truth, even though they might not live up to it. So, if you want the truth, you should know that it will first make you mad before it can set you free from something.

Inspiration Coffee: Wonder Counselor, I might wish to have the truth, in spite of my faults. However, if I want the truth, I must know that it will first make me mad before it can set me free from my problem. Thank you, Lord.

I imagine one of the reasons people cling to their hates so stubbornly is because they sense, once hate is gone, they will be forced to deal with pain. (James Baldwin (1924–1987), American writer, *Notes of a Native Son*) (Quotations, Hate, pg. 122)

Wi-Flavor: Hatred is the fuel that feeds the fire of controversies and fights. People like to cling to it tightly. You will learn that the reason for that is because they are afraid to deal with pain once hate is gone.

Wisdom Tea: Wisdom of God, hatred is the fuel that feeds the fire of fights and controversies. Sadly, I will learn that people often cling to it because they are afraid to deal with the pain once hate is gone. Thank you, Lord.

September 13

He who wishes to eat in the evening must be willing to work during the day. (Practical, Work, pg. 249)

In-Flavor: Some people assume they can eat without having to work because someone else will pay for it. But if you want to have an enjoyable retirement, you must be willing to work all your life.

Inspiration Coffee: Wonder Counselor, if I want to eat in the evening or enjoy a retirement, I must be willing to work during the day or all my life. I cannot assume someone else will pay for my meal or retirement. Thank you, Lord.

This is the punishment of a liar; he is not believed, even when he speaks the truth. (Talmud, Sanhedrin 29) (Quotations, Lies, pg. 162)

Wi-Flavor: A liar is so used to spreading lies and alternative facts that it becomes his/her second nature. You will learn that he/she might speak the truth later on, but no one will believe, and think he/she is "crying wolf."

Wisdom Tea: Wisdom of God, I must avoid being a liar and giving out lies and alternative facts in my daily talks. Otherwise, I might speak the truth later on, but no one will believe me at all. Thank you, Lord.

September 14

Character cannot be developed in ease and quiet. Only through experience of trial and suffering can the soul be strengthened, vision cleared, ambition inspired, and success achieved. (Helen Keller, *Helen Keller's Journal*) (Quotations, Character, pg. 36)

In-Flavor: A developed character means a strengthened soul, a cleared vision, and an inspired ambition. If you want to develop your character, you must be willing to experience trial and suffering.

Inspiration Coffee: Wonder Counselor, if I want to develop my character, I must be willing to experience trial and suffering. That character will give me a different soul, vision, and ambition, as listed above. Thank you, Lord.

Those who are inclined to compromise never make a revolution. (Kemal Atatürk (1881–1938), Turkish patriot and political leader) (Quotations, Revolution, pg. 239)

Wi-Flavor: It takes a special kind of person to be a revolutionary and keep the uprising going. If you are a person who is inclined to compromise, you will never make a revolution or enjoy a fight.

Wisdom Tea: Wisdom of God, if I am inclined to compromise, I will never make a revolution or enjoy a long fight, for it takes a special kind of person to be a revolutionary and keep the protest going. Thank you, Lord.

September 15

Hope is the thing with feathers that perches in the soul, and sings the tune without the words, and never stops at all; and sweetest in the gale is heard.
(Emily Dickenson (1830–86), *Poems*) (Quotations, Hope, pg. 235)

In-Flavor: Hope can perk up your soul and sing you the sweetest tune when you feel down. So, if you feel discouraged or want to give up, you need to rely on hope to help you find your mojo again.

Inspiration Coffee: Wonder Counselor, hope helps perk up my soul and sing me the sweetest tune when I feel depressed. If I feel discouraged, I need to count on hope to help me find the desire to live again. Thank you, Lord.

The simplest truths often meet the sternest resistance and are slowest in getting general acceptance. (Frederick Douglas (1817-1895), American abolitionist, "The Women's Suffrage Movement," The New National Era) (Quotations, Truth, pg. 284)

Wi-Flavor: The truth often meets a tough resistance at the beginning. The public might even be slow in accepting it. But you know that the truth will be highly praised and welcomed in the end.

Wisdom Tea: Wisdom of God, the simplest truth often meets stern resistance and the public is slow to accept it. But I know that the truth will be highly praised and warmly welcomed in the end. Thank you, Lord.

September 16

Put your heart, mind, intellect, and soul to your smallest acts. This is the secret of success.
(Sivananda Saraswati (1887–1963), Indian religious leader, "Exponent of Japa") (Quotations, Success, pg. 272)

In-Flavor: Some people might attribute success to good ideas, great planning, perfect performance, hard work, or even luck. But the real secret of success is your ability to take care of the smallest details.

Inspiration Coffee: Wonder Counselor, I might attribute success to good ideas, great planning, perfect performance, hard work, or luck. But the real secret of success is my attention to the smallest details. Thank you, Lord.

One wise man is better than forty fools; one moon sheds more light than myriads of stars.
(*Hitopadesha* (date unknown), Indian moral tales and aphorisms) (Quotations, Wisdom, pg. 306)

Wi-Flavor: A myriad of stars can get you to look up at the night sky. But one moon will help you see it clearly. Likewise, forty fools might catch your attention, but one wise person will convince you to follow him.

Wisdom Tea: Wisdom of God, one moon sheds more light than a myriad of stars on the night sky. Similarly, one wise person is better than forty fools and can help me resolve a difficult problem easily. Thank you, Lord.

September 17
Pray to God, but row for the shore. (Russian proverb) (Religious, Actions pg. 17)

In-Flavor: It does not hurt to ask for some divine help and unexpected miracles when you are in trouble. But you should keep on rowing for the shore while calling to God for help in tough times.

Inspiration Coffee: Wonder Counselor, it is alright for me to ask for divine help and miracles when I am in trouble. However, I should keep on rowing for the shore while praying to God for help in times of need. Thank you, Lord.

Violence is an admission that one's ideas and goals cannot prevail on their own merits. (Edward M. Kennedy, June 10, 1970, in Thomas P. Collins and Louis M. Savary's (eds.) *A People of Compassion*, 1972) (Religious, Aggression and Violence, pg. 22)

Wi-Flavor: People who do violent acts often carry them out with certain ideas and goals in mind. But you must know that those ideas and goals sadly did not prevail on their own before that.

Wisdom Tea: Wisdom of God, I must know that people who carry out violence had certain ideas and goals in mind. Sadly, those ideas and goals could not prevail on their own merits before that. Thank you, Lord.

September 18
Calamity is virtue's opportunity. (Seneca, *De Providentia*, 64 AD) (Religious, Adversity pg. 19)

In-Flavor: No one likes calamity or adversity, for it usually means stress, difficulty, work, sweat, tears, and heartache. But you should view calamity as an opportunity to practice your virtues.

Inspiration Coffee: Wonder Counselor, I certainly do not like calamity or adversity, because it often means stress, difficulty, work, sweat, and tears. But I should view it as an opportunity to practice my virtues. Thank you, Lord.

We advise all who feel hemmed in by a closed and stifling world to open the Old and New Testaments. They will there find vistas, which will liberate them, and the excellent food of the only true God. (Emmanuel Suhard, *The Church Today*, 1953) (Religious, Bible, pg. 56)

Wi-Flavor: You might feel hemmed in by life's burdens and the pressure of a stifling world. When that happens, you should open the Bible to give you refreshment and new vistas to journey on.

Wisdom Tea: Wisdom of God, I might feel hemmed in by life's burden and the pressure of a stifling world. But I must remember that when I feel like that, I should open the Bible to give me new vistas. Thank you, Lord.

September 19
One of the disconcerting facts about the spiritual life is that God takes you at your word.

(Dorothy Day, *The Long Loneliness*, 1952) (Religious, Commitment, pg. 89)

In-Flavor: In your spiritual life, you promise to love God and love your neighbors. God takes you at your word and trusts that you will keep your promise. Hopefully, you will stay committed to it.

Inspiration Coffee: Wonder Counselor, I may promise to love God and my neighbors in my spiritual life. I need to stay committed to it because God takes me at my word and trusts that I will keep it. Thank you, Lord.

The house of mourning teaches charity and wisdom. (St. John Chrysostom, *Homilies*, 388 AD) (Religious, Death, pg. 124)

Wi-Flavor: When you are in mourning, you usually try to act kindly and be charitable to people around you. You also know well your priorities and life lessons that you can pass on to the next generations.

Wisdom Tea: Wisdom of God, when I am in mourning, I usually try to act kindly and be charitable to others. I also know well my priorities and life lessons that I can pass on to the next generations. Thank you, Lord.

September 20
In my experience, there is only one motivation, and that is desire. No reasons or principles contain it or stand against it.

(Jane Smiley, *Ordinary Love*, 1989) (Religious, Desire, pg. 131)

In-Flavor: You can be motivated to begin a project and complete it by the threat of punishment or promise of reward. But the best motivation is your desire to embrace and finish it successfully.

Inspiration Coffee: Wonder Counselor, I can be motivated to begin a project and complete it by the threat of punishment or promise of reward. But the best motivation is my desire to do it and finish it gladly. Thank you, Lord.

Every kingdom divided against itself is laid waste, and no city or house divided against itself will stand. (Matthew 12:25) (Religious, Discord, pg. 140)

Wi-Flavor: Discord in a community creates division and fights among its members. But any kingdom or house divided against itself cannot stand. You need to restore unity and heal discord when possible.

Wisdom Tea: Wisdom of God, I must restore unity and heal any discord when possible, because discord causes division and fights in a community. Any kingdom or house divided against itself cannot stand. Thank you, Lord.

September 21

If everything is coming your way, you are probably in the wrong lane. Adversity and defeat are more conducive to spiritual growth than prosperity and victory. (John Steinbeck, 1967) (Religious, Failure and Defeat, pg. 176)

In-Flavor: In life, if everything is coming your way, you are perhaps in the wrong lane, for adversity and defeat are a part of life and a better way for your spiritual growth than prosperity and victory.

Inspiration Coffee: Wonder Counselor, I might not like adversities and defeats, but they are a part of life. They are also a better way than prosperity and victory to help me with my spiritual growth. Thank you, Lord.

All happy families are alike; each unhappy family is unhappy in its own way. (Leo Tolstoy, opening line of *Anna Karenina*, 1876) (Religious, Family, pg. 186)

Wi-Flavor: You might not realize this fact of life, but all happy families resemble one another and share many common virtues. In contrast, every unhappy family fights with each other over all kinds of things.

Wisdom Tea: Wisdom of God, I might not know that every unhappy family is unhappy in its own way. However, all happy families resemble one another and share the common goal of happiness. Thank you, Lord.

September 22

If you do not hope, you will not find what is beyond your hopes. (St. Clement of Alexandria, *Stromateis*, 193 AD) (Religious, Hope, pg. 235)

In-Flavor: Hope is the door that opens to a wonderful world of incredible miracles and great possibilities. Indeed, if you do not hope, you will not be able to experience what is beyond that door.

Inspiration Coffee: Wonder Counselor, hope shows me a wonderful world of incredible miracles and great possibilities. I have to have hope in my life to help me find what is beyond this door and celebrate it. Thank you, Lord.

Religious faith is not a storm cellar to which men and women can flee for refuge from the storms of life. It is, instead, an inner spiritual strength which enables them to face those storms with hope and serenity. It has the miraculous power to lift ordinary human beings to greatness in seasons of stress. (Sam Ervin, *Humor of a Country Lawyer*, 1983) (Religious, Faith, pg. 177)

Wi-Flavor: People often think religious faith is a cocoon that can shelter them from the storms of life. But it is really an inner spiritual strength to bring you hope and serenity in times of turmoil and stress.

Wisdom Tea: Wisdom of God, I might think of religious faith as a storm cellar that can shelter me from the storms of life. But it is really an inner spiritual strength to give me hope and serenity in tough times. Thank you, Lord.

September 23

He who loves brings God and the world together. (Martin Buber, *At the Turning*, 1952) (Religious, Love, pg. 304)

In-Flavor: In the Bible, God is depicted as love. The world certainly likes to have love in its life. If you live by the rule of love, you will be able to make God present in the world and draw it closer to God.

Inspiration Coffee: Wonder Counselor, I might know God is love, and the world wants to fill its life with more love. If I live by the law of love, I will make God more present in the world and bring it closer to God. Thank you, Lord.

There may be Peace without Joy, and Joy without Peace, but the two combined make Happiness. (John Buchan, *Pilgrim's Way*, 1940) (Religious, Happiness, pg. 221)

Wi-Flavor: Everyone wishes to have happiness and constantly searches for it. In the process, some find peace, while others joy. But if you combine those two, today you are told they make happiness.

Wisdom Tea: Wisdom of God, I constantly search for happiness and wish to have it. In my search, I find joy sometimes and peace other times. Today, I am told that those two combined make happiness. Thank you, Lord.

September 24

No pain, no gain; no thorns, no throne; no gall, no glory; no cross, no crown. (William Penn, *No Cross, No Crown*, 1669) (Religious, Pain, pg. 378)

In-Flavor: Pain or any form of hardship is a part of life and also a necessary contribution to success. If you want to experience an achievement, you must endure the difficulties and carry the cross for it.

Inspiration Coffee: Wonder Counselor, I might want to gain glory and experience success, but it only happens if I can endure difficulties and carry the cross. Pain or hardship is the condition for any success. Thank you, Lord.

Let us, like [Mary], touch the dying, the poor, the lonely and the unwanted according to the graces we have received and let us not be ashamed or slow to do the humble work. (St. Mother Teresa, *Life in the Spirit*, 1983) (Religious, Humility, pg. 254)

Wi-Flavor: Society is often afraid of and ignores the dying, the poor, and the unwanted. You are called to reach out to those outcast, touch them, and humbly serve their needs as a faithful servant of God.

Wisdom Tea: Wisdom of God, the world might forget about the dying, the poor, the lonely, and the unwanted. Today, I am encouraged to reach out to touch them and serve their needs as a humble servant. Thank you, Lord.

September 25

No dogma of religion is surer than this: if one would be close to God, he must suffer. (Walter Elliott, *The Spiritual Life*, 1914) (Religious, Suffering, pg. 539)

In-Flavor: The way to God and holiness demands a person to make sacrifices and suffer as a part of purification. If you want to be close to God, you will have to endure lots of suffering and sacrifices.

Inspiration Coffee: Wonder Counselor, religion is full of dogmas and beliefs. One of them I know for sure is that if I want to be close to God, I must suffer. So, the way to God for me is suffering and sacrifice. Thank you, Lord.

No one may forsake his neighbor when he is in trouble. Everybody is under obligation to help and support his neighbor as he would himself like to be helped. (Martin Luther, letter, November 1527) (Religious, Neighbor, pg. 361)

Wi-Flavor: The Golden Rule tells everyone to treat one another like a neighbor. Unfortunately, people often mistreat their neighbors and ignore them. You should not forsake your neighbors in trouble.

Wisdom Tea: Wisdom of God, the Golden Rule calls on me to treat everyone as my neighbor. Sadly, the world does not live up to this. Today, I am reminded to practice it and help my neighbor in trouble. Thank you, Lord.

September 26

We are judged by what we finish, not by what we start. (Wise, Accomplishment, pg. 7)

In-Flavor: Most people have a humble beginning and do not have much. But with God's help and hard work, they accomplish a great deal. Likewise, you are not judged by your start, but your finish.

Inspiration Coffee: Wonder Counselor, I might not have a good, clean start like the rich do. However, with your help and my hard work, I will accomplish a great result, which is the only thing that matters in the end. Thank you, Lord.

He that pities another remembers himself. (George Herbert, *Outlandish Proverbs*, 1640) (Religious, Pity, pg. 397)

Wi-Flavor: Some people do not have any compassion or concern in their treatment of others. But you are reminded to pity another in your daily decisions, because it shows that you remember yourself.

Wisdom Tea: Wisdom of God, it might not be my nature to have compassion and concern for others. However, I am encouraged to pity another in my daily decisions to show that I remember myself. Thank you, Lord.

September 27
The roots of happiness grow deepest in the soil of service.

(Wise, Happiness, pg. 69)

In-Flavor: Some people think wealth and glamor will make them happy. But true happiness comes from the fact that you have served your neighbors and made a difference in the lives of others.

Inspiration Coffee: Wonder Counselor, I might be convinced that wealth and glamor will make me happy. Truthfully, I am happy when I can serve my neighbors and make a difference in the lives of others. Thank you, Lord.

The source of peace is within us; so also the source of war. And the real enemy is within us, and not outside. The source of war is not the existence of nuclear weapons or other arms. It is the minds of human beings who decide to push the button and to use those arms out of hatred, anger, or greed.

(Dalai Lama, speech, Costa Rica, in the *Wall Street Journal*, June 17, 1989) (Religious, War, pg. 599)

Wi-Flavor: You might not realize that the real enemy or evil is within you and not outside. The source of peace is within you; so is the source of war. You are capable of peace, love, anger, and hatred.

Wisdom Tea: Wisdom of God, I may not realize that the source of peace and of war is within me. I am capable of peace, love, anger, and hatred. The real enemy or evil is within me and not outside. Thank you, Lord.

September 28
We are silent at the beginning of the day because God should have first word, and we are silent before going to sleep because the last word also belongs to God.

(Dietrich Bonhoeffer) (Wise, Priorities, pg. 109)

In-Flavor: Some people like to offer their day to God for guidance in the morning. Others enjoy an evening prayer to give thanks for a good day. You should do both and give God the first and last word.

Inspiration Coffee: Wonder Counselor, some like to ask God for guidance in the morning, while others want to give thanks to God in the evening. I should do both and let God have the first and last word. Thank you, Lord.

Let us run with perseverance the race that is set before us.

(Hebrews 12:1) (Religious, Patience, pg. 382)

Wi-Flavor: Humans do not have patience or resilience in their search for success. You are admonished to persevere amidst life challenges and be patient in your marathon of faith to get to the finish line.

Wisdom Tea: Wisdom of God, I might not have patience to achieve great success. However, I am advised to be patient in my faith marathon and persevere in my life challenges to get to the finish line. Thank you, Lord.

September 29

He who wants to make foot-prints in the sands of time must not sit down. (Wise, Work, pg. 151)

<u>In-Flavor</u>: Everyone likes to leave a great legacy and earn a deep admiration from the future generations. If you want the same, you must work hard on that goal every day and never stop doing it.

<u>Inspiration Coffee</u>: Wonder Counselor, I might want to earn a deep admiration from the future generations and leave behind a great legacy. If I do, I must work hard on it every day and never stop doing it. Thank you, Lord.

The advice of a wise man refreshes like water from a mountain spring. Those accepting it become aware of the pitfalls on ahead. (Proverbs 13:14) (Practical, Advice, pg. 8)

<u>Wi-Flavor</u>: A wise person possesses knowledge and life experience. If you are blessed to get advice from him/her, it refreshes you like spring water and helps you avoid pitfalls and dangers ahead.

<u>Wisdom Tea</u>: Wisdom of God, if I want to know about the pitfalls ahead and feel refreshed like a mountain spring, I need to have the advice of a wise man, who possesses knowledge and life experience. Thank you, Lord.

September 30

It takes courage to push yourself to places that you've never been before ... to test your limits, to break through barriers. (Wit, Unknown, pg. 2)

<u>In-Flavor</u>: You might like to be around familiar things and do your daily routines. But you must have courage and an adventurous spirit to push yourself to unknown places and test your limits.

<u>Inspiration Coffee</u>: Wonder Counselor, I may enjoy being around familiar things and having daily routines. However, I must have courage to test my limits and the desire to push myself to new places. Thank you, Lord.

Authority is like a bank account. The more you draw on it, the less you have. (Practical, Authority, pg. 20)

<u>Wi-Flavor</u>: Humans mistakenly assume their power or authority is unlimited and absolute. But you are reminded that authority is like a bank account, and you will drain it if you keep drawing on it.

<u>Wisdom Tea</u>: Wisdom of God, I may think authority or power is absolute and unlimited. Today, I am told that authority is like a bank account, which I will drain fast if I keep drawing on it. I need to stop that. Thank you, Lord.

OCTOBER

October 1
You do not test the resources of God until you attempt the impossible. (F. B. Meyer) (Practical, Ambition, pg. 13)

In-Flavor: You might know God has lots of resources and also miraculous power. The best way for you to find out what resources God might have is to attempt the impossible and ask God for help.

Inspiration Coffee: Wonder Counselor, I am told that God has miracle power and lots of resources. But if I want to know what resources God might have, I have to attempt the impossible and ask God for help. Thank you, Lord.

Most of us follow our conscience as we follow a wheelbarrow. We push it in front of us in the direction we want to go. (Billy Graham) (Practical, Conscience, pg. 40)

Wi-Flavor: People often compare conscience to a moral compass to show them where to go and what to do. Today, it is compared to a wheelbarrow that you push in front of you to clear and guide your way.

Wisdom Tea: Wisdom of God, I might think of my conscience as an inner voice to tell me what to do or a moral compass to show me the way. Today, it is compared to a wheelbarrow to clear my way. Thank you, Lord.

October 2
Louis Pasteur had nothing to work with but the germ of an idea. (Practical, Creativity, pg. 48)

In-Flavor: The best creation does not have to come from the greatest idea. Louis Pasteur only had an idea of a germ to create the famous pasteurization method. So, you can still be creative like him.

Inspiration Coffee: Wonder Counselor, I might think I need to have the greatest idea to come up with the best creation. Today, the story of Louis Pasteur tells me that I just need the germ of an idea to create something. Thank you, Lord.

Wise people sometimes change their mind, fools never! (Practical, Fools and Foolishness, pg. 82)

Wi-Flavor: The fool is often prideful and does not like to listen to others or change his/her way. But if you are a wise person, you will listen to various opinions and change your mind sometimes.

Wisdom Tea: Wisdom of God, fools often think they know everything and do not want to change their ways. But as a wise person, I need to listen to different opinions and sometimes change my mind. Thank you, Lord.

October 3

Success comes in cans; failure comes in can'ts. (Practical, Failure, pg. 70)

In-Flavor: Failure may be the result of various things, but it will definitely be so if you say you can't. On the other hand, success will come about if you believe you can do it and try hard to achieve it.

Inspiration Coffee: Wonder Counselor, if I begin any project with "I can't," I have already surrendered myself to failure. However, if I look at my dreams and say "I can," I will be not too far from success. Thank you, Lord.

There are better things ahead than any we leave behind.

(C. S. Lewis) (Practical, Future, pg. 92)

Wi-Flavor: You might regret things you did not do or did wrong in the past. However, you are reminded that there are still better things waiting ahead for you than anything you left behind.

Wisdom Tea: Wisdom of God, I might regret all the wonderful things I have had to leave behind. However, I am told that there are still better things waiting ahead in the future for me. Thank you, Lord.

October 4

Pray for faith that will not shrink when it is washed in the waters of affliction. (Practical, Faith, pg. 72)

In-Flavor: Affliction and disappointment are a part of life and something you do not have any control over. The best way for you to endure them is to rely on the higher power that comes through faith and prayer.

Inspiration Coffee: Wonder Counselor, I might not have any control over the water of affliction and pain as part of life. However, I must pray for strength that I will not shrink when I am washed in that water. Thank you, Lord.

The hope of good men is eternal happiness; the hopes of evil men are all in vain. (Proverbs 10:28)

(Practical, Hope, pg. 109)

Wi-Flavor: Evil people focus on this life, and their hopes are all in vain as they see them vanish before their eyes. But you will learn that the hope of good men is eternal happiness and more secure.

Wisdom Tea: Wisdom of God, the hopes of evil people are in vain and focused simply on the things of this world. However, the hope of good people is eternal happiness and beyond this world. Thank you, Lord.

October 5

For every minute you are angry, you lose sixty seconds of happiness. (Practical, Happiness, pg. 101)

In-Flavor: Anger can cause you to lose your inner peace, err in judgment, say hurtful things, do regrettable acts, and have other problems. But worst of all, it will steal from you lots of happy hours.

Inspiration Coffee: Wonder Counselor, I might not know that anger can cause me to say hurtful things, do regrettable acts, err in judgment, and lose inner peace. Worst of all, it makes me lose lots of happy hours. Thank you, Lord.

Discussion is an exchange of knowledge; argument is an exchange of ignorance. (Practical, Knowledge, pg. 131)

Wi-Flavor: It is hard for you to tell the difference between a lively discussion and a heated argument. But today, you learn that a discussion is an exchange of knowledge, while an argument is an exchange of ignorance.

Wisdom Tea: Wisdom of God, if I have a lively discussion with someone, it is surely an exchange of knowledge. But if I have a heated argument with someone, it is just an exchange of ignorance. Thank you, Lord.

October 6

Here are a dozen ways to celebrate joy: Complete what you start; enlarge your interests; laugh a lot; express gratitude to a friend; be kind, thoughtful, and caring; read the Bible daily; accent the positive; tell a friend you love him/her; extend a helping hand; jot down every morning five reasons to be happy; overlook pettiness and jealousy; yield your life to God. (Practical, Joy, pg. 121)

In-Flavor: Joy is the wonderful medicine for a worried, anxious heart. If you can find this gift, you will always be content and at peace amidst your daily chaos. You can celebrate it by a dozen ways.

Inspiration Coffee: Wonder Counselor, joy is a fine blessing that can change the mood of a chaotic day and a good medicine that can heal a worried, anxious heart. I can celebrate it by a dozen ways above. Thank you, Lord.

Love cures people — both the ones that give it and the ones who receive it. (Dr. Karl Menninger) (Practical, Love, pg. 145)

Wi-Flavor: You might hear about the magical power of love, but might not know that love cures people. When you share your love with others, you bring them healing and yourself feel good about that act.

Wisdom Tea: Wisdom of God, I might hear all about the power of love, but not know that love can cure people. If I can share it with others, I will bring them healing and I will certainly feel good about it. Thank you, Lord.

October 7
Work hard and become a leader; be lazy and never succeed. (Proverbs 12:24) (Practical, Leadership, pg. 137)

In-Flavor: Lazy people cannot get anything done and will never succeed at anything. But if you want to achieve something spectacular or become a great leader, you must work hard and never lose hope.

Inspiration Coffee: Wonder Counselor, if I am lazy, I cannot get anything done and will never succeed. However, if I want to succeed or be a great leader, I must work hard and keep my dream alive. Thank you, Lord.

A person's character is put to the test when he suddenly acquires or quickly loses a considerable amount of money. (Practical, Money, pg. 161)

Wi-Flavor: Money is an important factor of daily life. If you suddenly acquire or quickly lose a considerable amount of money, it will test your character and how you deal with material possessions.

Wisdom Tea: Wisdom of God, money is an important part of my life. If I suddenly acquire or quickly lose a huge amount of money, it will test my character and how I deal with material possessions. Thank you, Lord.

October 8
The pessimist sees the difficulty in every opportunity; the optimist sees the opportunity in every difficulty. (L. P. Jacks) (Practical, Optimism/Pessimism, pg. 177)

In-Flavor: The pessimist will always see the negative in everything, including every opportunity. However, the optimist will see the positive, even in difficulty. You must learn to be an optimist.

Inspiration Coffee: Wonder Counselor, if I am a pessimist, I will see only the negative and difficulty in every opportunity. But if I am an optimist, I will see the positive and great opportunity in every difficulty. Thank you, Lord.

God's promises are like the stars; the darker the night, the brighter they shine. (Practical, Promises, pg. 201)

Wi-Flavor: You get scared when things turn dark and wonder if God will come to help. You should know that God's promises for you are like the stars, which shine brighter when the night is darker.

Wisdom Tea: Wisdom of God, I wonder if God will still help me when my life turns dark with its problems. I must know that God's promise is like the stars, which shine brighter when the night is darker. Thank you, Lord.

October 9
Prayer is the key of the morning and the bolt of the night.
(Practical, Prayer, pg. 189)

In-Flavor: People pray to ask for something or help them with a problem. You may consider prayer as the key to open the morning door for you to opportunities and the bolt to safeguard you at night.

Inspiration Coffee: Wonder Counselor, prayer might be about inquiry. But I consider it as the key to open the morning door for me to opportunities and also the bolt to safeguard my evening door from danger. Thank you, Lord.

The best time to keep your shirt on is when you're hot under the collar. (Practical, Self-Control, pg. 209)

Wi-Flavor: When you find yourself getting hot and irritated under the skin, you should keep your shirt on to prevent yourself from breaking into hives. That is the best practice of self-control when you are angry.

Wisdom Tea: Wisdom of God, when I find myself getting hot and irritated about something, I must keep my shirt on to hold myself under control and prevent any irrational things from happening. Thank you, Lord.

October 10
The secret to success is to do the common things uncommonly well. (John D. Rockefeller Jr.)
(Practical, Success, pg. 211)

In-Flavor: Some people think there is a special formula for success. But actually, the secret to success is for you to do common things extremely well. You do not have to do extraordinary things to get success.

Inspiration Coffee: Wonder Counselor, I might think I have to do extraordinary things if I want to achieve success. Today, I am told that the secret to success is simply to do common things extremely well. Thank you, Lord.

The man of love follows the path of God—and shows affection to both the believer and the nonbeliever. (Muhammad Iqbal (1873–1938), Indian Muslim poet and philosopher) (Quotations, Conduct, pg. 46)

Wi-Flavor: It is sad to see people show affection and care only for folks of their own kind in faith or race. But if you are a person of love and follow the true path of God, you will show that love to everyone.

Wisdom Tea: Wisdom of God, if I am really a person of love and follow the true path of God, I will share my love with everyone. I should not show my love to only people of my own faith or race. Thank you, Lord.

October 11

Anytime you find the truth standing in your way, you may be sure you are heading in the wrong direction. (Practical, Truth, pg. 232)

In-Flavor: The truth is often considered to be the moral compass and guideline to keep a person on the right path. So, if you see it standing in your way, you must be heading in the wrong direction.

Inspiration Coffee: Wonder Counselor, I often consider the truth to be the moral compass and guideline to keep me on the right path. But if I see it standing in my way, I must be heading in the wrong direction. Thank you, Lord.

One must be poor to know the luxury of giving. (George Eliot (1819–1880), English writer) (Quotations, Gifts and Giving, pg. 107)

Wi-Flavor: If you are rich, you can afford to give away anything without considering it a luxury. However, if you are poor, you have to struggle for your daily necessities and will know the luxury of giving.

Wisdom Tea: Wisdom of God, the rich can afford to give things away freely without considering it a luxury. But if I am poor, I will have to struggle for my daily necessities and know the luxury of giving. Thank you, Lord.

October 12

The art of life lies in a constant readjustment to our surroundings. (Okakura Kakuzō (1862–1913), Japanese art critic and philosopher) (Quotations, Adaptability, pg. 4)

In-Flavor: There is no roadmap to show you how to navigate through the uncertainties of life. But life survival lessons tell you to be adaptable to and in a constant readjustment of your surroundings.

Inspiration Coffee: Wonder Counselor, my life does not have a roadmap to show me pitfalls and hurdles. But life survival lessons tell me to be adaptable to and in a constant adjustment of my surroundings. Thank you, Lord.

The greater you are, the more you must practice humility. (Ben Sira (190 BC), Hebrew scholar and philosopher, in Patrick Skehan's *The Wisdom of Ben Sira*) (Quotations, Humility, pg. 131)

Wi-Flavor: When you are rich, powerful, or famous, you will be tempted to be arrogant and look down on old friends and others. You must practice humility and not let those vanities get into your head.

Wisdom Tea: Wisdom of God, if I am rich, powerful, or famous, I will be tempted to look down on old friends and others. I must practice humility and not let those vanities change my character. Thank you, Lord.

October 13

The secret of contentment is knowing how to enjoy what you have, and to be able to lose all desires for things beyond your reach. (Lin Yutang (1895–1976), Chinese writer) (Quotations, Contentment, pg. 50)

In-Flavor: Most people do not feel content with their lives or satisfied with what they have. You should learn to be content by enjoying what you have and losing all desire for things beyond your reach.

Inspiration Coffee: Wonder Counselor, I must learn to be content with what I have and be grateful for it. I also need to lose all desire for more things in life. That is how I can show I am content with my life. Thank you, Lord.

It is Heaven's role to declare a man's destiny; it is man's role to shorten or lengthen his days. (Chinese proverb) (Quotations, Life, pg. 163)

Wi-Flavor: You might think it is Heaven's role to declare your destiny and your longevity. But actually, you will determine your days on earth by the way you take care of your body, soul, and spirit.

Wisdom Tea: Wisdom of God, it might be Heaven's role to declare my destiny. However, it is really me who determines the length of my days on earth by the way I take care of my body, soul, and spirit. Thank you, Lord.

October 14

Strength comes from waiting. (Jose Marti (1853–1895), Cuban patriot) (Quotations, Patience, pg. 199)

In-Flavor: Waiting for something is not a skill many people can master, for most people are impatient and impulsive. If you can wait patiently for something, you must have the divine strength.

Inspiration Coffee: Wonder Counselor, most people are impatient and cannot wait for anything. I must learn to wait patiently for something in order to show my incredible strength, which can only come from God. Thank you, Lord.

Revolution is a drama of passion. We did not win the people over by appealing to reason but by developing hope, trust, and fraternity. (Mao Zedong (1893–1976), Chairman of People's Republic of China) (Quotations, Revolution, pg. 243)

Wi-Flavor: A revolution like the Chinese Cultural Revolution did not happen by reasoning with the people. You will learn that it is a campaign of passion that appeals to hope, trust, and fraternity.

Wisdom Tea: Wisdom of God, a revolution does not come about by reasoning with the people. I will realize that it is a drama of passion that appeals to hope, trust, and fraternity with all the people. Thank you, Lord.

October 15

He who is able to conquer others is powerful; he who is able to conquer himself is more powerful. (Lao Tzu (604–531 BC), Chinese philosopher and founder of Taoism, *Tao Te Ching*) (Quotations, Power, pg. 211)

In-Flavor: It takes intense power and great resolve for a king to conquer another kingdom. But if you want to conquer yourself from bad habits, you need more motivation and better discipline.

Inspiration Coffee: Wonder Counselor, it takes careful planning and great resolve for a leader to conquer others. But if I want to conquer myself from darkness, I need much discipline and motivation to complete it. Thank you, Lord.

Seven characteristics distinguish the wise: he does not speak in the presence of one wiser than himself, does not interrupt, is not hasty to answer, asks and answers the point, talks about first things first and about last things last, admits when he does not know, and acknowledges the truth. (Talmud, Aboth 5:7) (Quotations, Wisdom, pg. 307)

Wi-Flavor: Wisdom is usually defined in terms of having knowledge and life experience. What you see above is a list of seven characteristics that distinguish the wise and help you be one.

Wisdom Tea: Wisdom of God, the list of seven characteristics above helps me distinguish the wise from the ordinary. If I want to be wise, I must own that list beside broad knowledge and experience. Thank you, Lord.

October 16

Let us have faith that right makes might; and in that faith let us dare to do our duty as we understand it. (Abraham Lincoln, speech, New York, February 21, 1859) (Religious, Right, pg. 491)

In-Flavor: Everyone likes to be right, but no one wants to carry on the duty that comes with it. So, you may believe that the one who is right is powerful, but you also need to follow through with your duty.

Inspiration Coffee: Wonder Counselor, everyone wants to be right, but no one wants to carry on the duty that follows. I might believe that the one who is right is powerful, but I also need to follow through with my duty. Thank you, Lord.

In violence, we forget who we are. (Mary McCarthy, *On the Contrary*, 1961) (Religious, Aggression and Violence pg. 23)

Wi-Flavor: When people become violent, they often forget everything about them and their surroundings. They act foolishly and irrationally. You need to avoid violence and always act peacefully.

Wisdom Tea: Wisdom of God, I need to avoid violence and act peacefully, even if the world might get violent and act foolishly. When the world acts that way, it often forgets who it is and its life mission. Thank you, Lord.

October 17

Do you know a hard-working man? He shall be successful and stand before kings! (Proverbs 22:29) (Wise, Success, pg. 126)

In-Flavor: If you are a hardworking person, you should never worry about being poor. More importantly, you will eventually end up being successful and glamorous as the result of your good work ethic.

Inspiration Coffee: Wonder Counselor, if I am a hardworking person, I should never worry about being poor, for my good work ethic will help me eventually be successful and glamorous before the world. Thank you, Lord.

A man has found himself when he has found his relation to the rest of the universe, and here is the Book [the Bible] in which those relations are set forth. (Woodrow Wilson, speech, May 7, 1911) (Religious, Bible, pg. 56)

Wi-Flavor: Your whole life is a constant search to learn about yourself and your life mission. You will succeed in that when you find your relation with the whole universe. The Bible will help you.

Wisdom Tea: Wisdom of God, my whole life is a constant search for my own identity and life mission. I will succeed with that when I find my relation with the whole universe. The Bible will help me. Thank you, Lord.

October 18

If you faint in the day of adversity, your strength is small. (Proverbs 24:10) (Religious, Adversity, pg. 18)

In-Flavor: Adversity and difficulty are certainly a part of human life. They are also important tests of character and resolve. So, if you become discouraged and fail those tests, you are just a wimp.

Inspiration Coffee: Wonder Counselor, adversity is a part of this life and an important test of my character and resolve. So, if I get discouraged and fail this test, my strength is too little, and I am simply a wimp. Thank you, Lord.

The true Christian is the true citizen, lofty of purpose, resolute in endeavor, ready for a hero's deeds, but never looking down on his task because it is cast in the day of small things. (Theodore Roosevelt, speech, December 30, 1900) (Religious, Christianity, pg. 77)

Wi-Flavor: A Christian is often defined in terms of beliefs, rules, and traditions. You see above how a Christian is viewed in simple terms. You are challenged to be a true Christian and live up to those terms.

Wisdom Tea: Wisdom of God, I often hear the definition of a Christian in terms of beliefs, traditions, and rules. I see above how a true Christian is viewed in simple terms. I am called to be a true Christian. Thank you, Lord.

October 19

As I have seen, those who plow iniquity and sow trouble reap the same. (Job 5:8) (Religious, Conduct and Behavior, pg. 95)

In-Flavor: The type of seed you sow and the kind of work you do will produce the exact same harvest. So, if you sow love and act kindly, you will receive the same back. The contrary is also true.

Inspiration Coffee: Wonder Counselor, I should know that the type of seed I sow and the work I do will produce the same harvest. So, if I sow love and act kindly, I will receive the same back, and vice versa. Thank you, Lord.

Death is what takes place within us when we look upon others not as gift, blessing, or stimulus but as threat, danger, or competition. (Dorothee Soelle, *Death by Bread Alone*, 1978) (Religious, Death, pg. 127)

Wi-Flavor: You might view death as the cessation of bodily and mental functions. However, today you are given a new definition of death if you see others as threat, danger, or competition.

Wisdom Tea: Wisdom of God, I often think of death as the end of bodily and mental functions. Today, I am told that death happens within us when we see others not as gift and blessing but as a threat. Thank you, Lord.

October 20

A sense of duty is moral glue, constantly subject to stress. (William Safire, in The *New York Times*, May 23, 1986) (Religious, Duty, pg. 147)

In-Flavor: Duty is the moral sense that the military often reminds you of. If you know your daily duties, you will understand your moral responsibilities to complete them. But that can make you feel stressed.

Inspiration Coffee: Wonder Counselor, duties are my moral responsibilities toward my home, country, or faith that can cause me stress. If I know my daily duties, I will see why I need to complete them. Thank you, Lord.

If you would be a real seeker after truth, it is necessary that at least once in your life you doubt, as far as possible, all things. (René Descartes, *Principles of Philosophy*, 1644) (Religious, Doubt, pg. 144)

Wi-Flavor: You are certainly familiar with the story of the doubting Thomas who wanted to know the truth about the risen Christ. If you are a real seeker of truth, you must doubt all things at least once in life.

Wisdom Tea: Wisdom of God, if I am a real seeker of truth, it is important that I doubt at least once and do not blindly believe all the time. That is how I can appreciate the truth and desire it a lot more. Thank you, Lord.

October 21

If ye do not recognize God, at least recognize His signs. (Al-Hallaj (858–922 AD), in A. J. Arberry's *Sufism*) (Religious, Finding God, pg. 188)

In-Flavor: God is everywhere in the whole of creation. You might not see God, but you can recognize his signs. When you are around God, great things happen. Therefore, you must find God every day.

Inspiration Coffee: Wonder Counselor, when I am around God, I feel peaceful and joyful, and lots of great things happen. That is why I need to find God and recognize his presence by his signs around me. Thank you, Lord.

Faith is obscure. By faith a man moves through darkness; but he moves securely, his hand in the hand of God. He is literally seeing through the eyes of God. (Walter Farrell, *The Looking Glass*, 1951) (Religious, Faith, pg. 177)

Wi-Flavor: You have heard the saying, "We walk by faith and not by sight." Faith is basically seeing through the eyes of God. You rely on faith to help you move through life, especially in the dark nights of your soul.

Wisdom Tea: Wisdom of God, I use faith to help me move through this life as if God holds my hands and guides me through darkness and the uncertainties of my life under the eyes of God. I feel good with its presence. Thank you, Lord.

October 22

A true Christian should have but one fear—lest he should not hope enough. (Walter Elliot, *The Spiritual Life*, 1914) (Religious, Hope, pg. 235)

In-Flavor: People have all kinds of fears that might inhibit them from living a joyful and fulfilling life. But as a true Christian, you should have but one fear: That is, you do not hope enough in this life.

Inspiration Coffee: Wonder Counselor, I may have all sorts of fears that might keep me from enjoying a happy and fulfilled life. However, I should have but one fear as a true Christian: That is, not hope enough. Thank you, Lord.

"I can forgive, but I cannot forget" is only another way of saying, "I will not forgive." A forgiveness ought to be like a cancelled note, torn in two and burned up, so that it can never be shown against the man. (Henry Ward Beecher, *Life Thoughts*, 1858) (Religious, Forgiveness, pg. 192)

Wi-Flavor: The saying above is not really forgiveness. Today, you are admonished to forget everything once you truly forgive someone. It is like tearing in two a cancelled note and burning it up.

Wisdom Tea: Wisdom of God, I might think I can forgive but cannot forget. But that attitude will never work. When I forgive someone, it is like tearing up a cancelled note and forgetting about it. Thank you, Lord.

October 23

If you have a particular faith or religion, that is good. But you can survive without it if you have love, compassion, and tolerance. The clear proof of a person's love of God is if that person genuinely shows love to fellow human beings. (Dalai Lama, *For the Love of God*, 1990) (Religious, Love, pg. 305)

In-Flavor: Some like to be associated with a particular faith or religion to help them be close to God. But the best way for you to show your love for God is to have love and compassion for a human.

Inspiration Coffee: Wonder Counselor, I might associate myself with a particular religion to help others see my love of God. But the best way for me to show my love for God is to have compassion for others. Thank you, Lord.

The supreme happiness of life is the conviction that we are loved. (Victor Hugo, *Les Miserables*, 1862) (Religious, Happiness, pg. 222)

Wi-Flavor: Happiness has been defined in various ways. Today, you learn that the supreme happiness of life is experienced when you feel that you are loved, for love brings you joy and completes everything.

Wisdom Tea: Wisdom of God, I can define happiness in a variety of ways. However, I will have the supreme happiness of life when I feel that I am loved, for love brings me joy and many other blessings. Thank you, Lord.

October 24

For without risk there is no faith, and the greater the risk, the greater the faith. (Søren Kierkegaard, postscript, *Philosophical Fragments*, 1846) (Religious, Risk and Safety, pg. 494)

In-Flavor: People put their faith in God for various reasons. You may risk part of your life or everything you have for divine blessings. But the more risk you take, the greater faith you must have in God.

Inspiration Coffee: Wonder Counselor, I put my faith in God and risk part of my life or everything for divine blessings and all kinds of reasons. I must know that the more risk I take, the greater faith I have in God. Thank you, Lord.

Poverty often deprives a man of all spirit and virtue. (Benjamin Franklin, *Poor Richard's Almanac*, 1757) (Religious, Poverty, pg. 404)

Wi-Flavor: You might know some hardships and sufferings that the poor have to endure. But today you will see that poverty can also deprive you of all spirit and virtues and push you to do bad things.

Wisdom Tea: Wisdom of God, if you are poor, you would have to endure hardships and sufferings. Today, I am told that poverty can also deprive me of all spirit and virtues and cause me to do bad things. Thank you, Lord.

October 25

No one draws closer to a knowledge of the truth than he who has advanced far in the knowledge of divine things, and yet knows that something always remains for him to seek. (St. Leo (390?–461 AD), "Sermon in Nativitate Domini, IX") (Religious, Truth, pg. 577)

In-Flavor: You can come closer to the knowledge of truth by advancing in the knowledge of divine things such as God, soul, spirit, or eternal life. You can also find it through mathematics and science.

Inspiration Coffee: Wonder Counselor, I can come closer to the knowledge of truth by advancing in knowledge of divine things like God and spirit. I can also search for it through mathematics and science. Thank you, Lord.

When Jesus says that we should turn the other cheek, he is telling us that we must not take revenge; he is not saying that we should never defend ourselves or others. ("The Kairos Document" (revised second edition), 1986) (Religious, Revenge, pg. 487)

Wi-Flavor: Jesus calls you to turn the other cheek when someone slaps you. He does not tell you to stop defending yourself or others; you must know that he just wants you not to take revenge.

Wisdom Tea: Wisdom of God, Jesus asks me to turn the other cheek when somebody slaps me on one. He does not ask me to stop defending myself or others; he just wants me not to take revenge. Thank you, Lord.

October 26

The three great essentials to achieve anything worthwhile are first, hard work; second, stick-to-itiveness; and third, common sense. (Thomas Edison) (Wise, Accomplishment, pg. 7)

In-Flavor: If you want to achieve something, you must keep these three essential elements—hard work, persistence, and common sense—mixed well together from the beginning to the end of the project.

Inspiration Coffee: Wonder Counselor, if I want to achieve something, I must keep these three essential elements—hard work, persistence, and common sense—mixed well together throughout the project. Thank you, Lord.

It is not a crime to be rich, nor a virtue to be poor. ... The sin lies in hoarding wealth and keeping it from circulating freely to all who need it. (Charles Fillmore, *Prosperity*, 1940) (Religious, Wealth, pg. 607)

Wi-Flavor: Society tends to condemn the rich and praise the poor. You must know that it is not a crime to be rich or a virtue to be poor. But sin lies in hoarding the wealth and keeping it from the needy.

Wisdom Tea: Wisdom of God, the world likes to condemn the rich and praise the poor. But I must know that it is not a crime to be rich or a virtue to be poor. Sin lies in hoarding wealth from the needy. Thank you, Lord.

October 27

It's more important to know where you're going than to see how fast you can get there. (Wise, Direction, pg. 41)

In-Flavor: You might not be able to wait patiently for something in this lightning-fast time. But it is much more important for you to know your destination than to see how fast you can get there.

Inspiration Coffee: Wonder Counselor, I might not want to wait patiently for anything in this fast-paced world. But it is more important for me to know my destination than to see how fast I can get there. Thank you, Lord.

Conscience is something inside that bothers you when nothing outside does. (Practical, Conscience, pg. 40)

Wi-Flavor: Conscience has been defined in many ways, but the best one is the inner voice that bothers you when nothing outside does. So, whenever you feel guilty or an inner nagging, that is your conscience.

Wisdom Tea: Wisdom of God, conscience has been considered the moral compass or the wheelbarrow going ahead of me. Today, I am told it is the inner voice that bothers me when nothing outside does. Thank you, Lord.

October 28

The really happy guy is the one who can enjoy the scenery even when he has to take a detour. (Wise, Happiness, pg. 69)

In-Flavor: If you have ever had to take a detour, you know how frustrating it is when that happens. But if you are truly a happy person, you can enjoy the scenery amidst that chaos.

Inspiration Coffee: Wonder Counselor, a detour can make me feel impatient and frustrated when I have to go through it. But if I am a really happy person, I can simply enjoy the scenery amidst that chaos. Thank you, Lord.

Cooperate! Remember the banana? Every time it leaves the bunch it gets skinned. (Practical, Cooperation, pg. 42)

Wi-Flavor: Cooperation and working together is the key for a long life and great success. So, if you leave the bunch and create division, you will face great hardship and get your life cut short.

Wisdom Tea: Wisdom of God, if I leave the bunch and create division like the banana, I will face great hardship and get my life cut short, for cooperation is the key to a long life and great success. Thank you, Lord.

October 29

He who puts God first will find God with him to the last. (Wise, Priorities, pg. 109)

In-Flavor: God is the last thing most people would think about in their lives. But if you choose to put God first in everything you do, you will find God throughout your life all the way to the end.

Inspiration Coffee: Wonder Counselor, God is the last thing many people would think about in their lives. If I choose to put God first in everything I do, I will find God throughout my life all the way to the end. Thank you, Lord.

A wise man makes his own decisions; an ignorant man follows public opinion. (Chinese proverb) (Practical, Decision Making, pg. 50)

Wi-Flavor: A lot of decisions these days have been made by gauging public opinion. But you must know that a wise person makes his/her own decisions, while an ignorant one follows public opinion.

Wisdom Tea: Wisdom of God, many decisions these days are made by gauging public opinion, like an ignorant person often does. But I know that a wise person makes his/her own decisions. Thank you, Lord.

October 30

If you can't alter the hardships in your life, change your attitudes toward them. (Wit, Spring & Summer)

In-Flavor: Hardships are part of life. But you must not let them overwhelm and stress you out. Instead, you should change your attitudes and view them as a test of your endurance and commitment.

Inspiration Coffee: Wonder Counselor, hardships are part of my life, and they can overwhelm and stress me out. If I cannot change them in my life, then I should change my attitudes toward them. Thank you, Lord.

An egomaniac is someone who's hard of listening. (Practical, Egotism, pg. 61)

Wi-Flavor: You might not have met an egomaniac, but it is someone who is hard of listening. All this person focuses on and talks excessively about is himself/herself. You must avoid being this type of person.

Wisdom Tea: Wisdom of God, I should avoid becoming an egomaniac who is hard of listening and obsessive about himself/herself. All this person concentrates on and talks excessively about is himself/herself. Thank you, Lord.

October 31

Courage does not always roar. Sometimes, it is the quiet voice at the end of the day saying, "I will try again tomorrow." (Wit, Unknown, pg. 2)

<u>In-Flavor</u>: You assume courage always takes on the form of a roaring lion when you act fearlessly. But it can also be the quiet voice at the end of a long day encouraging you: "I will try again tomorrow."

<u>**Inspiration Coffee**</u>: Wonder Counselor, I may assume courage takes on the form of a roaring lion when I act fearlessly. But it is also the quiet voice at the end of a long day saying, "I will try again tomorrow." Thank you, Lord.

A true friend is always loyal, and a brother is born to help in time of need. (Proverbs 17:17) (Practical, Friendship, pg. 83)

<u>Wi-Flavor</u>: Your brother or sister is around you from birth to help you in time of need. However, if you are blessed, you will find a true friend who is always loyal to you in any circumstance.

<u>**Wisdom Tea**</u>: Wisdom of God, my brother or sister is with me from birth to help me in time of need. However, if I am blessed, I will find a true friend who is always loyal to me in in any situation. Thank you, Lord.

NOVEMBER

November 1

Behold the turtle. He makes progress only when he sticks his neck out. (James Bryant Conant)
(Practical, Ambition, pg. 13)

In-Flavor: A turtle can make progress only when it risks its safety and sticks its neck out. Similarly, you cannot make progress and achieve your ambition unless you stick out your neck and take risks.

Inspiration Coffee: Wonder Counselor, a turtle makes progress by risking its safety and sticking its neck out. Likewise, I cannot make progress and achieve my dream unless I stick out my neck and take some risks. Thank you, Lord.

A gossip goes around spreading rumors, while a trustworthy man tries to quiet them.
(Proverbs 11:13) (Practical, Gossip, pg. 97)

Wi-Flavor: Rumors can create lies and innuendoes that might cause hurts and divisions. A gossip goes around doing that work. Meanwhile, if you are a trustworthy person, you will try to quiet those.

Wisdom Tea: Wisdom of God, a gossip goes around spreading rumors and creating lies and innuendoes that cause hurt and division. However, if I am a trustworthy person, I will try to quiet them. Thank you, Lord.

November 2

He who cannot endure tough times will not see good times.
(Practical, Endurance, pg. 63)

In-Flavor: Tough times can come from various challenges and push your endurance to its limit. If you fail that test and cannot make it through those times, you will not see the good times that follow.

Inspiration Coffee: Wonder Counselor, tough times could come from various challenges and push my endurance to its limit. If I fail that test and cannot make it through those times, I will not see the good times that follow. Thank you, Lord.

The first step to wisdom is silence; the second is listening. (Practical, Hearing, pg. 104)

Wi-Flavor: Wisdom is achieved after a life-long experience and a relentless search for knowledge over the years. But the first step for you to get there is to be silent. The second one is to listen well.

Wisdom Tea: Wisdom of God, in silence, I am able to let the voices of my conscience and you talk and pass on to me your wisdom. I also need to listen well to those voices to figure out what I must do next. Thank you, Lord.

November 3
Falling down doesn't make you a failure, but staying down does.
(Practical, Failure, pg. 70)

In-Flavor: You will surely fall down many times on your way to the mountaintop of success. But that does not make you a failure. What makes you a failure is if you decide to stay down.

Inspiration Coffee: Wonder Counselor, I will surely fail or fall down lots of times on my way up the mountain of success. But what really makes me a failure is if I decide to stay down permanently. Thank you, Lord.

Life without hope is a life without meaning.
(Practical, Hope, pg. 110)

Wi-Flavor: A life without meaning prevents you from waking up each day. You will end up with that life if you have no hope. Hope gives you reasons to live for and inspires you to overcome daily challenges.

Wisdom Tea: Wisdom of God, a life without hope leads me to a life without meaning that might prevent me from waking up each day. Hope gives me reasons to live for and inspires me to persevere. Thank you, Lord.

November 4
The heart is happiest when it beats for others.
(Practical, Happiness, pg. 101)

In-Flavor: You might be happy when you get what you want or when things turn out the way you hope. However, your heart is happiest when it beats for others or when it is at the service for others.

Inspiration Coffee: Wonder Counselor, I might be happy when I get what I want or when things go the way I wish. But my heart is happiest when it beats for others or when it is at the service for others. Thank you, Lord.

Faults are thick where love is thin.
(James Howell) (Practical, Love, pg. 145)

Wi-Flavor: When you do not have any love for someone, you will see a lot of faults with that person. On the contrary, when you love someone, you cannot see anything wrong with that person.

Wisdom Tea: Wisdom of God, if I do not have any love for someone, I tend to see a lot of faults with that person. But if I have just a little love for someone, I cannot see anything wrong with that person. Thank you, Lord.

November 5
Humor is the lubricating oil of business. It prevents friction and wins goodwill. (Practical, Humor, pg. 115)

In-Flavor: In the process of doing business, people might cause friction and make one another mad. You can reduce friction and win goodwill by using humor, for it helps lighten up the mood with laughs.

Inspiration Coffee: Wonder Counselor, in doing daily business, I might have caused friction and made some people mad. I can reduce that tension and win some goodwill by using humor and laughs. Thank you, Lord.

The exercise that wears most people out is running after cash. (Practical, Money, pg. 162)

Wi-Flavor: Everyone is encouraged to exercise daily and keep it up, despite any hurdles. However, you will learn that the exercise that might wear you out is running after cash, for it never ends.

Wisdom Tea: Wisdom of God, I exercise every day to keep up my good health. But I will realize that the exercise that might wear me out is running after cash, for it is exhausting and never ends. Thank you, Lord.

November 6
You can't judge another person until you've walked in his shoes. (Practical, Judgment, pg. 123)

In-Flavor: It is human nature to cast judgment and condemn one another. But you should not judge another person unless you have been in his/her shoes, for you do not know his/her situation.

Inspiration Coffee: Wonder Counselor, it is my human nature to judge and condemn other people. However, I should not do that without knowing their situations and walking in their shoes. Thank you, Lord.

We never know the love of the parent till we become parents ourselves. (Henry Ward Beecher) (Practical, Parents, pg. 182)

Wi-Flavor: Parents often get criticized and blamed for all kinds of negative things. However, you will have to admit that you never know the love of the parent until you become parent yourself.

Wisdom Tea: Wisdom of God, parents often get criticized and blamed for their work with their children. But I will never know the real love of the parent unless I have become a parent myself. Thank you, Lord.

November 7

He who cannot obey, cannot command. (Benjamin Franklin) (Practical, Leadership, pg. 138)

In-Flavor: Obedience is not a natural instinct, but a learned skill. A person can be trained to obey. If you wish to be a leader, you must know how to inspire others to obey, beginning with yourself.

Inspiration Coffee: Wonder Counselor, obedience is a skill I get through training and not an instinct I was given at birth. But if I wish to be a leader, I must know how to inspire myself and others to obey. Thank you, Lord.

To quarrel with a neighbor is foolish; a man with good sense holds his tongue. (Proverbs 11:12) (Practical, Quarrels, pg. 202)

Wi-Flavor: You might want to keep peace with your neighbors and avoid quarreling with them like a person with good sense. But a fool will pick a fight with his/her neighbors over everything.

Wisdom Tea: Wisdom of God, I may want to hold my tongue and keep peace with my neighbors like someone with good sense. However, if I am a fool, I will quarrel with my neighbors about many things. Thank you, Lord.

November 8

A pessimist says that anytime things appear to be going better, you have overlooked something. (Practical, Optimism/Pessimism, pg. 178)

In-Flavor: A pessimist usually see the negative in everything even when things appear to be going better. You should not be a pessimist and become critical of every little detail around you.

Inspiration Coffee: Wonder Counselor, a pessimist often sees the negative in everything, even when things appear to be going better. I must avoid being a pessimist and getting critical about every detail in my life. Thank you, Lord.

Whether you're on the road or in an argument, when you see red it's time to stop. (Practical, Self-Control, pg. 209)

Wi-Flavor: Self-control is a wonderful virtue that will serve you well if you know how to use it wisely in your life. So, it will tell you to stop whenever you see red on the road or in an argument.

Wisdom Tea: Wisdom of God, self-control is a magnificent virtue that will serve me well if I know how to use it wisely in my life. It will let me know to stop whenever I see red on the road or in an argument. Thank you, Lord.

November 9

If God shuts one door, he opens another. (Irish proverb) (Practical, Prayer, pg. 189)

In-Flavor: You will encounter failures or disappointments in your life. But do not be discouraged. Rather, in prayer, you should realize that when God shuts one door, he opens another one for you.

Inspiration Coffee: Wonder Counselor, I will surely see failures and disappointments in my life. However, I should not feel discouraged and forget that when God shuts one door, he opens another one for me. Thank you, Lord.

If you have good eyesight and good hearing, thank God who gave them to you. (Proverbs 20:12) (Practical, Thankfulness, pg. 221)

Wi-Flavor: Gratitude is a great virtue for you to carry along and practice daily. Some people might complain about everything, but you should thank God often if you have good eyesight and hearing.

Wisdom Tea: Wisdom of God, gratitude is a wonderful virtue for me to bring along and practice every day. However, I should thank God regularly and avoid complaining if I have good eyesight and hearing. Thank you, Lord.

November 10

A successful man keeps on looking for work after he has found a job. (Practical, Success, pg. 211)

In-Flavor: Anyone who already had a job does not need to look for work. However, if you want to be a successful person, you will never stop looking ahead and searching for more opportunities.

Inspiration Coffee: Wonder Counselor, I might think I will not need to look for work if I already have a job. But if I hope to be a successful person, I will never stop searching for more opportunities. Thank you, Lord.

Yesterday is a cancelled check; tomorrow is a promissory note; today is the only cash you have—so spend it wisely. (Kay Lyons) (Practical, Tomorrow/Today/Yesterday, pg. 228)

Wi-Flavor: You might keep looking back on yesterday with regrets, or you might look forward to the future with worries. But you must remember that today is what you need to focus on and do well.

Wisdom Tea: Wisdom of God, I might look back on yesterday with regrets or look forward to the future with worries. However, I must remember that today is the only thing I need to focus on and do well. Thank you, Lord.

November 11

Those who never retract their opinions love themselves more than they love truth. (Practical, Truth, pg. 233)

In-Flavor: In your search for the truth, you will make mistakes and say or do something regrettable. However, if you love the truth, you will humbly retract your opinions and correct your mistakes.

Inspiration Coffee: Wonder Counselor, in my search for the truth, I might make mistakes and say something regrettable. But if I love the truth, I will humbly retract my opinions and correct my mistakes. Thank you, Lord.

Be gentle to all and stern with yourself. (Teresa of Avila (1515–1582), Spanish nun, "Maxims for Her Nuns," in *Complete Works St. Teresa of Avila, Vol. 3*) (Quotations, Conduct, pg. 47)

Wi-Flavor: Today, you are asked to be gentle with others and stern with yourself. Sadly, you might do the opposite. You should learn to treat others better and hold yourself to a higher standard.

Wisdom Tea: Wisdom of God, I might be gentle with myself and stern with others around me in my daily life. I need to turn that around and try to be gentle to others while being tougher with myself. Thank you, Lord.

November 12

If a man hasn't discovered something that he would die for, he isn't fit to live. (Martin Luther King Jr.) (Quotations, Belief, pg. 25)

In-Flavor: It is a joyous blessing when a person can figure out his/her life mission. But if you have not figured out yours yet, you will not know what you should die for, and your life is meaningless.

Inspiration Coffee: Wonder Counselor, it is a great blessing if I have figured out my life mission. However, if I have not yet, I will not know what I should die for, and my life will be meaningless. Thank you, Lord.

A good deed will make a good neighbor. (Bantu proverb) (Quotations, The Golden Rule, pg. 112)

Wi-Flavor: Sometimes, neighbors might have a war with each other over the silliest things. However, if you review the Golden Rule, you will see that a good deed will make your neighbors happy.

Wisdom Tea: Wisdom of God, neighbors sometimes can have fights with one another over trivial things. But if I look over the Golden Rule, I will see that a good deed might make my neighbors happy. Thank you, Lord.

November 13

It is in supporting one another that two hands find strength. A thorny branch can only be cut if [the] left hand is helping. The right hand raised alone could not cut even a morsel of gristle. (Abdiliaahi Muuse (1890–1966), Somali sage, in a poem that has become a proverb) (Quotations, Cooperation, pg. 51)

In-Flavor: If you try to cut with one hand, you will see how difficult it is. Only by the support and cooperation of two hands can you find strength. One hand holds the branch, while the other cuts it.

Inspiration Coffee: Wonder Counselor, if I try to cut a branch with one hand, I cannot do it. One hand needs to hold it while the other cuts it. So, I will find strength in the support and cooperation of two hands. Thank you, Lord.

I look back on my life like a good day's work; it was done and I am satisfied with it. (Grandma Moses (1860–1961), American artist) (Quotations, Life, pg. 164)

Wi-Flavor: Some people regret things they should or should not have done. You should live your life to the fullest and look back on it like this: "It was a good day's work, and I am fine with it."

Wisdom Tea: Wisdom of God, I should live my life to the fullest and not regret things I should or should not have done. Then, I will say, "It was a good day's work, and I am satisfied with it." Thank you, Lord.

November 14

Life itself is a strange mixture. We have to take it as it is, try to understand it, and then to better it. (Rabindranath Tagore (1861–1941), Indian writer and philosopher) (Quotations, Life, pg. 166)

In-Flavor: Life is a strange mixture of good and bad, joy and sadness. You can never understand it completely. Most of it remains a mystery. You take it as it is, cherish it, and try to make the best of it.

Inspiration Coffee: Wonder Counselor, life is a strange mixture of joy and sadness, good and bad. I try to understand it, but it remains a mystery. All I can do is take it as it is, cherish it, and make the best of it. Thank you, Lord.

Sacrifice is not something that comes from outside. It is something that comes from inside, being born in our hearts. (*The Li Chi*, 200 BC, a compilation of Confucian writings) (Quotations, Sacrifice, pg. 248)

Wi-Flavor: You might see people carry out many acts of sacrifice for their families, churches, or country every day. But the actual sacrifice itself takes place inside them, as they have to give up lots of things.

Wisdom Tea: Wisdom of God, I might see people carry out countless acts of sacrifice for their families, churches, and country. But the real sacrifice takes place inside of a person by giving up lots of things. Thank you, Lord.

November 15

It is better to win the peace and to lose the war. (Bob Marley (1945–1981), Jamaican singer) (Quotations, Peace, pg. 201)

In-Flavor: If you have ever been in a war, you will know how destructive it can be. One side might claim it has won the war, but truthfully, everyone loses in a war. It is better for you to win the peace.

Inspiration Coffee: Wonder Counselor, everyone likes to win and does not hesitate to engage in countless fights. But everyone loses in a fight. So, it is better for me to win the peace and lose the war. Thank you, Lord.

Speaking the truth to the unjust is the best of holy wars.
(Muhammad) (Quotations, Truth, pg. 285)

Wi-Flavor: Holy wars have been conducted with threats and swords to spread certain beliefs or religions. But you must know that the best of holy wars is the one in which you speak the truth to the unjust.

Wisdom Tea: Wisdom of God, holy wars have happened between various religions with swords and spears. But I must remember that the best of holy wars is conducted by speaking the truth to the unjust. Thank you, Lord.

November 16

Our greatest glory is not in never falling but in rising every time we fall. (Confucius, *Analects*) (Quotations, Perseverance, pg. 202)

In-Flavor: People might pick certain events, like their induction into a hall of fame, as their greatest glory. Yours should be about perseverance in adversity and the ability to rise again every time you fall.

Inspiration Coffee: Wonder Counselor, I will surely fall and encounter many failures in my life. However, my greatest glory will be my perseverance in adversity and the ability to rise again every time I fall. Thank you, Lord.

He who knows others is learned; he who knows himself is wise.
(Lao Tzu, *Character of Tao*) (Quotations, Wisdom, pg. 307)

Wi-Flavor: You might get mixed up between knowledge and wisdom. But you must realize that knowledge comes from everything you might learn about others, while wisdom is the result of knowing yourself.

Wisdom Tea: Wisdom of God, I might not be able to tell knowledge from wisdom. But knowledge comes from everything I might learn about others, while wisdom is the result of knowing myself well. Thank you, Lord.

November 17

Without the bitter suffering, we cannot rise above others. (Chinese proverb) (Quotations, Suffering, pg. 273)

In-Flavor: Most people do not like suffering and will do anything to eliminate it. But you should view suffering as the training ground to strengthen you and help you rise above future challenges.

Inspiration Coffee: Wonder Counselor, I might not like suffering and will do anything to avoid it. But I should consider it as the training ground to strengthen and help me rise above future challenges. Thank you, Lord.

A soft answer turns away wrath, but a harsh word stirs up anger. (Proverbs 15:1) (Religious, Anger pg. 27)

Wi-Flavor: If you want a fight, all you have to do is use some harsh words that will stir up anger in someone. But if you use some soft answers, you can calm people down and divert a potential fight.

Wisdom Tea: Wisdom of God, if I want a fight, all I need to do is use some harsh words on someone to stir up anger. But if I use some soft answers, I will calm people down and divert a potential fight. Thank you, Lord.

November 18

If you have not clung to a broken piece of your old ship in the dark night of the soul, your faith may not have the sustaining power to carry you through to the end of the journey. (Rufus M. Jones, *The Radiant Life*, 1944) (Religious, Adversity pg. 19)

In-Flavor: Adversity often causes everyone to cringe. But for the believer, you should consider it as one of the best ways for you to gain strength to sustain yourself through to the end of the faith journey.

Inspiration Coffee: Wonder Counselor, adversity can scare people. However, I should view it as one of the great ways for me to strengthen my faith and help carry me through to the end of my life journey. Thank you, Lord.

Whatever makes men good Christians makes them good citizens. (Daniel Webster, speech, December 22, 1820) (Religious, Christianity, pg. 78)

Wi-Flavor: A secular society does not think there is any value in faith or religion. What it does not realize is that whatever makes people good Christians also makes them good citizens. You better believe it!

Wisdom Tea: Wisdom of God, a secular society might think there is no value in faith or religion. However, I must realize that whatever makes people good Christians also makes them good citizens. Thank you, Lord.

November 19

On Judgment Day, God will not ask to what sect you belonged, but what manner of life you led. (I. M. Kagan, *Chofetz Chaim*, 1873) (Religious, Conduct and Behavior, pg. 95)

In-Flavor: Human beings are often preoccupied with a brand name. However, you should know that on Judgment Day, God is only concerned about your past life manners and not your faith denomination.

Inspiration Coffee: Wonder Counselor, the world might be fascinated with a brand name. But I must know that on Judgment Day, God will not care about my faith denomination, but my past life manners. Thank you, Lord.

Next to the care of our own souls, a right education of our children is greatest. (John Bellers, *Epistles to Friends Concerning Education*, 1697) (Religious, Education, pg. 152)

Wi-Flavor: You should take good care of your soul because it is the most valuable part of yourself. Similarly, you ought to give your children a right education because they are a precious treasure.

Wisdom Tea: Wisdom of God, I should take great care of my soul because it is the most valuable part of myself. Also, I must give my children a right education because they are a precious national treasure. Thank you, Lord.

November 20

But I say to you, Love your enemies and pray for those who persecute you, so that you may be sons of your Father who is in Heaven; for he makes his sun rise on the evil and on the good, and sends rain on the just and the unjust. (Matthew 5:44–45) (Religious, Enemy, pg. 157)

In-Flavor: It is in our human nature to love our family, friends, and anyone who loves us. But as a Christian, you are encouraged and challenged to love your enemies and pray for your persecutors.

Inspiration Coffee: Wonder Counselor, it is my human nature to love my family, friends, and people who love me. But as a Christian, I am encouraged to love my enemies and pray for my persecutors. Thank you, Lord.

Without faith[,] man becomes sterile, hopeless, and afraid to the very core of his being. (Erich Fromm, *Man for Himself*, 1947) (Religious, Faith, pg. 177)

Wi-Flavor: Faith brings lots of benefits. In case you do not know, it gives you a source of spiritual refreshment, something to look to beyond this life, the courage to do the right things, and much more.

Wisdom Tea: Wisdom of God, I must know that faith can give me a good source of spiritual refreshment, something to look to beyond this life, the courage to do the right things, and many more great benefits. Thank you, Lord.

November 21

The man who does not need God will not find God. (George Brantl, *Catholicism*, 1962) (Religious, Finding God, pg. 188)

In-Flavor: The Bible reports that the sick, the broken, the poor, and the lost searched for God because they needed God. Likewise, if you want God for something, you just need to search, and you will find God.

Inspiration Coffee: Wonder Counselor, people who experienced miracles in the Bible needed God and searched for divine help. Similarly, if I need God to do something for me, I will find God to help me. Thank you, Lord.

No sin is too big for God to pardon, and none too small for habit to magnify. (Bahya ben Joseph ibn Pakuda, *Hobot HaLebabot*, 1040 AD) (Religious, Forgiveness, pg. 192)

Wi-Flavor: Some people cannot fathom how God can forgive their outrageous sins and help them overcome their bad habits to find a new life. But if you truly repent, God is ready to pardon you.

Wisdom Tea: Wisdom of God, my sin can start out as a bad habit and become a huge problem over time. However, if I truly repent, God can forgive even my outrageous sins and help me find a new life. Thank you, Lord.

November 22

The miserable have no other medicine, but only hope. (William Shakespeare, *Measure for Measure*) (Religious, Hope, pg. 237)

In-Flavor: People take hope for granted and do not exploit its great potential. The miserable, however, have nothing else but hope to survive. So, you should maximize the power of hope for your own benefits.

Inspiration Coffee: Wonder Counselor, I might take hope for granted and not know how to maximize its great potential. Today, I am reminded that the miserable have no other medicine but hope to survive. Thank you, Lord.

An hour spent in hate is an eternity withdrawn from love. (Ludwig Börne (1786–1837), *Fragmente und Aphorismen*, no. 191) (Religious, Hatred, pg. 223)

Wi-Flavor: You must know that love can bring you lots of wonderful things. Sadly, hatred keeps that from happening. Remember that an hour you remain in hate is an eternity you are away from love.

Wisdom Tea: Wisdom of God, I must realize that love brings me lots of wonderful things, while hatred keeps that from happening. So, if I remain in hate for an hour, I will be away from love for eternity. Thank you, Lord.

November 23

No one who is a lover of money, a lover of pleasure, or a lover of glory, is likewise a lover of mankind; but only he who is a lover of virtue. (Epictetus, *Enchiridion*) (Religious, Love, pg. 306)

In-Flavor: You are always tempted to be a lover of money and pleasure. But if you are a lover of virtue, you will naturally be a lover of mankind, for you will care about other people more than yourself.

Inspiration Coffee: Wonder Counselor, I am tempted to love money, pleasure, and glamor every day. However, if I want to be a lover of mankind, I have to reject those temptations and be a lover of virtue. Thank you, Lord.

Most men find in Jesus a reflection of their own ideals. (Grandville Hicks, *Eight Ways of Looking at Christianity*, 1926) (Religious, Jesus Christ, pg. 272)

Wi-Flavor: Jesus wants you and everyone to live in God's love. He also wants to heal, help, feed, and save everyone in the world. Like most people, you may find in Jesus a reflection of your own ideals.

Wisdom Tea: Wisdom of God, I want to love God and my enemies. I also wish to heal, help, feed, and save my neighbors. So, I find in Jesus a reflection of my own ideals and try to practice them. Thank you, Lord.

November 24

I object to violence because when it appears to do good, the good is only temporary; the evil it does is permanent. (Mahatma Gandhi, *Selections from Gandhi*, 1945) (Religious, Nonviolence, pg. 362)

In-Flavor: When people do not get what they want, they often resort to violence to get it. But Gandhi wants to inspire you to reject violence and find other, more peaceful ways to achieve your goals.

Inspiration Coffee: Wonder Counselor, when I do not get what I want, I might resort to violence to get it. Today, I am advised to reject violence and find other, more peaceful ways to achieve my goals. Thank you, Lord.

When we live at each other's mercy, we had better learn to be merciful. (William Sloan Coffin, *Living the Truth in a World of Illusions*, 1985) (Religious, Mercy, pg. 324)

Wi-Flavor: People like others to be merciful to them, but they do not often act that way. You must remember that when you live at others' mercy, you had better learn to be merciful to everyone.

Wisdom Tea: Wisdom of God, I might hope people are merciful to me, but I sometimes do not act the same. I must know that when I live at others' mercy, I had better learn to be merciful to everyone. Thank you, Lord.

November 25

If the Creator had a purpose in equipping us with a neck, he surely meant for us to stick it out.
(Arthur Koestler, *Encounter*, 1970) (Religious, Risk and Safety, pg. 494)

In-Flavor: Most people are afraid of taking risks or sticking their necks out for something good. But if the Creator gave you a neck, you are called to stick it out and take some risks to achieve your success.

Inspiration Coffee: Wonder Counselor, I might be afraid of sticking my neck out to do something good. But I should know that I must stick it out and take risks for my success if the Creator gave me a neck. Thank you, Lord.

A decent person's provision for the poor is the true test of civilization. (Samuel Johnson, in Boswell's *Life of Samuel Johnson*, 1772) (Religious, Poverty, pg. 405)

Wi-Flavor: The first-world countries often brag about their level of civilization by their high living standard. But the true test of civilization is the provision and treatment you show to the poor.

Wisdom Tea: Wisdom of God, the first-world countries often talk about their level of civilization by their high living standard. But the true test of it is the provision and treatment I show to the poor. Thank you, Lord.

November 26

It is one thing to wish to have truth on our side, and another to wish sincerely to be on the side of truth. (Richard Whately, *On the Love of Truth*, 1825) (Religious, Truth, pg. 580)

In-Flavor: Everyone likes to be around the truth and have the truth on their side. That way, they are right. However, it will be tougher for you to convert yourself to the side of truth and enjoy being there.

Inspiration Coffee: Wonder Counselor, I might like to have the truth on my side in a debate to make sure I am right. But I must know that it is better to convert myself to the side of the truth and love it there. Thank you, Lord.

The hunger for love is much more difficult to remove than the hunger for bread. (St. Mother Teresa, in *Time* magazine, December 4, 1989) (Religious, Poverty, pg. 407)

Wi-Flavor: The poor are hungry for bread, and you will find enough bread to feed them and end that problem. But you will see that it is much tougher to find enough love to end the hunger for love.

Wisdom Tea: Wisdom of God, I might find enough food to feed the people who are hungry for bread. However, I will see that I may not find enough love to help people who are hungry for love around me. Thank you, Lord.

November 27

When your adversaries tell you that you can't go any farther, just tell them to look behind you and see how far you've come.
(Wise, Accomplishment, pg. 7)

In-Flavor: Your adversaries will try to discourage and keep you from going any farther. However, if you want to accomplish the rewards ahead, you just have to tell them to see how far you have come.

Inspiration Coffee: Wonder Counselor, my adversaries will try to discourage and keep me from going any farther. But if I want to accomplish great rewards, I have to tell them to see how far I have come. Thank you, Lord.

To know what is right and not to do it is the worst cowardice.
(Confucius, *Analects*) (Religious, Right, pg. 491)

Wi-Flavor: Everyone hates to be called a coward. But you will be that person if you do not do what you know is right. The best way for you to learn about right or wrong is with the help of God and religion.

Wisdom Tea: Wisdom of God, I learn about right and wrong through religion and moral rules. If I know what is right and do not do it, I am the worst coward. I must do it and avoid being that person. Thank you, Lord.

November 28

Happiness is like a potato salad—when shared with others, it's a picnic. (Wise, Happiness, pg. 69)

In-Flavor: Some people view happiness as a personal and exclusive thing and keep it all to themselves. But if you see happiness like a potato salad, it should be shared with others to make a fun picnic.

Inspiration Coffee: Wonder Counselor, I might think of happiness as a personal thing and keep it all to myself. However, if I see it like a potato salad, then it should be shared with others to create a fun picnic. Thank you, Lord.

Tragedy is a tool for the living to gain wisdom, not a guide by which to live. (Robert F. Kennedy, speech, March 18, 1968) (Religious, Wisdom, pg. 617)

Wi-Flavor: People do not like tragedy, and pray that they will not have to deal with it. So, it makes sense that you might not see tragedy as guide for daily living. But it is a tool for you to gain wisdom.

Wisdom Tea: Wisdom of God, I might not like tragedy, which is not a good guide for my daily living. But I have to admit that it is great tool for me to gain wisdom and life lessons to survive this life. Thank you, Lord.

November 29

Problems are opportunities in work clothes. (Henry Kaiser) (Wise, Problems, pg. 111)

In-Flavor: No one likes problems, and would want nothing to do with them. However, you should consider problems as opportunities in work clothes and use them to help you grow and be better.

Inspiration Coffee: Wonder Counselor, I surely do not like problems and would do anything to avoid them. But I must see them as opportunities in work clothes and use them to help me grow and be better. Thank you, Lord.

Have two goals: wisdom—that is, knowing and doing right—and common sense. Don't let them slip away, for they fill you with living energy and bring you honor and respect. (Proverbs 3:21–22) (Practical, Aim, pg. 10)

Wi-Flavor: You might see the value of wisdom, for it helps you know and do the right things. But you often do not value common sense. Yet, both of them will fill you with living energy and bring you honor.

Wisdom Tea: Wisdom of God, I need to value wisdom, which gives me lifelong knowledge, and common sense, which tells me what to do now. Both will fill me with living energy and bring me great honor. Thank you, Lord.

November 30

The Lord has some wonderful things to display if we will allow our lives to be used as His showcase. (Wit, Spring & Summer)

In-Flavor: The Lord definitely has a lot to reveal and share with you. One of those is his miraculous power. If you allow your life to be used as his showcase, you will see lots of his miracles every day.

Inspiration Coffee: Wonder Counselor, the Lord has a lot to reveal and share with me. If I allow my life to be used as his showcase, I will see a lot of his wonderful miracles and great exhibits every day. Thank you, Lord.

Don't talk so much. You keep putting your foot in your mouth. Be sensible and turn off the flow! When a good man speaks, he is worth listening to, but the words of fools are a dime a dozen. (Proverbs 10:19–20) (Practical, Bores and Boredom, pg. 23)

Wi-Flavor: You are advised to talk less and listen more, for you might put your foot in your mouth if you talk too much. Besides, it is worth listening only to a good man speaking and not to the words of a fool.

Wisdom Tea: Wisdom of God, I am admonished to talk less and listen more to avoid putting my foot in my mouth. Besides, it is worth listening only to the talk of a good man and not the words of a fool. Thank you, Lord.

DECEMBER

December 1

The good man asks advice from friends; the wicked plunge ahead—and fall. (Proverbs 12:26) (Practical, Change, 25)

In-Flavor: Humans have learned from each other and past generations in order to avoid mistakes. Likewise, you should ask for advice from friends before moving forward. Otherwise, you will fall when plunging ahead.

Inspiration Coffee: Wonder Counselor, people have learned from each other and past generations in order to avoid failures. Similarly, I should ask advice from friends before plunging ahead like the wicked do, and fall. Thank you, Lord.

People who are all wrapped up in themselves usually make pretty small packages. (Practical, Egotism, pg. 61)

Wi-Flavor: Some people are so egotistical and self-centered that they do not care about anyone else. You are warned to avoid being like them. They make no difference to the world except small packages.

Wisdom Tea: Wisdom of God, some people focus only on themselves and become just small packages in the eyes of the world. I should reach out to help the needs of others and leave behind a big footprint. Thank you, Lord.

December 2

You can tell when you are on the right road—it's all uphill. (Practical, Direction, pg. 54)

In-Flavor: Sometimes, it is difficult to tell the right way as you face all kinds of distractions and try to make it through life. If you want to know you are on the right road to success, it is usually uphill.

Inspiration Coffee: Wonder Counselor, I cannot tell if I am on the right road sometimes, due to all the distractions and confusion in life. But I know that I am on right road to success when it is all uphill. Thank you, Lord.

He who walks in when others walk out is a true friend. (Practical, Friendship, pg. 84)

Wi-Flavor: When you encounter a problem, some of your friends might walk away and abandon you. But that is the test of true friendship. A true friend will walk in or stick around with you to the end.

Wisdom Tea: Wisdom of God, a test of true friendship happens when I encounter a problem. A true friend will walk in and stay with me to the end, while others will walk out and abandon me in time of need. Thank you, Lord.

December 3

If the enemy can't puff you up with pride, he will try to dampen your spirit by discouragement. It's his best tool! (Practical, Discouragement, pg. 56)

In-Flavor: Pride might cause you to underestimate your enemy and become overconfident. If he/she does not exploit your pride, he/she will discourage you in order to dampen your spirit and make you give up easily.

Inspiration Coffee: Wonder Counselor, my enemy might puff me up with pride to make me overconfident and underestimate him. Or, he can dampen my spirit with discouragement and make me give up easily. Thank you, Lord.

A gossip can give you all the details without knowing any of the facts. (Practical, Gossip, pg. 98)

Wi-Flavor: A gossip can spread all kinds of rumors and innuendoes that might hurt others. You must avoid being a gossip or stop this person, because he/she does not know all the facts of an issue.

Wisdom Tea: Wisdom of God, I must avoid being a gossip or stop this person, because he/she does not know all the facts, for a gossip can spread rumors and innuendoes that might wrongly hurt others. Thank you, Lord.

December 4

Christian faith helps us to face the music, even when we don't like the tune. (Practical, Faith, pg. 72)

In-Flavor: Adversity is a part of life, and sometimes, it can be overwhelming and difficult for you to handle. But Christian faith gives you the right way to face it and helps you learn to deal with it.

Inspiration Coffee: Wonder Counselor, life adversity can be tough and overwhelming for me to handle. But Christian faith tells me how to face the music and helps me learn to deal with it. Thank you, Lord.

Hope is putting faith to work when doubting would be easier. (Practical, Hope, pg. 110)

Wi-Flavor: You might know that faith helps point you to hope and gives your life purpose. However, you might not realize that hope helps you put faith to work and encourages you to achieve the final reward.

Wisdom Tea: Wisdom of God, faith gives me my life purpose and helps me to keep on hoping. However, it is hope that helps me put faith to work and encourages me to reach for the final reward. Thank you, Lord.

December 5
We have two ears and only one tongue in order that we may hear more and speak less.
(Diogenes) (Practical, Hearing, pg. 104)

In-Flavor: Most people find it hard to listen to God and others. But they have no problem expressing their opinions. If you truly understand the Creator's intention, you will speak less and hear more.

Inspiration Coffee: Wonder Counselor, some people can express their opinions but have a tough time listening to God and others. If I truly understand the Creator's intention, I will speak less and hear more. Thank you, Lord.

Getting wisdom is the most important thing you can do! And with your wisdom, develop common sense and good judgment.
(Proverbs 4:7) (Practical, Judgment, pg. 122)

Wi-Flavor: People usually focus on getting wisdom and forget everything else. You are reminded to develop common sense and good judgment after that, for they make you complete in your daily life.

Wisdom Tea: Wisdom of God, I might think I should focus only on getting wisdom. I should know that I also need to develop common sense and good judgment to make my daily life complete. Thank you, Lord.

December 6
To feel sorry for the needy is not the mark of a Christian—to help them is. (Practical, Help, pg. 106)

In-Flavor: It is easy for people to say they care for the needy and then do nothing about it. If you truly want to show your Christian love for the poor, then roll up your sleeves and do something for them.

Inspiration Coffee: Wonder Counselor, it is easy for me to say that I care for the needy and then do nothing. But if I really want to show my Christian love for the poor, then I need to do something for them. Thank you, Lord.

How does a man become wise? The first step is to trust and reverence the Lord! Only fools refuse to be taught. Listen to your father and mother. What you learn from them will stand you in good stead; it will gain you many honors. (Proverbs 1:7–9) (Practical, Learning, pg. 139)

Wi-Flavor: It is rare that you are shown how to become wise. First, you need to trust and reverence the Lord, the source of wisdom. Next, you listen and learn from your parents. Then you keep on learning.

Wisdom Tea: Wisdom of God, I am told how to become wise by putting my trust and reverence in the Lord, listening and learning from my parents, and continuing to learn throughout my life. Thank you, Lord.

December 7

You can judge a man not only by the company he keeps but by the jokes he tells. (Practical, Judgment, pg. 123)

In-Flavor: People are good at putting on disguises and hiding their true identity. They want to appear to be nice but are truly ugly inside. Still, you can learn about a person by his friends and his humor.

Inspiration Coffee: Wonder Counselor, I might find it difficult to judge someone. However, today I am told to learn more about a person by watching the company he keeps and the jokes he tells. Thank you, Lord.

Those who hope for a happy marriage will do well to remember that in wedding[,] the we comes before the I. (Practical, Marriage, pg. 150)

Wi-Flavor: It takes two people to form a marriage union. You must know that a happy marriage demands that the couple work together as a team and put their common goals before individual needs.

Wisdom Tea: Wisdom of God, I may not realize that a marriage needs two people. So, a happy marriage demands a couple to work as a team and put their common goals before individual interests. Thank you, Lord.

December 8

Leadership is the courage to admit mistakes, the vision to welcome change, the enthusiasm to motivate others, and the confidence to stay out of step when everyone else is marching to the wrong tune. (E. M. Estes) (Practical, Leadership, pg. 138)

In-Flavor: Everyone wants to be the boss. But they do not admit mistakes, embrace change, motivate others, and stand tall for justice. If you want to be a leader, you must learn to do all the things above.

Inspiration Coffee: Wonder Counselor, Everyone wants to be the boss. But if I want to be a leader, I must learn to admit mistakes, embrace change, motivate others, and fight for justice in any situation. Thank you, Lord.

A fool thinks he needs no advice, but a wise man listens to others. (Practical, Hearing, pg. 103)

Wi-Flavor: You should not be a fool who thinks he/she does not need any advice or to hear no one else's opinions. But you should be a wise person who values others' advice and listens to people's feedback.

Wisdom Tea: Wisdom of God, I must avoid being a fool who thinks he needs no advice or values no one else's opinions. Rather, I should try to be a wise person and listen to others' advice. Thank you, Lord.

December 9
An optimist is one who makes the best of it when he gets the worst of it. (Practical, Optimism/Pessimism, pg. 178)

In-Flavor: You may define an optimist in various ways, but one definition of it is someone who makes the best out of the worst situation. If you have that attitude and determination, you are an optimist.

Inspiration Coffee: Wonder Counselor, some people like to complain about everything or freak out when things turn bad. However, I want to be an optimist who can make the best out of the worst situation. Thank you, Lord.

True prayer is a way of life, not just in case of an emergency.
(Practical, Prayer, pg. 188)

Wi-Flavor: People usually pray when they want something from God or they face an emergency. But you must know that true prayer is your way of life or a daily routine that you cannot survive without it.

Wisdom Tea: Wisdom of God, some people pray only if they face an emergency or want God to do something. But I must see prayer as my way of life or a daily routine to help me survive this life. Thank you, Lord.

December 10
Seven days without prayer makes one weak. (Practical, Prayer, pg. 190)

In-Flavor: Prayer is the sacred time for believers to renew their spiritual strength and ask God to help them with their needs. If you cannot do that once a week, your spirit will be hungry and weak.

Inspiration Coffee: Wonder Counselor, I must remember that prayer is an important time for me to ask God for help and recharge my spiritual strength. If I go through a week without prayer, I will be weak. Thank you, Lord.

The only way to get the best of an argument is to avoid it.
(Dale Carnegie) (Practical, Quarrels, pg. 203)

Wi-Flavor: When people engage in quarrels and arguments, they are much more interested in being right and winning. However, you must realize that the only way to get the best argument is to avoid it.

Wisdom Tea: Wisdom of God, I might want to be right and win all arguments that I engage in with others. However, I must know that the only way for me to get the best of an argument is to avoid it. Thank you, Lord.

December 11
A successful man is one who can lay a firm foundation with the bricks that others throw at him.
(David Brinkley) (Practical, Success, pg. 211)

In-Flavor: People get angry easily over everything and spend their whole lives trying to even the score. But if you want to succeed, you will make use of everything to achieve it, even the insults of your critics.

Inspiration Coffee: Wonder Counselor, people get angry easily and will spend their whole lives trying to get even. However, if I want to succeed, I need to make good use of everything I have, including the insults of my critics.

A wise teacher makes learning a joy; a rebellious teacher spouts foolishness. (Proverbs 15:2) (Practical, Teaching, pg. 214)

Wi-Flavor: A teacher helps his/her students acquire knowledge and virtues that benefit them. If you are a wise teacher, you make learning fun. But if you are a rebellious teacher, you make it overwhelming.

Wisdom Tea: Wisdom of God, if I am a wise teacher, I will make learning fun and help my students acquire virtues and knowledge that benefit them. But if I am a rebellious teacher, I will make it a chore. Thank you, Lord.

December 12
Hard work brings prosperity; playing around brings poverty.
(Proverbs 28:19) (Practical, Work, pg. 247)

In-Flavor: Prosperity often comes from hard work and some luck while poverty is the result of laziness. So, if you want to see prosperity and avoid poverty, you must work hard and stop playing around.

Inspiration Coffee: Wonder Counselor, hard work will bring prosperity while playing around will result in poverty. So, if I want to see prosperity and avoid poverty, I must work hard and stop playing around. Thank you, Lord.

The Lord grants wisdom! His every word is a treasure of knowledge and understanding. For wisdom and truth will enter the very center of your being, filling your life with joy. (Proverbs, pg. 2:6-10) (Practical, Wisdom, pg. 236)

Wi-Flavor: The Lord is the source of wisdom and a wonderful treasure of knowledge. His every word will bring you great understanding and fill your life with joy and finest blessings. You must search for him.

Wisdom Tea: Wisdom of God, you are the source of truth and a wonderful treasure of knowledge. Your every word will bring me great understanding and fill my life with joy and wonderful blessings. Thank you, Lord.

December 13

If there is no dull and determined effort, there will be no brilliant achievement. (Hsün Tzu (310–220 BC), Chinese philosopher) (Quotations, Effort, pg. 76)

In-Flavor: Most brilliant achievements are the result of toil, sweat, great ideas, and determined effort. If you want to see spectacular achievements, you must have a good work ethic and relentless effort.

Inspiration Coffee: Wonder Counselor, most brilliant achievements are the result of determined effort, toil, sweat, and great ideas. If I want to see that, I must have a good work ethic and relentless effort. Thank you, Lord.

Envy is a worm that gnaws and consumes the entrails of ambitious men. (Pachacutec Inca Yupanqui, Incan ruler (1438–1471)) (Quotations, Envy and Jealousy, pg. 79)

Wi-Flavor: Envy, or jealousy, is one of the deadly sins that gnaw and consume your inner self and make you overlook your blessings. It stirs up unhealthy desires to crave what your neighbor has.

Wisdom Tea: Wisdom of God, envy (or jealousy) is one of the deadly sins that gnaws and consumes my inner self. It makes me overlook my blessings and crave what my neighbor has. Thank you, Lord.

December 14

Do the common thing in an uncommon way. (Booker T. Washington, *Daily Resolves*) (Quotations, Nonconformity, pg. 191)

In-Flavor: People make a name for themselves by doing the impossible or creating something unique. If you want to be remembered, you must try to do common things in an uncommon way.

Inspiration Coffee, Wonder Counselor, some people make a name for themselves by doing the impossible or something unique. If I want to be known, I must do common things in an uncommon way. Thank you, Lord.

No man is a true believer unless he desires for his brother that which he desires for himself. (Muhammad) (Quotations, The Golden Rule, pg. 112)

Wi-Flavor: The faithful often forget about their neighbors on their way to Heaven. But the Golden Rule reminds you that if you are a true believer, you must desire for your neighbor what you desire for yourself.

Wisdom Tea: Wisdom of God, the faithful often forget about their neighbors as they search for the way to Heaven. But if I am a true believer, I must desire for my neighbor what I desire for myself. Thank you, Lord.

December 15
To keep a lamp burning, we have to keep putting oil in it.
(St. Mother Teresa) (Quotations, Perseverance, pg. 202)

In-Flavor: A lamp will stop burning and be extinguished if you do not keep putting oil in it. Similarly, if you do not keep filling up your lamp of faith with kind words and caring acts, it will slowly burn out.

Inspiration Coffee: Wonder Counselor, a lamp will be extinguished if I do not keep putting oil in it. Likewise, if I do not keep filling up my lamp of faith with kind words and caring acts, it will eventually burn out. Thank you, Lord.

Ignorance alone is the prime cause of all misery.
(Chandrasekhara Bharati Swamigal (1892–1954), Hindu sage) (Quotations, Ignorance, pg. 136)

Wi-Flavor: If you suffer from the virus of ignorance, it will keep you from the well of knowledge. But you can free yourself from that misery by finding joy in learning and putting an end to ignorance.

Wisdom Tea: Wisdom of God, if I suffer from the virus of ignorance, I will be in great misery. However, I can free myself from that problem and virus by finding joy in learning and love of knowledge. Thank you, Lord.

December 16
Everyone has talent. What is rare is the courage to follow the talent to the dark place where it leads.
(Erica Jong (b. 1942), American writer, "The Artist as Housewife: The Housewife as Artist," in *Ms.* magazine, October 1972) (Quotations, Talent, pg. 275)

In-Flavor: The creator has given everyone unique and various talents to do different things. You should learn to use your talents for the common good and have the courage to make good use of them.

Inspiration Coffee: Wonder Counselor, I have been given unique talents and gifts to do various things. I should learn to use my talents for the common good and have the courage to make good use of them. Thank you, Lord.

Woman reaches love through friendship; man reaches friendship through love.
(Muhammad Hijazi (twentieth century) Iranian writer and politician, *Hazar Sokhan* (*A Thousand Sayings*)) (Quotations, Men and Women, pg. 181)

Wi-Flavor: Love is your deepest feeling for someone, while friendship is simply your rapport with someone. You will see that a woman reaches love through friendship, while a man does the opposite.

Wisdom Tea: Wisdom of God, love is my deepest feeling for someone, while friendship is just a relationship. So, I will realize that women reach love through friendship, while men do the opposite. Thank you, Lord.

December 17

Affliction is able to drown out every earthly voice ... but the voice of eternity within a man it cannot drown. (Søren Kierkegaard, *Christian Discourses*, 1847) (Religious, Adversity pg. 19)

In-Flavor: Affliction has a way to silence every earthly voice. But if you listen to the voice of eternity within you, you know it cannot be silenced and will keep calling you to live up to your potential.

Inspiration Coffee: Wonder Counselor, affliction knows how to drown out every earthly voice. However, if I listen to the voice of eternity within me, I know it cannot be silenced and will call me to be good. Thank you, Lord.

Sticks in a bundle are unbreakable. (Bondei (Kenyan) proverb) (Quotations, Unity, pg. 289)

Wi-Flavor: You might be able to break all the sticks individually, but you cannot do that when they are in a bundle. So, if you unite together, nobody can break you. If you are divided, you will be destroyed.

Wisdom Tea: Wisdom of God, I may be able to break all the sticks individually, but not when they are in a bundle. Likewise, if I remain united with others, nobody can break us. Thank you, Lord.

December 18

Conscience is the perfect interpreter of life. (Karl Barth, *The Word of God and the Word of Man*, 1957) (Religious, Conformity, pg. 98)

In-Flavor: Life remains a mystery, despite the relentless human effort to discover it. If you truly want to know what life communicates, listen to your conscience, which is the perfect interpreter of life.

Inspiration Coffee: Wonder Counselor, my life is full of dreams but remains a mystery. If I truly want to know what it tries to tell me, I just need to listen to my conscience, which is the perfect interpreter of life. Thank you, Lord.

It has been women who have breathed gentleness and care into the harsh progress of mankind. (Elizabeth II (b. 1926), English queen) (Quotations, Women, pg. 308)

Wi-Flavor: Humans have made great progress and coarse contributions to creation. But you should know that it has been women who have smoothed things out and given gentle care.

Wisdom Tea: Wisdom of God, humans have made great progress to creation. However, I should know that it has been women who have smoothed things out and given gentle care. Thank you, Lord.

December 19

If your enemy is hungry, feed him; if he is thirsty, give drink; for by so doing you will heap burning coals upon his head.
(Romans 12:20) (Religious, Enemy, pg. 157)

In-Flavor: Human nature would tell you to hate your enemy and treat him badly. But the Bible would call on you to love your enemy, feed him, and care for him. That way, you make him wonder and change.

Inspiration Coffee: Wonder Counselor, human nature would make me hate my enemy and treat him badly. But the Bible calls on me to love my enemy, feed him, and care for him to win him over to my side. Thank you, Lord.

He who is slow to anger has great understanding, but he who has a hasty temper exalts folly.
(Proverbs 14:29) (Religious, Anger, pg. 28)

Wi-Flavor: Anger and a hot temper often come from misunderstandings and cause lots of destruction. However, if you are slow to anger, you will have great understanding and avoid folly.

Wisdom Tea: Wisdom of God, anger and a hot temper often bring misunderstandings and hurt. However, if I am slow to anger, I will have great understanding and avoid folly and destructive acts. Thank you, Lord.

December 20

Nobody hath found God by walking his own way. (Guru Ram Das, in M. A. Macauliffe's *The Sikh Religion*) (Religious, Finding God, pg. 189)

In-Flavor: Everyone loves to find God, for God will show them the way and give them all the wonderful blessings they might need. But if you want to find God, you have to follow God's way, not your way.

Inspiration Coffee: Wonder Counselor, I love to find God every day so that God can show me the way and give me many blessings. But if I want to find God, I will have to follow God's way, not my way. Thank you, Lord.

The eye is the lamp of the body. So, if your eye is sound, your whole body will be full of light.
(Matthew 6:22) (Religious, Body and Soul, pg. 57)

Wi-Flavor: You need to take care of your eye because it is the lamp of the body. If your eye is good, it will radiate light throughout your entire body. But if it is bad, your whole body will be in darkness.

Wisdom Tea: Wisdom of God, I need to take good care of my eye and let it radiate light brightly like the lamp of the body. If it is bad, it cannot shine, and my whole body will be in darkness. Thank you, Lord.

December 21

Ideals are like stars; you will not succeed in touching them with your hands. But like the seafaring man on the desert waters, you choose them as your guides, and following them you will reach your destiny. (Carl Schurz, address, Boston, April 18, 1859) (Religious, Ideals, pg. 258)

In-Flavor: Ideals are like stars that inspire a person to dream big and aim high amidst daily challenges. You must have some ideals to guide you to your destiny, even though you might not reach them.

Inspiration Coffee: Wonder Counselor, ideals are like stars that inspire me to dream big and aim high, despite my daily challenges. I must have some ideals to guide me to my destiny on this life journey. Thank you, Lord.

The Church sometimes forgets that at least part of her divine commission is "to comfort the afflicted and to afflict the comfortable." (John E. Large, *The Small Needle of Doctor Large*, 1962) (Religious, Church, pg. 80)

Wi-Flavor: The Church is usually good at comforting the afflicted and caring for the suffering. But you might not know that it is afraid to afflict the comfortable or wake up the complacent.

Wisdom Tea: Wisdom of God, I may know that the Church is often good at comforting the afflicted and the suffering. But it is often afraid to afflict the comfortable and wake up the complacent. Thank you, Lord.

December 22

Love of men leads to the love of God. (Hindustani proverb) (Religious, Love, pg. 307)

In-Flavor: Some people think they can love God without having to love their fellow men first. If you truly love God, you must begin by loving your neighbors, then that love will lead you to the love of God.

Inspiration Coffee: Wonder Counselor, some think they can love God without having to love their fellow men. But if I really love God, I must love my neighbors first, and then it will lead me to the love of God. Thank you, Lord.

No man has the right to despair, since each was the messenger of a thing greater than himself. Despair was the rejection of God within oneself. (Antoine de Saint-Exupéry, *Flight of Arras*, 1942) (Religious, Despair, pg. 133)

Wi-Flavor: Despair is a rejection of God within yourself and a big problem in this secular world. But you should not fall into despair, because you are one of the messengers with a special mission from God.

Wisdom Tea: Wisdom of God, despair is my rejection of you—and a big problem in this secular world. I should not fall into despair, because I am one of the messengers with your special mission. Thank you, Lord.

December 23
In love, we find joy which is ultimate because it is the ultimate truth.
(Rabindranath Tagore, *Creative Unity*, 1922) (Religious, Love, pg. 311)

In-Flavor: People who experience love in their hearts will ultimately find joy in their lives, for joy is the ultimate truth. So, if you really want to have joy in your life, you must first fill it with love.

Inspiration Coffee: Wonder Counselor, I will find joy, which is the ultimate truth, if I can experience love in my heart. So, if I truly want to have joy in my life, I must fill it with love. Thank you, Lord.

A child that is early taught that he is God's child, that he may live and move and have his being in God, and that he has, therefore, infinite strength at hand for the conquering of any difficulty, will take life more easily, and probably will make more of it.
(Edward Everett Hale (1822–1909), in E. D. Starbuck's *Psychology of Religion*) (Religious, Education, pg. 152)

Wi-Flavor: You must know that early education is key to the confidence, resiliency, and success of a child. If you are taught early that you are God's child, you will handle life easily and make more of it.

Wisdom Tea: Wisdom of God, I know that early education is key to the confidence, resiliency, and success of a child. If I am early taught that I am God's child, I will handle life easily and make more of it. Thank you, Lord.

December 24
If you take no risks, you will suffer no defeats. But if you take no risks, you win no victories.
(Richard M. Nixon, in *U.S. News & World Report*, March 30, 1987) (Religious, Risk and Safety, pg. 494)

In-Flavor: Some people are afraid to take risks because they do not want to deal with defeats and losses. But if you want to experience victories, you must take risks and learn to handle defeats graciously.

Inspiration Coffee: Wonder Counselor, I may be afraid to take risks because I cannot handle defeat and loses. But if I want to experience victories, I must take risks and learn to deal with defeats graciously. Thank you, Lord.

Faith is not an easy virtue. But in the broad world of man's total voyage through time to eternity, faith is not only a gracious companion, but an essential guide.
(Theodore M. Hesburgh, in *The Way*, June 1963) (Religious, Faith, pg. 178)

Wi-Flavor: Faith is not an easy virtue to keep up daily. However, you will learn that it is not only a gracious companion but also an essential guide to help you on your voyage through time to eternity.

Wisdom Tea: Wisdom of God, faith is a wonderful virtue to have. I will learn that it is not only a gracious companion but also an essential guide to help me on my voyage through time to eternity. Thank you, Lord.

December 25

Virtue, like art, constantly deals with what is hard to do, and the harder the task the better success.

(Aristotle, *The Nicomachean Ethics*, 340 BC) (Religious, Virtue, pg. 593)

In-Flavor: Virtue is difficult for a person to master. It not only requires your commitment and sacrifice but also brings lots of blessings. If you want to make virtue a part of your life, you must see it like that.

Inspiration Coffee: Wonder Counselor, virtue can be difficult for me to master because it requires my commitment and sacrifice. However, I must know that it also brings lots of blessings to my life. Thank you, Lord.

Force may subdue, but Love gains; and he that forgives first wins the laurels. (William Penn, *Some Fruits of Solitude*, 1693) (Religious, Forgiveness, pg. 193)

Wi-Flavor: You might find it hard to practice forgiveness in your daily life. But remember that anyone who forgives first wins the laurels. When you forgive, you show love and let go of all past wrongdoings.

Wisdom Tea: Wisdom of God, I might know that it is difficult to practice forgiveness in my daily life. However, when I forgive first, I win the laurels and let go of all past wrongdoings by showing my love. Thank you, Lord.

December 26

Dreaming instead of doing is foolishness, and there is ruin in a flood of empty words.

(Ecclesiastes 5:7) (Wise, Action, pg. 8)

In-Flavor: Having an idea and dreaming about it is a good start for an awesome achievement. But if you do not do anything about it, it is useless and empty. So, act on your dream and make it a reality.

Inspiration Coffee: Wonder Counselor, having an idea and dreaming about it is a good start on the way to success. But if I do not act on my dream and make it a reality, it is foolish and simply an empty idea. Thank you, Lord.

Let a man overcome anger by kindness, evil by good. ... Victory breeds hatred, for the conquered is unhappy. ... Never in the world does hatred cease by hatred; hatred ceases by love.

(Buddha (563–483 BC), quoted in Radhakrishnan's *Indian Philosophy*) (Religious, Hatred, pg. 223)

Wi-Flavor: When you celebrate a victory, it brings out hatred from the conquered. But you can only put an end to hatred by love, anger by kindness, and evil by good. If you can do that, you are truly a victor.

Wisdom Tea: Wisdom of God, I can only put an end to hatred by love, anger by hatred, anger by kindness, and evil by good. I also need to know that victory brings out hatred in the conquered. Thank you, Lord.

December 27

People who have nothing to do are quickly tired of their own company. (Jeremy Collier) (Wise, Idleness, pg. 75)

In-Flavor: Most people keep themselves busy with work or other activities to help them avoid boredom. So, if you want to avoid idleness and boredom, keep yourself busy with work and volunteering acts.

Inspiration Coffee: Wonder Counselor, idleness can make me bored and involved in many problems. So, if I want to avoid idleness and boredom, I should keep myself busy with work and volunteering acts. Thank you, Lord.

The simple expression of the publican, "God, be merciful to me a sinner," was sufficient to open the floodgates of the Divine compassion. (St. John Climacus (525–600 AD), *Climax*) (Religious, Mercy, pg. 324)

Wi-Flavor: You recall how Moses bargained with God to spare a sinful city. But today, you learn that the simple expression of "God, be merciful to me, a sinner" opens the floodgates of the divine compassion.

Wisdom Tea: Wisdom of God, Moses bargained with God to seek mercy and spare a sinful city. Today, I learn that the simple expression of "God, be merciful to me, a sinner" receives the divine compassion. Thank you, Lord.

December 28

Young man, it's wonderful to be young! Enjoy every minute of it! Do all you want to; take in everything, but realize that you must account to God for everything you do. (Ecclesiastes 11:9) (Wise, Responsibility, pg. 120)

In-Flavor: Many youths think they are invincible and, hence, keep on acting irresponsibly. It is alright for you to have the adventurous spirit of the young and enjoy every minute of it. But act responsibly.

Inspiration Coffee: Wonder Counselor, many youths think they are invincible and keep on acting irresponsibly. I surely can have the spirit of the young and enjoy every minute of it, but I need to act responsibly. Thank you, Lord.

Zeal is fit only for wise men, but is found mostly in fools. (Thomas Fuller, *Gnomologia*, 1732) (Religious, Zeal, pg. 640)

Wi-Flavor: Fools tend to do things without much thinking and eagerly make many empty promises. But if you are a wise person, you have enough knowledge and life experience to take on a task with zeal.

Wisdom Tea: Wisdom of God, if I am a wise person, I will have knowledge and life experience to take on a task with zeal. But fools tend to do things without thinking and eagerly make empty promises. Thank you, Lord.

December 29

A man may make many mistakes, but he isn't a failure until he starts blaming others. (Wit, Spring & Summer)

In-Flavor: All humans make mistakes, which might cause disappointment and discouragement. You will surely do the same, but you should turn those into learning opportunities and stop blaming others.

Inspiration Coffee: Wonder Counselor, I will surely make mistakes that might get me disappointed and discouraged. But I should turn those into learning opportunities and stop blaming others. Thank you, Lord.

He who wishes to revenge injuries by reciprocated hatred will live in misery. (Baruch Spinoza, *Ethics*, 1677) (Religious, Revenge, pg. 488)

Wi-Flavor: Revenge is a vicious circle that can imprison you and make you miserable. If you wish to revenge past injuries by reciprocating hatred, you should know that you might constantly live in misery.

Wisdom Tea: Wisdom of God, revenge is a vicious circle that can imprison me and make me miserable. If I wish to revenge past injuries by reciprocating hatred, I will constantly live in misery. Thank you, Lord.

December 30

When life gives you scraps, make quilts. (Wit, Unknown, pg. 9)

In-Flavor: Life might deal you a bad hand and give you one disappointment after another. But if you are an optimistic and creative person, you will be able to turn those scraps into many beautiful quilts.

Inspiration Coffee: Wonder Counselor, life might deal me a bad hand and give me many disappointments. However, if I am optimistic and creative, I will be able to turn those scraps into many beautiful quilts. Thank you, Lord.

Go Godward: thou wilt find a road. (Russian proverb) (Religious, Paths, pg. 381)

Wi-Flavor: Sometimes, people head down the wrong path that leads to a dead end. However, if you go Godward and follow God's way, you will always find a path. And God will lead you to your destination.

Wisdom Tea: Wisdom of God, a wrong path will lead me into danger and perhaps a dead end. But if I go Godward and follow God's way, I will find a path that leads me to my true destination. Thank you, Lord.

December 31

Consult not your fears but your hopes and your dreams. Think not about your frustrations, but about your unfulfilled potential. Concern yourself not with what you tried and failed in, but with what it is still possible for you to do. (Pope John XXIII)

In-Flavor: Humans tend to fixate on things like fears, frustrations, and failures. But those will lead you to discouragement and depression. You better focus on hopes, dreams, opportunities, and possibilities.

Inspiration Coffee: Wonder Counselor, some people like to fixate on fears, frustrations, and failures. But those will bring me discouragement. I better focus on hopes, dreams, opportunities, and possibilities. Thank you, Lord.

He who has learned to pray has learned the greatest secret of a holy and happy life. (William Law, *Christian Perfection*, 1926) (Religious, Prayer, pg. 417)

Wi-Flavor: The secret of a holy and happy life is to be around God forever. Hence, everyone looks forward to the eternal life. Meanwhile, the best way for you to achieve that life is through prayer.

Wisdom Tea: Wisdom of God, the secret of a holy and happy life is to be around God as long as possible. So, the best way for me to achieve that life on earth is through prayer. Thank you, Lord.

Index to Issues

Borrow: *June 18*
Brain: *January 7, July 13*
Brilliant achievement: *December 13*
Broken spirit: *April 6*
Brother/sister: *January 13, October 31*
Burning lamp: *December 15*
Busy person: *January 29*
Calamity: *May 16, September 18*
Care: *December 18*
Cause: *March 10*
Cautious people: *April 16*
Challenge: *May 21*
Chance: *March 28, June 29*
Change: *January 3, February 20, April 29, May 29, October 2*
Character: *January 14, February 3, February 4, February 22, March 2, July 10, August 10, August 23, September 14, October 7*
Charity: *March 17, April 18, July 21, September 19*
Cheating: *June 2*
Cheerful heart: *April 6*
Cheerfulness: *March 10*
Child of God: *December 23*
Children: *January 9, May 18, June 20, November 19*
Choice: *June 23, August 16*
Choosing: *June 22*
Christian: *March 3*
Christian life: *July 18*
Christmas: *July 31*
Church: *December 21*
Civilization: *November 25*
Cleansing: *June 1*
Clergy: *January 11, July 22*
Climb: *July 27*
Clinging to a broken piece: *November 18*
Closing door: *November 9*
Coach: *May 9*
Cobwebs of the heart: *May 8*
Comfort: *January 22, February 23, April 15, July 20*

Comfort the afflicted: *December 21*
Commanding: *November 7*
Commitment: *March 3, March 25, April 2, September 19*
Committee: *March 14*
Common sense: *January 8, February 9, April 5, October 26, November 29, December 5*
Common thing: *December 14*
Companion: *July 5*
Company: *December 7, December 27*
Compassion: *March 19, March 22, April 19, May 19, August 10, October 23*
Competition: *September 10*
Compromise: *September 14*
Conceit: *February 29, March 30, April 29, June 7*
Condemn: *July 19*
Conduct: *June 18*
Confidence: *March 26, May 2, May 30, June 14*
Conquered: *December 26*
Conquering: *October 15*
Conquest: *January 19*
Conscience: *January 19, March 20, July 1, July 18, July 31, August 19, August 31, October 1, October 27, December 18*
Contented mind: *June 16*
Contentment: *June 19, October 13*
Conversation: *March 7*
Cooperation: *January 4, March 29, June 2, July 2, October 28, November 13*
Correction: February 5, March 31, April 1
Courage: *February 26, April 15, April 20, May 20, May 26, June 14, July 2, August 2, September 30, October 31, December 16*
Courtesy: *July 12*
Coveting: *March 21, May 16, June 24*
Cowardice: *November 27*

Creation: *March 17*
Creativity: *September 2, October 2*
Creed: *March 17*
Crisis: *February 15, August 23*
Cross: *September 24*
Crown: *September 24*
Cruelty: *February 7*
Curing: *October 6*
Daily life: *February 19*
Dark night of the soul: November 18
Dead: *June 24*
Death: *March 4, March 22, April 5, July 20, October 19*
Deceit: *August 5*
Decent person: *November 25*
Decision-making: *March 27, April 27, May 31, October 29*
Decisiveness: *August 26*
Defeat: *March 18, April 17, May 16, May 21, June 21, July 22, August 19, September 10, September 21, December 24*
Defending: *October 25*
Dehumanizing: *April 21*
Desire: *August 18, September 20, October 13, December 14*
Despair: *December 22*
Despise: *July 28*
Destination: *January 2, October 27*
Destiny: *January 23, February 11, October 13, December 21*
Determination: *March 4, June 12*
Determined effort: *December 13*
Detour: *October 28*
Devil: *March 20, April 5, April 20, May 20, June 22*
Difficulty: *October 8*
Diplomacy: *August 1*
Directing: *May 10*
Direction: *May 28, August 27, September 1, October 1, October 27, December 2*
Discipline: *July 20*
Discontent: *June 11*
Discord: *September 20*

Discouragement: *January 4, February 4, March 4, April 3, May 3, May 17, December 3*
Discussion: *October 5*
Disheartening: *May 26*
Dishonest: *April 10*
Dislike: *May 28*
Display: *November 30*
Divine attribute: *June 5*
Divine compassion: *December 27*
Divine things: *October 25*
Division: *September 20*
Do my best: *January 2, January 5*
Doing: *July 6, September 4, December 26*
Doing right: *July 14*
Doubt: *October 20, December 4*
Dreaming: *February 12, June 26, December 26, December 31*
Drowning: *June 1*
Duty: *May 14, October 16, October 20*
Dwelling place: *April 28*
Dying: *May 24, September 24*
Earnestness: *March 16*
Earthly voice: *December 17*
Easy: *April 29*
Eating: *September 13*
Education: *January 24, July 11, August 15, November 19, December 23*
Egomaniac: *October 30*
Egotism: *December 1*
Elect: *July 23*
Eloquence: *April 19*
Emotion: *February 13, March 26*
Empty: *June 10*
Empty word: *December 26*
Encouragement: *February 4*
End: *August 31*
Endeavor: *October 18*
Endurance: *June 3, July 3, November 2*
Enemy: *January 22, February 26, March 15, August 26, September*

11, October 22, November 21, December 25

Fraternity: *October 14*

Free will: *June 22*

Friend: January 6, February 4, March 1, May 5, June 19, July 1, September 6

Friendship: *February 7, April 3, September 5, September 6, October 31, December 16*

Frustration: *December 31*

Fulfillment: *May 1*

Future: *June 1, June 4, June 15, July 2, August 3, August 20, September 3, October 3*

Gain: *September 24*

Gaining wisdom: *November 28*

Gate: *June 25*

Generosity: *July 4*

Gentleness: November 11, December 18

Getting: *June 14, August 4*

Giving: *June 13, June 14, June 18, July 4, July 14, August 4, October 11*

Giving away: *March 7*

Giving up: *July 20*

Goal: *July 27, July 28, August 28, September 17, November 29*

God: *April 21, May 23, May 27, August 6, August 19, September 23, September 25*

Going Godward: *December 30*

Golden rule: *January 16, December 14*

Good: *June 19, November 24, December 26*

Good Christian: *November 18*

Good citizen: *November 18*

Good conscience: *February 21*

Good day's work: *November 13*

Good deed: *July 21, November 12*

Good eyesight: November 9

Good hearing: *November 9*

Good judgment: *February 9, August 4, December 5*

Good leader: *May 2*

Good man: *December 1*

Good neighbor: *January 13, November 12*

Good time: *November 2*

Goodness: *March 22, July 7, August 17*

Goodness of God: *March 25*

Goods: *August 22*

Goodwill: *November 5*

Gossip: *January 7, November 1, December 3*

Gracious companion: *December 24*

Graduate: *January 9*

Gratitude: *January 14*

Gravity: *March 16*

Great: *October 12*

Great leader: *May 2*

Great person: *March 12*

Great thing: *April 11*

Greatest glory: *November 16*

Greed: *May 12, May 24, June 24, September 27*

Grief: *September 6*

Grindstone: *July 30*

Groan: *August 30*

Growing: *June 26*

Guide: *April 26, November 28, December 21*

Guilt: *June 12*

Habit: *June 6, November 21*

Hand: *February 27*

Hand of God: *October 21*

Happiness: *February 8, February 14, March 8, April 4, May 1, July 5, July 12, July 23, August 12, August 21, August 22, September 23, September 27, October 5, October 6, October 23, November 28*

Happy and holy life: *December 31*

Happy family: *September 21*

Happy heart: *November 4*

Happy living: *September 5*

Happy person: *October 28*

Hard work: *July 16, October 7, October 17, October 26, December 12*

Hardship: *October 30*

Harmony: *May 14*

Harsh word: *November 17*

Harvest: *April 7, May 3, August 25*

Haste: *February 9*

Hasty temper: *December 19*

Hatred: *January 27, February 3, February 19, February 26, May 4, July 15, September 12, September 27, November 22, December 26*

Healer: *June 9*

Healing: *June 23*

Hearing: *May 5, December 5*

Heart: *July 13*

Heart of a child: *March 12*

Heartbreak: *July 16*

Heat: *February 2*

Heaven: *February 1, February 23, April 23, June 25*

Hell: *May 24, June 25*

Help: *January 6, February 6, February 29, March 6, May 31, June 2, August 13, September 25, December 6*

Hero: *February 23, May 16*

Hoarding wealth: *October 26*

Holding tightly: *July 4*

Holiness: *July 24*

Holy war: *November 15*

Home: *August 5*

Honesty: *June 2, July 3*

Honor: *June 17, August 13, November 29*

Hope: *July 16, July 18, July 23, August 13, August 20, September 15, September 22, October 4, October 14, October 22, November 3, November 22, December 4, December 31*

Hope addict: *September 9*

Hopelessness: *November 20*

Horse sense: *January 8*

Hospitality: *April 19*

Hot: *October 9*

House of the Lord: *February 18*

Human nature: *August 18*

Human spirit: *August 23*

Humble work: *September 24*

Humility: *July 29, October 12*

Humor: *April 6, May 6, June 5, November 5*

Hunger for bread: *November 26*

Hunger for love: *November 26*

Hunger of the soul: *August 27*

Hurtful act: *January 16*

Idea: *July 6, September 17, October 2*

Ideal: *January 3, February 14, November 23, December 21*

Idleness: *January 22, January 29, December 27*

Igniting: *June 13*

Ignorance: *January 17, October 5, December 15*

Ignorant person: *October 29*

Image of God: *March 22*

Immortality: *March 26, May 27*

Imperfection: *May 26*

Imploring: *May 22*

Impossibility: *January 11, October 1*

Inability: *April 2*

Infection: *June 26*

Inferiority: *August 25*

Infinite strength: *December 23*

Injustice: *April 12, May 3*

Inner spiritual strength: *September 22*

Instinct: *August 19*

Insult: *May 4*

Intelligence: *March 3*

Interest: *June 10*

Interest of friend: *July 31*

Interpreter of life: *December 18*

Inward reservoir: *June 25*

Jealousy: *March 21, May 21, June 2, June 21, June 30, September 5, December 13*

Jesus Christ: *November 23*

Joke: *December 7*
Journey: *May 11*
Joy: *February 21, March 23, August 5, September 6, September 23, October 6, December 11, December 12, December 23*
Judging: *September 26, November 6*
Judgment Day: *March 24, November 19*
Judgment: *January 7, January 28, February 17, February 25, March 13, March 26, December 7*
Jury: *June 6*
Justice: *March 18, April 12, April 16, April 24, May 3, May 27, June 3, June 5, July 4, September 7*
Justifying: *May 6*
Key: *October 9*
Killing: *February 18, March 31*
Kind speech: *September 11*
Kindness: *February 7, February 16, March 7, March 16, April 7, April 19, May 7, June 6, July 7, August 6, December 26*
Kiss of Jesus: *May 15*
Kitchen: *February 2*
Kneeling: *April 7*
Knowledge: *January 20, April 23, May 13, May 23, June 7, June 23, August 4, August 16, September 4, October 5, November 16*
Labor: *January 22*
Lamp of the body: *December 20*
Last word: *July 25, September 28*
Laugh: *April 30, July 12, October 6*
Laughter: *May 8, June 8*
Law: *March 19*
Lay down one's life: *January 23*
Laziness: *April 8, June 27, July 5, August 7, September 3, September 8, October 7*
Leadership: *January 8, February 27, March 8, March 16, April 1, October 7, November 7, December 8*
Leap of faith: *March 5*

Learning: *January 9, March 17, April 9, May 29, June 13, July 11, November 16, December 6, December 11*
Leaving behind: *October 3*
Leisure: *July 11*
Liar: *September 13*
Liberation: *May 13*
Lie: *May 25, June 26, July 3, July 13, August 14*
Life: *February 12, March 4, May 6, June 24, July 30, August 21, November 13, November 14*
Life meaning: *May 17*
Life preserver: *January 6*
Light: *December 20*
Liking: *September 5*
Limb: *August 2*
Limit: *September 30*
Listening: *August 28, October 30, November 2, November 30, December 8*
Listening to parents: *December 6*
Little people: *March 30*
Living: *September 11, November 12*
Living energy: *November 29*
Living example: *April 25*
Living model: *April 26*
Loneliness: *March 22, July 25, September 24*
Longevity: *October 13*
Looking down: *May 31*
Looking for work: *November 10*
Losing the war: *November 15*
Losing: *February 3, May 30, June 29*
Love of parent: *November 6*
Love: *January 23, February 17, February 22, March 23, March 24, April 11, April 24, May 4, May 24, June 4, June 17, June 24, June 28, July 6, July 15, July 16, July 24, July 31, August 5, August 17, August 21, September 5, September 23, October 6, October 23, November 20, November 22, December*

16, December 22, December 23, December 25, December 26
Lover of glory: *November 23*
Lover of mankind: *November 23*
Lover of money: *November 23*
Lover of pleasure: *November 23*
Lover of virtue: *November 23*
Loving Christ: *January 29*
Loyalty: *August 6, October 31*
Luck: *August 30*
Lust: *May 24*
Luxury: *October 11*
Magnanimity: *March 16*
Maintenance: *February 10*
Marriage: *January 10, February 10, April 6, May 5, August 24, December 7*
Master: *March 23, June 26*
Meaning: *November 3*
Measure: *January 28*
Medicine chest: *June 18*
Meek: *May 7*
Men and women: *February 15, December 16*
Mercy: *January 18, January 29, June 5, November 24, December 27*
Mercy of God: *March 25*
Merit: *January 27*
Messenger: *December 22*
Might: *October 16*
Mighty oak: *July 3*
Mind: *March 19*
Miraculous power: *September 22*
Misdeed: *March 11*
Misery: *November 22, December 15, December 29*
Mission field: *April 11*
Misstep: *February 28*
Mistake: *February 5, March 9, March 28, April 9, May 29, June 4, June 15, August 8, December 29*
Money: *February 18, March 23, April 25, July 7, August 5, August 6, September 6, October 7, November 5*

Monster: *June 24*
Moon: *September 16*
Moral choice: *February 25*
Moral law: *August 19*
Moral ruin: *May 18*
Moral upheaval: *August 23*
Moses: *April 18*
Mother: *January 11, February 11, March 5, May 2*
Motivation: *May 6, May 9, June 6, July 1, July 7, September 20, December 8*
Mountain: *April 10*
Mourning: *September 19*
Mouth: *August 7*
Move mountains: *January 25*
Music of the soul: *April 30*
Music: *February 27, March 8, May 26, December 4*
Mystery: *July 26*
Nagging: *June 4*
Nation: *May 22*
Negative: *April 5*
Neighbor: *March 21, March 29, May 25, August 25, September 25*
New beginning: *August 31*
New idea: *September 2*
Night: *January 17*
Noise: *March 27*
Nonconformity: *December 14*
Nut: *July 3*
Obedience: *June 28, November 7*
Obstacle: *March 13, July 24, August 28*
Odd: *June 29*
Omen: *February 20*
One's own way: *January 21*
Open mind: *January 15*
Opening: *April 23, November 9*
Opinion: *January 7*
Opportunity: *June 9, June 15, July 5, July 8, July 29, August 8, August 29, September 18, October 8, November 29*

Optimist: *March 10, September 9, October 8, December 9*
Ordinary person: *March 2*
Our day: *September 9*
Overcautious: *May 1*
Overconfidence: *May 30*
Overlooking: *November 8*
Pain: *March 22, May 27, August 22, September 12, September 24*
Pardon: *November 21*
Parents: *January 9, June 23, July 22, November 6*
Passion: *February 13, May 25, October 14*
Past: *January 31, July 8*
Path of God: *October 10*
Patience: *January 30, March 14, April 15, May 26, September 28, October 14*
Peace: *March 25, April 16, April 26, May 27, June 17, June 27, July 27, September 23, September 27*
Peace of mind: *July 27*
Pearl: *August 22*
People of good quality: *June 8*
Persecution: *August 26, November 20*
Perseverance: *March 11, September 28, November 16, December 15*
Persistence: *January 1, February 9, March 11, April 10, July 30*
Person of love: *October 10*
Pessimist: *October 8, November 8*
Physical capacity: *April 18*
Picnic: *November 28*
Pitfall: *September 29*
Pity: *September 26*
Plan: *May 10, June 10, July 9*
Playing: *July 12, December 12*
Pleasure: *May 27*
Plowing: *September 4, October 19*
Plunging ahead: *December 1*
Poor: *September 24, October 11, October 26, November 25*
Possibility: *April 21, December 31*

Potato salad: *November 28*
Poverty: *July 15, July 17, July 25, September 8, October 24, November 26, December 12*
Power: *March 26, April 13, April 22, June 19, August 16, August 30, October 15*
Praise: *July 1, July 7*
Prayer: *January 12, January 31, February 12, February 27, March 6, March 18, March 26, April 7, April 11, April 27, June 17, July 21, August 9, September 10, October 9, November 9, December 9, December 10*
Prayer group: *March 14*
Praying: *January 24, July 12, August 16, August 25, September 17, November 20, December 31*
Prejudice: *May 28*
Preparation: *January 10, February 10, March 12, May 11, August 8*
Presence of God: *July 24*
Present: *June 4, June 15, July 2, August 3*
Present pleasure: *August 3*
Preserve social standing: *April 16*
Pretense: *April 3*
Prevailing: *September 17*
Pride: *January 15, May 7, June 7, December 3*
Principle: *August 12*
Problem: *February 15, April 12, May 12, June 5, November 29*
Progress: *January 26, March 17, March 29, July 26, August 24, November 1*
Progress of mankind: *December 18*
Promise: *June 11, September 7, October 8*
Promised Land: *July 19*
Propaganda: *June 3*
Prophesy: *February 22*
Prosperity: *September 21, December 12*

Proving: *April 3*
Public opinion: *October 29*
Purpose: *April 8, October 18*
Quarrel: *January 13, March 10, May 4, July 10, November 7, December 10*
Quietness: *February 13, March 7*
Quiet voice: *October 31*
Quilt: *December 30*
Race: *March 17*
Rage: *May 24*
Reading: *July 12*
Readjustment: *October 12*
Reaping: *August 15, October 19*
Reciprocated hatred: *December 29*
Recognizing: *October 21*
Redeemed: *July 23*
Reform: *April 16*
Refreshing: *June 3*
Rejection of God: *December 22*
Rejoice: *August 30*
Relationship: *May 14, June 14, October 17*
Religion: *July 13, August 27, October 23*
Religious denomination: *November 19*
Remembering: *September 26*
Repairing: *February 10*
Reputation: *May 8, June 8, July 8, July 10, August 10, September 11*
Resistance: *September 15*
Resources of God: *October 1*
Respect: *January 16, May 12, June 28, August 13, November 29*
Responsibility: *January 1, December 28*
Resting: *April 23*
Retirement: *April 13, August 9*
Retracting: *May 15, November 11*
Revenge: *October 25, December 29*
Reverence: *December 6*
Revolution: *September 14, October 14*
Reward: *July 7*

Rich: *February 8, May 8, October 26*
Right: *April 29, May 3, October 16, November 27*
Right road: *December 2*
Righteous: *August 9*
Rising: *November 16, November 17*
Risk: *August 24, October 24, November 1, November 25, December 24*
Road: *June 25*
Rolling up sleeves: *June 27*
Root: *April 1*
Ruin: *December 26*
Rumor: *November 1*
Ruthlessness: *May 19*
Sacrifice: *January 25, November 14*
Saint: *February 23, March 25, April 25, June 20*
Salvation: *February 1*
Satan: *January 31*
Saying: *January 28*
Science: *April 19*
Scrap: *December 30*
Search light: *July 1*
Season: *April 8*
Seasons of stress: *September 22*
Secrecy: *April 14*
Secret of life: *April 24*
Seeking: *April 22*
Self-control: *August 8, September 8, October 9, November 8*
Self-disciplined: *January 19*
Self-expression: *September 8*
Selfishness: *February 24*
Self-reliance: *February 20*
Sensible person: *April 12*
Serenity: *May 27, June 25, July 17, September 22*
Servant: *February 21, March 23*
Service: *July 31, September 27*
Shame: *February 28, March 22, September 2*
Sharing: *August 21, November 28*
Ship: *March 16*
Shirtsleeves: *February 2*

Showcase: *November 30*
Sickness: *May 28*
Signs: *October 21*
Silence: *March 15, March 27, September 28, November 2*
Simpleton: *April 12*
Sin: *April 14, November 21*
Sincerity: *March 16*
Slander: *January 27*
Sleeping: *March 6, June 20, September 28*
Small packages: *December 1*
Small things: *April 11*
Smallest acts: *September 16*
Society: *May 18*
Soft answer: *November 17*
Solidarity: *April 24*
Sorrow: *May 29*
Soul: *April 28, June 23, September 14*
Sowing: *August 15, September 4, October 19*
Speaking: *December 5*
Speaking the truth: *November 15*
Speech: *May 15*
Spirit: *March 26, May 23, October 24*
Spiritual growth: *September 21*
Spiritual life: *September 19*
Spiritual salvation: *January 18*
Spirituality: *July 26*
Squabble: *May 29*
Star: *September 16, December 21*
Start: *September 26*
Staying down: *November 3*
Sterile: *November 20*
Stern: *November 11*
Sticking: *October 26*
Sticking the neck out: *November 25*
Stifling world: *September 18*
Storm: *April 1*
Storm cellar: *September 22*
Storms of life: *September 22*
Stranger: *April 19*
Strength: *January 5, January 14, April 18, June 14, October 14, October 18, November 13*

Stress: *October 20*
Striking: *August 17*
Strong: *March 31, April 20, August 16*
Struggle: *April 24*
Study: *August 8*
Sturdy tree: *March 31*
Succeed: September 1
Success: *January 11, January 30, February 11, February 28, March 13, March 28, April 4, April 17, May 16, June 15, June 30, July 16, August 14, August 27, September 14, September 16, October 3, October 7, October 17, December 25*
Successful person: *November 10, December 11*
Suffering: *January 20, July 23, August 23, September 14, September 25, November 17*
Supporting: *September 25, November 13*
Sustaining power: *November 18*
Talent: *December 16*
Talking: *May 5, November 30*
Teaching: *June 13, December 11*
Teamwork: *March 29, April 28*
Temperament: *February 22*
Temptation: *January 19*
Tenacity: *May 13, June 12, July 11*
Test: *October 7*
Thankfulness: *January 14, February 14, March 8, November 9*
The world: *April 16*
Thinking: *April 4, July 12, August 24*
Thinking ahead: *August 2*
Thirst: *May 11, July 9*
Thought: *March 27*
Threat: *October 19*
Time: *April 8, April 30, May 9, May 29, June 9, June 15, July 12, July 14, August 9, August 29*
Timid: *August 14*
Today: *November 10*
Together: *July 2*

Tolerance: *April 6, June 28, July 28, August 15, October 23*
Tomorrow: *April 8, August 11, September 4, November 10*
Top: *January 6*
Tough times: *November 2*
Tragedy: *November 28*
Training: *June 20*
Transcending: *July 18*
Transforming: *April 22, August 12*
Trial: *March 9, September 14, December 31*
Trip: *May 11, May 13*
Triumph: *June 3*
Trouble: *January 10, January 12, March 6, April 4, May 9, September 25*
True believer: *December 14*
True Christian: *October 18, October 22*
True citizen: *October 18*
True friend: *December 2*
Trust: *October 14, December 6*
Trustworthy person: *November 1*
Truth: *March 21, March 22, April 14, April 16, April 25, July 13, August 14, September 12, September 13, September 15, October 11, October 25, November 11, November 26, December 12*
Truth seeker: *October 20*
Tune: *December 4*
Turning: *August 17*
Ultimate truth: *December 23*
Unbreakable: *December 17*
Uncommon way: *December 14*
Unconsciousness: *August 25*
Unfulfilled potential: *December 31*
Unhappy family: *September 21*
Unity: *January 4, August 29, December 17*
Unjust: *November 15*
Unraveling: *September 10*
Unrepentant: *August 11*
Unwanted: *July 25*

Uphill: *December 2*
Vain: *October 4*
Valor: *March 18*
Victory: *January 17, July 22, August 29, September 21, December 24, December 26*
Viewpoint: *July 11*
Violence: *February 19, August 17, September 17, October 16, November 24*
Virtue: *March 5, March 16, April 15, July 28, August 22, September 18, October 24, December 25*
Vision: *January 26, February 24, August 18, September 14*
Vistas: *September 18*
Voice: *March 20, March 27*
Voice of eternity: *December 17*
Waiting: *October 14*
War: *September 27*
Way of life: *December 9*
Wealth: *February 16, May 16, June 16, July 15*
Wearing: *March 28*
Wearing down: *June 29*
Weaving: *March 28*
Wedding anniversary: *April 6*
Welcoming change: *December 8*
Wheelbarrow: *October 1*
Wicked: *August 9, December 1*
Wilderness: *July 19*
Wile: *June 22*
Will: *March 4, March 9, March 18, March 20, April 18, April 26, April 27, May 17*
Wind: *May 28*
Window: *March 25*
Winning: *January 17, May 30, June 29*
Winning the peace: *November 15*
Winter: *May 7, June 8*
Wisdom: *January 15, January 30, February 8, February 9, February 13, March 3, March 15, April 2, April 30, May 10, June 1, July*

12, July 29, August 2, August 4, August 16, August 22, September 19, October 15, November 2, November 16, November 29, December 5, December 12

Wise person: *March 2, July 5, July 17, September 16, September 29, October 2, October 29*

Witness: *April 14*

Women: *January 20, February 15, December 18*

Word: *January 4, March 10, April 9, July 8*

Work: *January 12, January 24, January 27, January 30, February 11, February 25, March 14, April*

13, May 18, June 9, June 16, July 12, July 17, August 30, September 13, September 29, October 2

Work of God: *April 7*

World: *March 17, September 23*

Worst person: *January 15*

Wrath: *November 17*

Wrong: *April 29, July 19*

Wrong direction: *October 11*

Wrong lane: *September 21*

Yesterday: *November 10*

Youth: *March 26, April 26, December 28*

Zeal: *April 19, May 14, June 13, December 28*

Books for sale

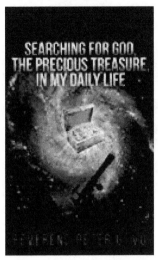

$11.95 (Spiritual Reading)

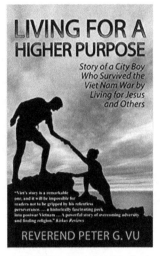

$13.95 (Inspirational Reading)

$17.95 (Adult Daily Devotion)

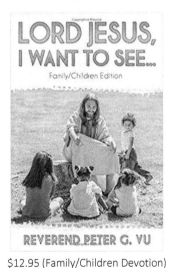

$12.95 (Family/Children Devotion)

A great gift for you & others. Thank you for your support.